THE COLUMBIA GUIDE TO

Modern Japanese History

THE COLUMBIA GUIDES TO ASIAN HISTORY

THE COLUMBIA GUIDE TO

Modern Japanese History

Gary D. Allinson

COLUMBIA UNIVERSITY PRESS

NEW YORK

Columbia University Press
Publishers Since 1893
New York   Chichester, West Sussex
Copyright © 1999 Columbia University Press
All rights reserved
Library of Congress Cataloging-in-Publication Data
Allinson, Gary D.
The Columbia guide to modern Japanese history / Gary D. Allinson.
p.   cm.   — (The Columbia guides to Asian history)
Includes bibliographical references and index.
ISBN 0-231-11144-4 (alk. paper)
1. Japan—History—1868–   I. Title. II. Series
DS881.9.A75   1999
952.03—dc21   99-10678

Casebound editions of Columbia University Press books are
printed on permanent and durable acid-free paper.
Printed in the United States of America
c 10 9 8 7 6 5 4 3 2 1

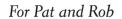

For Pat and Rob

CONTENTS

INTRODUCTION

The Columbia Guide to Modern Japanese History is a convenient learning tool and reference source for readers with little or no background in Japanese studies. This introduction describes the contents of the guide and illustrates how it can be used. Before turning to those matters, however, I first will explain my approach to the history of modern Japan.

APPROACH

Japan is rightly known as the first Asian nation to develop successfully as an economic power. Although many people attribute Japan's economic might to its rapid growth in the postwar era, its economic development actually was a long, slow process that began in the eighteenth century and accelerated in the late nineteenth when Japan entered the early stages of an industrial revolution. Changes were sporadic in the first half of the twentieth century. Then rapid growth between 1955 and 1973 made Japan a secure member of the world's economic superpowers and one of the United States' most important trading partners.

Beyond its importance as an economic power, Japan deserves attention for other reasons. Japanese history has several features that distinguish it from the histories of other nations. For example, in contrast with the United States, Japan has an ancient history; even its written records date from the eighth century. Its history has also been very unstable. The country experienced long periods of rule under a sedate aristocracy and even longer periods when it was beset by chaos incited by bloodthirsty warriors. In the past 140 years alone, Japan has endured revolution, imperialism, war, poverty, occupation, peace, development, and affluence. During its tumultuous history, Japan has witnessed the evolution of many institutions, customs, relationships, and achievements that differ dramatically from those of the United States and other countries. By appreciating the unusual ways in which Japan has evolved historically, we can better understand the content and meaning of our own history.

But we not only learn more about ourselves by studying Japan. We also learn more about a society that is inherently fascinating. Japan's political institutions and practices, its literature and ideas, its social conventions, and its economic institutions all have distinctive features. Sometimes Japanese institutions seem to employ more oppressive ways of conducting human behavior, but at other times they seem to provide opportunities that maximize human potential or structures that cushion social distress. Japan is too complex, and its history has been too diverse and unstable, to permit easy labeling as a good or evil, liberating or oppressive, society. Instead, by finding out more about its constantly changing diversities, we recognize how exciting the thrill of intellectual discovery can be and how challenging the search for understanding can become.

This book confines its treatment to the history of modern Japan, with the year 1850 as our beginning point. In this respect, "modern" refers to the most recent period in Japan's history, one that has some coherent, objective elements, such as Japan's participation in international diplomacy, its integration as a centralized nation-state, its development as an industrialized economy, its evolution into an urban society, and its entry into a kind of global cultural exchange. Historians have usually dated the onset of Japan's modern era from 1853, when Commodore Matthew Perry steamed into Japanese waters, or 1868, when Japan's modern political revolution began. Thus, by using the year 1850 as our point of departure, we can better illustrate the characteristics of the older system of premodern Japan just before it crumbled and more sharply define the base from which modern Japan evolved.

This use of the term *modern* derives from a commonsense understanding of the word, meaning "recent" or "contemporary." No attempt is made here to imply the many, more subjective meanings of *modern, modernity*, or *modernization*, as the two latter terms, especially, have taken on highly controversial overtones in recent academic debates. Modernity, for example, can refer to a subjective state of mind; designate specific movements associated with art, architecture, and literature; and identify a social condition. Modernization has equally subjective meanings, often implying progressive change that occurs when copying a good society or the measurable achievements that take place when a country is developing toward an ideal end. Events in the world since the early 1970s have profoundly undermined confidence in this unilinear vision of progress, however, so the term *modern* in this volume modifies "Japanese history" solely in order to mark a time period. Use of the term *modern* is not meant to convey any subjective judgments about Japan's modernity or its modernization. Those issues will be discussed in the Historical Narrative, both directly and indirectly.

History is another seemingly simple term that can invite controversy. This volume also employs a commonsense definition of *history*: changes that actually occurred in the past, in contrast with writing about those changes. This book assumes that such events and changes did occur and that we can know them through written, visual, and material sources that have survived into the present. We recognize that historical facts are highly controversial and that historians can differ among themselves about these facts owing to their personalities, rhetoric, definitions, perspectives, nationalities, and so on.

In this work, the facts have been selected, presented, and interpreted by an American in late middle age who has studied Japan for more than thirty years, lived there for four, and visited frequently. As the sole author of this work, I think of myself as a moderate with no ideological ax to grind, and I believe that *left-wing, right-wing, liberal,* and *conservative* are terms that must be used very carefully in discussions of Japanese politics. I am dismayed by "Japan bashers," conspiratorial thinkers who can find nothing good to say about the country, and I am also skeptical about "chrysanthemums," Japan lovers who sometimes overlook its shortcomings. Finally, I believe that there is, and has been, a real world out there (as opposed to games with language that may or may not describe it) — a world, moreover, that we can and should understand.

Theoretically, history includes all changes that took place in the past. But because of the limits of space and my expertise, this volume is confined to five facets of Japan's recent past: its external relations, domestic political affairs, economic developments, social changes, and the general characteristics of its culture and ideas, broadly conceived. It was not possible to deal with such topics as art, architecture, dance, science, sculpture, sports, martial arts, theater, or the tea ceremony, except occasionally in passing. The topics that are covered, however, do offer readers a comprehensive overview of the key events and changes in Japan's modern history.

To summarize, this book is based on the assumption that readers can and should understand something about five important facets of the history of Japan since 1850, in order to acknowledge Japan's importance, to learn more about the Japanese and ourselves, and to appreciate the distinctiveness of the subject itself.

CONTENTS AND USE

This guide is divided into four parts: Historical Narrative, Topical Compendium, Resource Guide, and Appendix. How readers use the guide will depend on their aims, and no brief introduction can possibly anticipate all of their objectives. The following comments describe the contents of each part, how they relate to one another, and how readers can take advantage of this book.

The Historical Narrative, part I, offers a comprehensive overview of five aspects of Japan's history since 1850: external relations, domestic politics, economic development, social change, and cultural life. It is organized chronologically into four periods of roughly equal length: 1850–1889, 1890–1931, 1932–1973, and 1974 to the present.

Readers can use the narrative in several ways. If they wish to obtain a comprehensive understanding of the period since 1850, they can read through the entire narrative from beginning to end. Some readers may be interested in only one aspect of Japan's recent history, such as its social changes or its economic development. These readers can easily find the pertinent section under each period and focus on that topic across the span of years since 1850. Other readers may want to know about a certain period in Japan's modern history, such as the wartime era. They can turn immediately to the segment treating the years between 1932 and 1973. In these and many other ways, the Historical Narrative serves as a flexible source for the history of modern Japan.

Part II, the Topical Compendium, is divided into thirteen categories, such as political leaders, economic institutions, and female writers. The 150 items that appear in the compendium consist of terms mentioned briefly in the Historical Narrative. One purpose of the compendium is to offer fuller, more detailed information about those leaders, institutions, writers, and the like. A second purpose is to provide this detailed information in a format that complements the more fragmented analysis in part I. The compendium does this by organizing the entries under each topical category according to chronological criteria. This arrangement enables readers to trace, for example, the sequence of political leadership, the evolution of economic institutions, or the development of a female literary voice.

One special feature of the compendium deserves further comment. It includes two categories for authors, men and women, for a total of thirty entries. Each entry recounts the writer's life history, relates that history to the author's work, and lists (either some or all) of the author's translated novels, novellas, and short stories. These entries serve several purposes. They provide a sequence of biographies that can be read in tandem with the Historical Narrative to shed more light on the cultural, intellectual, social, and gender history of modern Japan. Used in this way, the separate entries are especially helpful in illustrating the diversity of life experiences in Japan since 1850 and revealing the differences between prominent men and women with respect to their family backgrounds, education, and personal histories. The entries also provide sketches of fictional works that can be used as another source for understanding Japan's modern history. Finally, they serve a bibliographical purpose by listing the authors' works in English translation.

Readers can therefore use the Topical Compendium in a variety of ways. The quickest way for readers to find detailed information on a former prime minister, a major corporation, or a prize-winning author, is to go to the index and find the page on which the entry begins. Readers with more time should turn directly to the section in the Topical Compendium that discusses Political Leaders to find the specific prime minister; Business Associations, Enterprises, and Firms to find the corporation at issue; or Female Writers to find the prize-winning author. Readers with even more time who wish to identify a prime minister, corporation, or author in a broader historical context are invited to read through the entire segment on political leaders, businesses, or writers. In so doing, they will develop a deeper understanding of the prime minister's predecessors and successors, the corporation's historical evolution within the Japanese business world, and the writer's contributions in the larger context of Japanese literature. The Topical Compendium can thus be used flexibly as a complement to the Historical Narrative, as a separate source in its own right, and as a guide to fictional works helpful to understanding Japan's modern history.

Part III, the Resource Guide, is divided into three sections, the first and longest of which is an annotated bibliography of Japanese history. The bibliography includes many of the best and most authoritative books on modern Japan available in English; these are also the studies on which much of the Historical Narrative is based. These sources will enable interested readers to go well beyond the contents of this single volume to explore the history of modern Japan in greater depth and detail.

The second section of the Resource Guide describes fourteen feature films and four documentaries that offer particularly illuminating views of modern Japan. The third and final section of the Resource Guide identifies some of the electronic resources that were available for Japan when this volume was completed. Because such resources are still in their infancy, they are less well developed than electronic resources in other fields. Moreover, the format, content, and availability of such sources change swiftly and constantly, making this segment of the Resource Guide suggestive at best.

To reiterate a point made earlier, one type of written source on modern Japan appears not in part III but in part II. Works of Japanese literature–novels, novellas, and short stories—that are available in English translation appear in this book under the names of individual authors in the Topical Compendium. Thus, if readers want to know which novels by Natsume Sōseki are available in English, they should turn to Natsume Sōseki under Male Writers in the Topical Compendium. This entry lists Sōseki's translated novels according to their English-language titles, followed (in parentheses) by the date of publication of the original Japanese version.

The fourth and final part of this guide, the Appendix, contains several types of material. It provides either part or all of key documents in the history of modern Japan, such as its constitutions, a chronology of Japanese political and economic history between 1850 and the present, a list of prime ministers since 1885, and quantitative data on such phenomena as population growth, the gross national product, export and import volumes, and changes in Japan's trade partners over time. The Appendix thus complements both the Historical Narrative and the Topical Compendium.

PART I

Historical Narrative

The following narrative is a chronological and topical survey of Japan's modern history divided into four periods of about equal length: 1850 to 1889, 1890 to 1931, 1932 to 1973, and 1974 to the present. Within each period, the narrative treats five aspects of Japan's history: external relations, domestic political affairs, economic developments, social changes, and cultural life.

The four parts of the narrative can be read in sequence as a continuous account of Japan's modern history. In this respect, they trace Japan's evolution from a poor, isolated, authoritarian, agrarian state into an affluent, engaged, pluralistic, consumer society over the course of 150 years. Read in this fashion, the narrative relates a tale with strongly progressive overtones.

The narrative can be read in a second manner as well, as highlighting the discontinuities in Japan's modern history and drawing attention to the difficult, volatile, halting developments during the past century and a half. From this perspective, each of the four periods is characterized by a different, overriding historical challenge. Between 1850 and 1889, Japan's central objective was how it could avoid colonization by the expansionist powers of western Europe and North America. Having largely escaped that fate by the 1890s, Japan faced another challenge through the early decades of the twentieth century: How could it impose political unity on a fractious society undergoing rapid change in an unruly international environment? Japan never did resolve this challenge before one of the most tumultuous periods in its modern history began. Between 1932 and 1973 Japan underwent a series of wrenching changes: depression, foreign conquest, war, occupation, recovery, and growth. Nonetheless, one overriding concern shaped Japan's history throughout this period: the achievement of economic development. By the early 1970s Japan had successfully addressed this concern, only to find itself confronted with a new, and still unresolved, dilemma: What kind of society should Japan become, given its affluence?

The following narrative thus superposes the rhetorics of continuity and discontinuity, chronicling a tale of development and progress that has made Japan one of the most affluent countries in the world. At the same time, the narrative interweaves another tale that stresses how costly, difficult, and circuitous this path to material achievement has been.

The narrative begins with a sketch of Japan in 1850 and ends with another of Japan in 2000, both depicting a day in the life of two hypothetical figures. These sketches illustrate many features of Japanese life that are explained from different perspectives elsewhere in the narrative. First, the sketches portray the conditions of material life, such as diet, clothing, housing, work habits, leisure pursuits, and consumer preferences, as well as modes of transportation and communication. Second, they describe key social relationships, especially those between men and women as husbands and wives, between parents and children, and between families and the larger society. Third, the sketches offer some sense of people's political positions and ideas. Fourth, they convey what French historians call *mentalités*, the thoughts of common folk about life and its struggles. Fifth, the sketches disclose some intriguing changes in naming practices in Japanese history. Sixth and finally, the two sketches illustrate how the material, social, political, and mental worlds of average Japanese have changed over the past century and a half.

CHAPTER ONE

Preserving Autonomy, 1850–1889

JAPAN IN 1850

In 1850, a day in the life of a typical male head of household began early. Rising at 5:30 A.M., Tarō turned back the thin cotton quilt that covered him and crawled along the floor of his small room until he found the straw garment he used to keep the rain off and the cold out. Even in late summer, there was a chill in the mountain air. He threw the garment over his back to cover the tightly cinched cotton sash wrapped around his waist. In the cooking area beside the sleeping room, his wife had put out a bowl of gruel made from barley and rice. She had risen an hour before, and had already left for the mountainside to collect twigs for the fire and, if she was lucky, some mushrooms to sell to wealthier neighbors. Making short work of the gruel, Tarō grabbed a cone-shaped straw hat from the peg near the door and slipped on a pair of fraying straw sandals.

His main task for the day was to bundle together a load of reed mats and carry them to a nearby market town for sale. This year's rice crop had demanded the usual attention. Tarō and his wife had spent long days caring for the rice seedlings: transplanting them, controlling the water supply to the fields, weeding between the rows, and keeping pests away. Now that the crop was maturing, they had some spare time to cut and dry the reeds and shape and produce the mats that richer families used to cover the floors of their expensive houses. It would take Tarō most of the day to walk to and from the market and try to sell his mats. By the time he had bundled his load together, his wife had returned to care for the children and to continue her household tasks.

In their mid-thirties now, Tarō and his wife had only two children, a daughter aged ten and a son aged six. He regretted the loss of a second daughter, who had died in infancy from a severe cough made worse by malnutrition, and that of a third daughter. Hoping desperately for a boy, they had had the midwife dispose of her. They realized they could not afford to bring up a second girl on the scarce resources from their tiny holding plus a couple of rented parcels. Putting these thoughts aside and leaving his wife to feed, clothe, and oversee the children, Tarō departed.

Nestled in a valley several hundred feet above the plain below, Tarō's village was about ten miles from the market town. His trek today would carry him through numerous small villages like his, dotted among paddy fields still green with the maturing rice stalks. The market town served as a commercial center for these villages, providing a dazzling array of products brought in from elsewhere in the region and more distant parts. Sitting astride the Tōkaidō, a major land route connecting the shōgun's capital in the east with the imperial capital in the west, the town seemed a bustling mass of humanity that left Tarō both stimulated and exhausted.

Shops and stables, restaurants and inns, entertainment spots and drinking places all offered their own kind of stimulus. Even after he had sold his bundle of mats to a wholesaler in town, Tarō could never afford more than a bowl of noodles and a pot of tea at a dingy restaurant. But this did give him a chance to watch the wealthy landlords enjoy the offerings of other, more appealing establishments. It was even more exciting when a lord, making his biannual journey to the shōgun's capital, arrived in town with his retinue. The proud, jaunty samurai who traveled with him blustered about, commanding servants to stable their horses, find them rooms, provide their food, and generally entertain their needs. When they entered town, Tarō cowered at their domineering ways and marveled at the expensive silk garments they wore. Surely, he thought, men of such deportment and fortune deserved the powers that society bestowed on them.

Nonetheless, Tarō also wondered sometimes whether the lord and his companions overstepped their bounds. More than once he had been startled to see heads doused in saltwater standing on the ends of large pikes at the main entrance to the market. He realized that it was necessary to keep thieves in check. But sometimes the heads were those of hardworking peasants who had merely gathered to protest their heavy taxes during hard years. Tarō was not sure that such harsh punishment was really necessary. Nor was he sure that a few sword-bearing samurai should be the ones to make that judgment. But for him there was no value in such speculation, and he got up from his seat at the restaurant to begin his return journey. The jangle of humanity and the bustle of the town, along with the perplexing problems it posed in his mind, had already tired him out.

Tarō took another path out of town to vary the landscape of his return. Before long he had arrived at the high walls of a wealthy landlord's estate and soon entered a thriving village. On the right and left he passed large sheds, each with a score of young women sitting at looms and weaving cotton cloth. He had heard of the wealthy landlords who could afford to build sheds, buy cotton, pay workers, and reap profits from such ventures. The large mansion and the stone warehouses in the compound he had just passed confirmed the prosperity that such industry produced. In his own modest way, Tarō, too, was industrious, but it seemed that no amount of industry would bring him within reach of men like the landlord in this village.

With the sun now falling, Tarō remembered what he still had to do. Tomorrow one of the major annual festivals in his village would begin, and he had promised both the village headman and the local priest to help with the preparations at the shrine site. He also realized that today's arduous trek had not brought him much money, because he would give most of what he had earned from the sale of his mats as a contribution to the shrine. Such contributions made it difficult for him to get ahead, but he took satisfaction in knowing that his money and assistance were buying goodwill from the headman, the priest, and other villagers. For him and his family, this was valuable compensation in its own right, because it reaffirmed the cooperation and community on which their survival depended.

Tarō finished sooner than expected at the shrine and rushed to get home. He knew that his wife and children would be waiting expectantly, because he often bought fresh fish from a vendor in the market town. Tonight they would enjoy a special dinner with this rare addition to their usual diet of mixed rice and barley, pickled vegetables, and tea.

His wife eagerly accepted the fish and started to grill it on their small brazier. While Tarō played with his son, the daughter struggled with her work nearby. Her mother was teaching her to spin cotton, a skill that would enhance her marriage prospects and also make some money for the family. In addition, the task would keep the daughter busy. Her grandmother had died recently, and she was still recovering from the loss. She had never known her other grandmother or her grandfathers because like so many elders in the village, they had died in their forties before she was born. But she had been close to Tarō's mother, and Tarō and his wife thought that the spinning would be useful as a distraction.

By the time the family had finished dinner, the sun had set. Tarō wished he could read the children a bedtime story, but neither he nor his wife had had any formal education, and he was not a good storyteller. His wife was, however. She told yet again a folktale about a young salt maker who, through hard work, had become rich. His wife then tucked the children under their thin cotton quilt beside the padded mat on which she and Tarō slept. The long day ended as they fell asleep thinking about tomorrow's festivities.

Our perspective on Japan in 1850 changes when we turn from the microscopic niche that Tarō occupied to a macroscopic view of Japanese society as a whole. In formal terms, Japan was an authoritarian, martial society that still maintained some of the trappings of an aristocratic and monarchical state. In informal terms, it was a society in which the industrious and enterprising habits of merchants and farmers were finding a larger place. It was also a society in which the acquisitive and hedonistic activities of city dwellers formed an awkward counterpoint to the austere stability that ruling groups sought to preserve.

The formal features of Japan in 1850 were the enduring product of a political and military settlement gradually reached in the late 1500s and the early 1600s. Before this time, hundreds of regional military forces had fought one another to acquire control of land and human resources. Those battles began in the 1400s and continued into the 1500s. In the late 1500s two warriors in succession raised large armies that gave them even greater powers over their peers. Gradually they formed alliances; the fighting subsided, and peace emerged. In 1603 a third warrior family, a kind of successor to the previous two, accepted the title of *shōgun*. Thereafter, until the shōgunate resigned its powers in 1867, it occupied the paramount political position in Japan.

The shōgun all were successive heads of a military house known as the Tokugawa. Throughout the Tokugawa era (1600–1868), this family directly governed one-fourth of the productive agricultural land in Japan, commanded the largest military force, conducted Japan's external relations, and shaped its political and legal practices. Through its house government, the Tokugawa family ruled from a castle in the city of Edo (known after 1868 as Tōkyō) in eastern Japan.

Even though the Tokugawa house enjoyed many powers and privileges, it was not the ruler of a centralized, unitary state, for Japan was a highly fragmented political entity during the Tokugawa era. The Tokugawa house actually shared power with some 260 lesser military lords known as *daimyō*. Each daimyō functioned within his own domain as an autonomous lord, maintaining his own army, levying his own taxes, and making and executing his own laws. These lesser lords together controlled the remaining three-fourths of Japan's agricultural land, over which the shōgun in Edo had virtually no direct political, legal, or financial authority.

In 1850 Japan thus had developed a partly centralized political system. Although the Tokugawa house was the preeminent power in the land, it shared power with many other, lesser lords, some of whom were related by blood to the Tokugawa house and had been loyal allies for more than two centuries. A second group had been long-standing allies as well, and the Tokugawa house relied on their support to deter threats to its power from the remaining third group among the daimyō. This third group consisted of lords who had not sworn fealty to the Tokugawa until after 1600. The main daimyō in this group had domains in far western Japan that were referred to as the "outer domains." The reliability of these outer domains was always suspect, however, given their location and history. Events in the 1860s confirmed their unreliability, but in 1850 this carefully balanced system of shared power still endured largely unchanged after more than two centuries.

A group of warriors known as *samurai* assisted both the shōgun and the daimyō in the conduct of their administrative and military affairs. The term *samurai* had first appeared several centuries earlier in reference to warriors in the service of a lord. During the Tokugawa era, the position of samurai became hereditary, with fathers passing on the title to their eldest sons. Samurai were identified by the two swords they carried, one long and one short. They actually fulfilled a variety of roles, serving not just as warriors and administrators but also as physicians, educators, poets, financial officers, and trading agents. In formal terms, this group had the third highest status in the country after the even higher-ranking daimyō and shōgun. In nearly every domain, the samurai had to live in dwellings situated in the lord's castle town and thus they formed a landless, military aristocracy. Together with their dependents, they made up about 6 percent of Japan's total population.

The lingering features of an aristocratic and monarchical state persisted in 1850 in the form of an imperial court in the ancient capital of Kyōto, located in west central Japan. Since the last decade of the 700s, Kyōto had been the residence of the emperor and a hereditary court aristocracy, although between the 700s and the late 1500s, the powers of the throne waxed and waned. Other groups, especially military houses, often usurped the real powers of the throne, but none had ever dared to try to eliminate the imperial institution itself. This remained the case under the Tokugawa. In theory and in ritual practice, the emperor conferred the title of shōgun on the head of the Tokugawa house. In reality, however, the imperial house acted at the behest of the Tokugawa because it played no real role in the affairs of state, had no army of its own, had no sources of income (except what the Tokugawa gave it), and performed only ceremonial functions. Consequently, the Tokugawa political system functioned as a dual sovereignty in which the Tokugawa house or shōgun exercised real political, military, and diplomatic power and the imperial house in Kyōto exercised only ritual and symbolic authority.

The society over which these political groups wielded their influence was formally divided into a rural mass and an urban populace. Landless tenants, peasants, and more prosperous farmers living in small farming villages comprised 80 to 85 percent of the country's total population and derived their income largely from the land. Rice and other cereal grains, often grown in irrigated paddy fields, were the main commodities in the economy and the staples of the Japanese diet. By law, villagers had to reside permanently in their settlements and could travel beyond the village only with written permission from a headman.

Commoners inhabiting the towns and cities were known as *chōnin*. They were expected to reside permanently in designated urban areas and were not allowed to travel through the countryside, except with written permission. Most *chōnin* were merchants or artisans who produced goods—such as housewares, clothing, and processed foods—for the consumer market. They then sold these goods to urban consumers, who were either other *chōnin* like themselves or warrior families residing in castle towns. *Chōnin* made up barely 10 percent of the total population in 1850, and most of them resided in the largest cities of Edo, Kyōto, and Ōsaka or in the many castle towns.

The other unusual feature of Japanese society in 1850 was that it was almost entirely closed off from the outside world. Since the 1630s, the shōgun had successfully kept foreigners away from residence in Japan or encroachment on Japanese soil, with two exceptions. A score of Dutch merchants and a few thousand Chinese merchants were allowed to live in a special district in the city of Nagasaki (in far western Japan) where they were licensed to carry on a small-scale and closely monitored international trade. Otherwise, the shōgun had largely managed to repel the inflow of goods, people, and ideas from the outside and virtually to eliminate the exit of people and goods from Japan.

Viewed in this way, Japanese society in 1850 fit into a kind of straitjacket that appeared to impede change and foster stability. A large body of military figures kept in check a much larger mass of commoners who seemed content to accept their stations in life while an archaic monarchy and aristocracy languished in Kyōto.

Such stability was deceptive, however, and the formal character of Japanese society actually masked a great deal of informal change taking place beneath the surface. Change affected nearly every group in Japan. The Tokugawa house continually overspent its revenues and so was gradually wearing out its welcome. The daimyō also tended to overspend, forcing them both to increase their taxes and to reduce some of their outlays. The higher taxes rankled the peasantry and provoked protest movements, and the cuts in outlays lowered the samurai's incomes and alienated them. This in turn caused them to question the wisdom of hereditary rule and the financial notions of their lords.

In the large cities a culture of industry and enterprise was emerging. Spurred by prosperous merchants, this culture was premised on the expansion of commercial and economic activity, and it nurtured an acquisitive consumer culture that was gradually reaching more deeply into Japanese society. The same culture also underwrote the hedonistic commoner behavior that flourished in the entertainment quarters of the largest cities.

The spirit of enterprise and industry also extended to the rural areas. Wealthy farmers were especially susceptible to the inducements and examples of urban merchants, and they began investing in protoindustrial ventures, pawn broking, and regional commerce. As the wealthy farmers took the lead in promoting economic development, more peasants and landless tenants were drawn into an economy oriented toward markets for both raw and processed agricultural goods. By the 1800s, the rural population everywhere was engaged in the part-time employments created by this expanding, cash-based, market activity.

By 1850 even the seclusion on which the system of Tokugawa political rule was based found itself at risk. For decades, certain groups operating through the island of Tsushima in far western Japan had carried on a thriving informal commerce with Korea and the Asian continent. Well-informed observers in Edo and key castle towns understood that foreign powers were encroaching on Chinese sovereignty and that they posed a potential threat to Japanese sovereignty as well. These same people also worried about the activities of Russian representatives who had been interested in northern Japan for several decades. With more foreign commercial ships sailing near Japanese waters all the time, the prospect for continued seclusion seemed dim. But in 1850, just what the future held still remained unclear.

POLITICAL REVOLUTION

Foreign crises occurring amid domestic turbulence finally led to a revolution in 1868. Known as the Meiji Restoration, this long-term political renovation produced sweeping changes throughout Japan. Revolutionary leaders drawn from the old samurai class seized power at the center, sweeping aside the shōgun and then eliminating the daimyō and their domains. They created new structures of political authority that laid the foundations for a modern, centralized nation-state. Their anxiousness and diligence to keep the foreign powers at bay were for the sake of the nation and the emperor, a young man who ascended the throne as a teenager in 1867, his princely demeanor distinguishing the next forty-five years of Japan's history.

Left to their own devices, the informal changes occurring beneath the surface in late Tokugawa Japan might eventually have produced a significant transformation. But the importance of domestic change was dramatically heightened in the 1850s when foreign powers from North America and western Europe began to impose their will on Japan. The leading authority on the collapse of the Tokugawa house observed that "radical escalation in foreign aggressiveness extracted commensurate concessions from Edo and set in motion political, sociocultural, and ecological changes that are still unfolding a century and a half later."[1]

Commodore Matthew Calbraith Perry of the United States Navy was the symbol of this foreign pressure, owing to his insistence in 1853 that the Japanese government sign a treaty on his return visit in 1854. Faced with Perry's political pressure and confronted with evidence of his superior military technology, representatives of the shōgun knuckled under. They grudgingly agreed to allow an American representative to reside on Japanese soil while a commercial treaty was negotiated. Townsend Harris, a patrician Yankee down on his luck, arrived in 1856 to fill this position. Two years later shōgunal representatives concluded the Treaty of Amity and Commerce with the United States.

The provisions of the treaty were few but significant. Japan would henceforth allow the United States to conduct trade and harbor vessels in six ports, three of which had already been open to American commerce for four years. They were Nagasaki, Shimoda (a small fishing village southwest of Edo), and Hakodate (a castle town situated on the southern tip of Hokkaidō). The three new ports were Niigata (on the coast of western Japan), Kobe (at the head of the Inland Sea near Kyōto), and Yokohama (then only a small village south of Edo). In addition, the United States would be allowed to trade with Japan in accordance with the low tariffs set by the treaty. Finally, the United States won the right to extraterritoriality. A common provision in treaties of the nineteenth century, extraterritoriality ensured that foreign nationals residing—in this case, on Japanese soil—would be subject to the laws of their own land, not Japan's. In the next few years, several European powers, including Great

Britain and France, signed similar treaties with Japan. For the first time in more than two centuries, Japan had begun diplomatic and commercial intercourse with Europe and America.

Almost immediately, the treaties created a storm of protest in Japan. Initially, domestic groups vented their opposition in isolated incidents, including attacks by individuals or small numbers of samurai on foreigners and representatives of the shōgun. For example, Ii Naosuke, a high-ranking shōgunal official who had signed the 1858 treaty, was assassinated in 1860. Gradually, however, the opposition broadened. More and more samurai began to cut their ties to their home domains and to gather together in guerrilla-like bands, often in the Kyōto area. During the early 1860s, some of these groups tried to foment uprisings in the countryside by calling the peasantry to arms. But they never succeeded, and they always faced death or imprisonment when captured by the shōgun's forces or allies of the Tokugawa.

More ominous were the other political disturbances. Sometimes these were fairly inconsequential actions that merely taunted authorities and had no well-defined political objectives. **Ee ja nai ka²** movements were typical. These movements would occur when drunken revelers at city festivals or on religious pilgrimages in the countryside would misbehave en masse, chide the authorities, and resist crowd control. Other popular disturbances had more significant implications. Increasingly after 1850, poor peasants in rural areas would band together against rich farmers and attack their property. These **uchikowashi**, or "trashings," were symptomatic of the sense of malaise and unease among the agrarian populace that bespoke a lack of regard for authority more generally. The most threatening popular political activity consisted of **insurrections**, which brought together armed protesters in the thousands, drawn from all ranks of society—from samurai to priests to the poorest peasants. The insurrections often challenged authorities with armed violence and sometimes resulted in widespread unrest that crossed domain boundaries and implicitly challenged the very foundations of the political system.

Recognizing this widespread unease, talented, aggressive, and concerned samurai from domains in western Japan gathered for discussions in the mid-1860s aimed at creating an alliance to overthrow the Tokugawa house. Most of these men were only in their early thirties, though some already held important positions in their domain administrations, won through talent and achievement and not heredity. They were concerned about the country's political instability and even more concerned about the long-term consequences of Japan's opening to the West because they saw the shōgunate as weak and vacillating, unable to stem the foreign expansion. Regarding this as a threat to both Japan's political autonomy and its cultural integrity and rallying around the cry of "revere the emperor and expel the barbarian," they joined together to unify Japan under the banner of imperial rule.

The two key domains that formed the anti-Tokugawa alliance were Satsuma and Chōshū, both in far western Japan. Their leaders were **Ōkubo Toshimichi** and **Saigō Takamori** from Satsuma and **Kido Kōin** from Chōshū. In promoting their cause, the leaders of the Satsuma-Chōshū coalition sought support from the court in Kyōto. **Iwakura Tomomi**, a young aristocrat deeply opposed to the 1858 treaty, joined them. He provided an essential link with the emperor, his advisers, and court aristocrats whose support would be needed when restoring imperial government.

Tensions rose steadily after 1866 between the shōgun and his emerging opposition. Satsuma and Chōshū used their domain treasuries to purchase guns from British sources; the shōgun relied on an alliance with France to improve his military position. On both sides, new armies were raised that relied on members of the samurai class for leadership and also, for the first time in centuries, recruited commoners into the lower ranks. A series of military skirmishes took place as both sides vied for superiority, especially in the area around Kyōto in west central Japan.

Given the magnitude of the changes it wrought, the Meiji Restoration seemed at first to be relatively quick and conflict free. In 1867, when the tide turned against the shōgun and his forces, he chose to step down rather than invite broader conflict. The last Tokugawa shōgun resigned in October 1867, and in early January 1868, leaders from Satsuma and Chōshū proclaimed the Restoration—that is, the emperor's official return to his position of supreme authority. Later that month, military forces still loyal to the shōgun protested this change by engaging in battle a combined Satsuma-Chōshū force at Toba-Fushimi near Kyōto. The Satsuma-Chōshū forces quickly prevailed, thereby quashing the greatest military threat to their takeover of political rule. Other small forces loyal to the shōgun continued to fight a rearguard action in parts of eastern and northeastern Japan for another year, but they, too, were eventually suppressed. In a matter of months, therefore, the core of the Tokugawa political system had been removed and a new imperial government had been established in its place under the control of young samurai from the outer domains.

Because these new leaders had no fixed plan for rule when they won power, the following years were dominated by frequent experiment and change. The new government made one of its first public pronouncements in April 1868 when the emperor announced the Meiji Five-Article Oath (see under Documents in part IV). This purposely vague declaration alluded to the prospects for more representative forms of government but did not specify what these would be. Already, two things were becoming clear. First, the emperor would be reigning as a public symbol of authority but would not be ruling in his own right. Second, the young samurai who had participated in the Restoration would be controlling the emperor and making the political decisions.

Consequently, the sweeping political reforms taking place between 1868 and 1889 were essentially imposed on Japan by an oligarchy unchecked by representative political institutions and operating largely free from the constraints of public opinion. Under such circumstances, the oligarchs could have used their power and position to enrich themselves and their families. Indeed, some Japanese political leaders in the late nineteenth century did become wealthy men, but many others died virtually penniless. Nearly all of them, though, resisted the lure of personal wealth in order to do what they thought best for the nation as a whole. This often meant restricting freedoms and liberties, and the oligarchs' methods were sometimes harsh and authoritarian. Many of them detested opposition and compromise and fought tenaciously to retain power. But by the time they had passed from the scene, these new leaders had left Japan with a political and legal system that compared favorably with that of Germany, if not with those of Great Britain and France.

One of the Meiji government's first tasks was to dismantle the old order, which it did in gradual steps over a decade. In 1869 the new government prevailed on the daimyō to cede it their domains and authority. Two years later the government began to abolish the former domains and to reorganize the nation into new administrative units called *prefectures*. Along with these changes, the new government conducted a land survey that uncovered sizable pieces of untaxed land, registered all cultivated land for tax and legal purposes, and laid the foundation for the new state's revenue base.

The government initially paid stipends to most of the former samurai, but it soon found this a heavy financial burden. In the early 1870s, therefore, it began cutting off its support of the samurai, leading to the impoverishment of numerous members of the old ruling class. Finally, in 1876 the government ended all stipends to former samurai but cushioned the blow by offering them a one-time payment in the form of government bonds. Some samurai invested the bonds wisely in the new banks created for the purpose, but others quickly spent their rewards. In the following year, 1877, a large contingent of unhappy, former samurai gathered in Kyūshū in southern Japan to stage an armed rebellion against the new state, whereupon the government dispatched its new army and ruthlessly suppressed the rebels. Thereafter, the Meiji government encountered no armed resistance from its own citizens.

The years 1877 and 1878 marked a critical turning point in the government's leadership. One of the three samurai leaders of the Restoration, Saigō Takamori, lost his life in the rebellion, opposing the government he had once helped create. In the same year, Kido Kōin died of physical debilities, and in 1878 Ōkubo Toshimichi was assassinated by a disgruntled former samurai. New men, slightly younger than these three, now entered the government. They also were former samurai and had been close lieutenants of their predecessors. Several, including **Itō Hirobumi**, **Yamagata Aritomo**, and **Inoue Kaoru**, hailed from Chōshū. Others, such as **Matsukata Masayoshi**, came from Satsuma. And one, **Ōkuma Shigenobu**, came from the former domain of Hizen. These men assumed the more constructive duties of creating the new institutions of the Meiji state.

While still in his twenties, Yamagata Aritomo had assisted in forming the mixed samurai-peasant armies in the Chōshū domain that ultimately prevailed over shogunal forces in the battles of the Restoration. After the Restoration he was a leader in organizing a modern army. Alert to developments in Europe at the time, he adopted features of French training and German organization. In 1877 his new army faced and passed its first test when it prevailed over the samurai rebels in Kyūshū. In the following years he established army academies to train an officer corps, expanded a standing force that quickly became the most proficient in Asia, and, on behalf of the army, competed for resources and power in struggles at the center of government.

During this period, lacking abundant military resources, possessing a tiny industrial base, and facing many demands at home, the Meiji leaders limited Japan's foreign adventures. In 1874 the government did send an expeditionary force to the island of Taiwan, ostensibly to retaliate against locals who had attacked Japanese nationals. This was essentially a saber-rattling exercise that sent notice to China, Britain, and France that if necessary, Japan would use force to deal with diplomatic controversies in Asia. Five years later, in 1879, the Japanese government arbitrarily seized control of the Ryūkyū Islands (south of Kyūshū) and incorporated them into the new state as the prefecture of Okinawa. The government of China—which also claimed the islands—protested then and later, but to little avail. In 1895 China finally conceded the loss of the islands in the settlement ending the Sino-Japanese War.

Japan's domestic matters, however, demanded even greater attention during this time. Yamagata Aritomo took an interest in local government, and during the 1880s he played a leading role in instituting a new system of sub-national administration. After the former 260-odd domains were abolished, the country was divided into prefectures, which initially numbered just over forty. The prefectures were viewed as agents of national government, and their governors were national civil servants appointed while serving in the Ministry of Home Affairs. Accordingly, the prefectures—and also the cities, towns, and villages—had little political autonomy. Although high-status male residents were allowed to elect executives and small councils, in both the municipalities and the prefectures, mayors and councilmen were answerable to the national government.

Itō Hirobumi concentrated on the structure of the state and its constitution. Since the 1870s the leadership felt the necessity of drawing up a constitution that created representative bodies. Some of this pressure came from domestic opponents of the Meiji leaders. Acting through the loose, shifting coalition of parties known as the **Freedom and People's Rights Movement**, these governmental outsiders called for more representative institutions. Foreign powers also wanted Japan to put in place a "modern" legal and political system before they renegotiated their treaties and renounced their claims of extraterritoriality.

Throughout the 1880s, therefore, Itō devoted considerable attention to creating a constitution. He traveled to Europe to consult with legal authorities in person and to examine constitutional systems in practice and ended up adopting the views of Austrian legal theorists and German constitutional practitioners. As the basis for the new constitution, Itō helped create a new peerage (or nobility) in 1884, introduced a system of cabinet government in 1885, and instituted the Privy Council (high-ranking advisers to the emperor) in 1888. With these preliminaries completed, Itō had the emperor promulgate the Meiji Constitution on February 11, 1889, the mythic anniversary of the founding of the first imperial dynasty.

The Meiji Constitution (see under Documents in part IV) concentrated in the hands of the emperor the executive, legislative, diplomatic, and military powers of state. Because the emperor was the head of state, he would accept the proceedings of the legislature as merely advisory; he alone could declare war and sign treaties; and he was the commander in chief of the armed forces. In theory, at any rate, his powers were supreme, but in practice, they were not. The former samurai who really controlled the reins of power consistently pushed the emperor into the background, where he exercised only symbolic authority and some powers of coordination and persuasion. By controlling the prime ministership and all cabinet posts and excluding the emperor from cabinet meetings, these former samurai served effectively as leaders of state. Although they disagreed about the roles and powers of the legislature, they were generally content to limit its authority. They also managed the nation's diplomatic affairs by keeping the emperor at arm's length when wars were declared and fought and when treaties were negotiated. Furthermore, the leaders of the army and navy guaranteed that they, not the emperor, would determine strategic plans and battle operations.

The Meiji oligarchs used the emperor adroitly as a public, ceremonial figure to back up their power, and they carefully exploited the "imperial will" (the often secret approval of the emperor) to reinforce their policies. In this way, the Meiji Constitution—despite the appearance it conveyed of concentrated power—actually created a political system in which authority was diffused among many formal groups, including cabinet members, legislators, military figures, privy councillors, and, as time wore on, others, too. This set the scene for constant political contention after 1889, as we will see in the next two chapters.

ECONOMIC RENOVATION

The Japanese phrase *fukoku kyōhei*, meaning "enrich the nation and strengthen the military," summarizes the primary aims of the Meiji government. We have already seen how Yamagata Aritomo achieved one part of these objectives by creating a modern army. At the same time his associates from Satsuma were creating a modern navy. Other government leaders took up the task of enriching the nation, by adopting a range of policies that built on a broad foundation for economic growth already in place by the late Tokugawa period. These government policies shaped economic developments between 1868 and 1889, but the contributions of business leaders from the private sector were equally important.

Many legacies from the Tokugawa era provided a basis for more rapid developments in the Meiji period: a spirit of enterprise, widespread entrepreneurship, commercial institutions, trading networks, capital savings, some protoindustrial enterprises, financial mechanisms, and a responsive labor force.

The spirit of enterprise was evident throughout Japanese society long before 1868, identified by an eagerness to pursue economic gain, an ambition to explore new economic opportunities, and a willingness to work long and hard to achieve one's objectives. Merchants in large cities demonstrated this spirit of enterprise by spotting new commodities in demand, encouraging producers to make them, and developing markets in which to sell them. Wealthy farmers in rural areas displayed the spirit of enterprise when they used their profits from agricultural endeavors to purchase more land; to build warehouses, weaving sheds, and sake breweries; and to develop commercial enterprises in rural districts. Even the poorest tenant farmers showed a spirit of enterprise by maximizing the returns from their small, intensively farmed plots of land and using their spare time and labor to produce other goods for the market, such as the mats that Tarō wove.

Entrepreneurship appeared when such persons took risks to enter new business ventures. Urban merchants were never sure that a new commodity would actually appeal to consumers, so they were taking risks in finding producers and developing marketing networks to bring such commodities to cities for sale. Rural farmers took risks to build sake breweries and warehouses, because they could never be sure that they would find skilled laborers to staff the breweries or adequate rice supplies to fill the warehouses. Even the tenant farmers weaving reed mats took risks because they were never assured an adequate return on the time and labor they invested. Although some aspects of the legal and political setting inhibited economic activities during the Tokugawa era, the spirit of enterprise and widespread evidence of entrepreneurship emerged nevertheless. In addition, the Meiji state not only removed many of these obstacles to commerce, but it also encouraged such positive attitudes and behavior.

Commercial institutions and trading networks were two by-products of entrepreneurship during the Tokugawa era. The largest cities of Edo, Kyōto, and Ōsaka had witnessed the emergence of large merchant houses as early as the 1600s, one of the most famous of which was the **Mitsui enterprise**. It had originated as a firm selling used clothing and later sold new clothing through shops in Kyōto and Edo that were precursors to modern department stores. Even later, but well before the Restoration, the Mitsui enterprise developed money exchange and financial services capabilities. Mitsui was only one of thousands of commercially successful merchant establishments that lined the streets of the big cities and the major castle towns long before 1868. These shops were in turn dependent on intricate domestic trade networks that radiated from the major cities into production regions throughout Japan. These networks carried demand signals and organizational inducements to rural producers and brought finished goods back to the cities.

During the Tokugawa period, capital for investment purposes accumulated in the hands of prosperous urban merchants and wealthy rural farmers, and even in the face of arbitrary exactions by political authorities and high volatility in regional markets, some business establishments and households were able to increase their wealth. Many of them put their capital to good use well before 1868, expanding it even further. Others preserved their capital and found even more lucrative outlets for it in the more friendly economic environment that followed the Restoration.

Protoindustrial enterprises were one form of investment that attracted the capital of wealthy farmers. Common among these were sake breweries and weaving sheds, small enterprises employing a labor force of perhaps twenty to forty men or women. They were located in rural villages, often at some distance from major urban centers, and they used only manually operated, not mechanically driven, equipment. As in Europe in the eighteenth and early nineteenth centuries, small manufacturing establishments like these signaled the arrival of broader production capabilities and wider consumer markets.

Credit facilities and financial services were essential even to a premodern agrarian economy. During the Tokugawa era Japan developed sophisticated mechanisms for extending credit, whether it went to the poorest tenant in a remote village or a large merchant house in a major city. In this way, people developed a feeling of trust, which is essential to meeting contractual obligations in a commercial and industrial society. Moreover, many individuals and business firms possessed the skills necessary to make complex financial transactions and ensure that they were carried out accurately and faithfully. In this area, too, the Meiji state was able to enhance and expand its legacies from the Tokugawa era.

A final gift of the pre-Meiji economy was a large labor force that was responsive to economic inducements. Most of this labor force resided in rural villages and included both men and women. Both sexes had proved to be highly responsive to economic opportunity in rural districts, by engaging in a wide range of farm side employments and also by moving easily to new sites of production (such as sake breweries and weaving sheds) when there were job openings. This mobile, responsive, and diligent labor force was an invaluable asset when factory-based manufacturing expanded in the 1880s and afterward. Indeed, according to one scholar, "Japan's human capital and the ability to use resources economically may have constituted more of the 'secret' [to its economic success] than technology and other factors on which economic historians focus their attention."[3]

Despite the many assets already available to the Japanese economy, this summary of the Tokugawa legacies reveals some deficiencies as well. Transportation facilities, for example, were ill suited to a modern industrial economy, as much rural trade was still carried on horseback or by men on foot. Wheeled vehicles were rare, and there was no railway system in 1868. Although the maritime commerce on the coast was thriving, Japan had no oceangoing commercial fleet. Nor did it have a steam-driven, mechanical industrial complex. Moreover, it had a limited resource base in raw materials and virtually no institutions for the conduct of international trade. Finally, before 1868 the Japanese economy did not have a single public authority capable of coordinating the nation's economic activities and promoting its policies of growth. Thus the Meiji state devoted much time and effort to rectifying just these deficiencies, through a complex mix of policies that shifted over time.

These policies emerged through collective discussions among the various leaders of the Meiji state, and they were implemented through ministries of the central government. One of the most important of these was the **Ministry of Finance**. Originally established in 1869, the Finance Ministry was given broad authority to raise revenues, devise national budgets, make expenditures, and supervise and regulate financial institutions. The Ministry of Home Affairs also played a role in carrying out national economic policy, overseeing the funding and construction of public works. Finally, the Ministries of the Army and Navy promoted industrial production through their management of military arsenals and naval shipyards.

Developing a modern system of transportation and communication was a high priority for the Meiji state. The national government used its own resources to construct major trunk lines connecting the new capital of Tōkyō with major cities in western and northeastern Japan. It also stimulated private interests to build shorter branch lines that provided intra- and intercity traffic for both goods and people, and by 1889 almost two thousand miles of track were in operation. The government also fostered the development of an oceangoing merchant marine, though more through subsidies and favoritism than through direct investment. It did this by selling, at deep discounts, once government-owned ships to private parties and by granting monopoly rights to favored firms for mail traffic along key routes. The national government also took the lead in instituting in the 1870s a modern postal system and a nationwide telegraph system.

The Meiji state improved the quality of the existing financial institutions by creating a modern banking system. The Daiichi Bank (1873), the Mitsui Bank (1876), and the Yasuda Bank (1879) were three of the earliest and most important of the national banks chartered under the new system. The government also underwrote some of the capital costs of the Yokohama Specie Bank when it was established in 1880 to serve as the country's principal bank for foreign exchange. In 1882 the government also created and financed a new central bank, the Bank of Japan, which became the bank of currency issue and the major depository for government tax funds, operating under the close supervision of the Ministry of Finance.

The Meiji government also promoted economic development through the direct ownership and management of industrial enterprises, hoping that this would form the basis for a modern industrial economy. One of the first examples of this economic policy was the Tomioka Silk Mill, which was opened in 1872 to demonstrate how to spin and weave silk using the latest equipment imported from abroad. Other factories followed, making glass, cement, and bricks; spinning cotton; and brewing beer. The government also opened coal mines at numerous locations, especially on the islands of Hokkaidō and Kyūshū, and the state assumed the management of a shipyard located in Nagasaki.

The foregoing ventures in transportation, finance, and manufacturing denoted a policy approach that was active, promotional, and participatory. The central government identified sectors to develop and often participated directly through financing or management or both. In some cases, especially transportation and finance, these policies worked reasonably well, but in manufacturing, they did not. Often there were no markets for the products of these factories, and they quickly encountered financial problems that became a burden for the government, which was soon forced to reexamine its policies. By the early 1880s, therefore, the state embarked on a new approach to industrial development that reversed its former position and foreshadowed a different relationship between the state and the private sector.

During the 1870s, in its eagerness to promote economic change, the government overextended its capacities. It spent more than it brought in, making up the difference either through borrowing (occasionally abroad) or by printing money. These policies, however, led to high rates of inflation that threatened to cause widespread economic distress. Gradually in the early 1880s, the minister of finance, **Matsukata Masayoshi**, adopted deflationary policies aimed at cutting inflation, reducing the amount of currency in circulation, and paying off government debt.

One important element of Matsukata's policies was the sale of government enterprises. Between 1884 and 1889, the government sold twenty-three coal mines, shipyards, factories, textile mills, and other industrial enterprises to private parties. A few of these enterprises were sold at considerable profit to the government, but in most cases, the private parties were able to buy them on generous terms at prices far below their original cost. As a result, the government's actions had the effect of subsidizing what today would be called *start-up costs* for favored parties in the private sector.

The list of private parties that benefited from these sales eventually read like a "who's who" of Japanese big business. Many of the coal mines and a major shipyard in Nagasaki were purchased by the **Mitsubishi enterprise**, then operating under the leadership of **Iwasaki Yatarō**. For decades, the former government-owned mines served as the financial lifeblood of the Mitsubishi group, and the shipyard made it one of the country's most important manufacturers. **Ōkura Kihachirō** bought the Sapporo brewery from the government during this period and added it to his growing commercial empire. Furukawa Ichibei bought a number of mines central to the development of his industrial conglomerate, and Kawazaki Shōzō purchased a shipyard that laid the foundation for **Kawasaki Heavy Industries**, one of the oldest and largest manufacturing combines in modern Japan.

By selling these enterprises to private firms, the Japanese government largely withdrew from the direct ownership and management of manufacturing enterprises. It did retain control of the military arsenals and naval shipyards, however, and it later owned and managed a major steel mill. But in nearly every other respect, the government adopted a new strategic approach to economic development that gave considerable initiative to the private sector while reserving for the national government the roles of guide, facilitator, and provider of infrastructure. Subsequently, the government and private industry—for the most part—worked in tandem to enrich the nation.

Fortunately for Japan, the country had plenty of private entrepreneurs who responded enthusiastically to these opportunities. Some of them were long-standing merchant houses, such as the Mitsui enterprise, which expanded during this period into banking, mining, textile making, and international trade. Another long-standing business firm, the **Sumitomo enterprise**, took advantage of its historic expertise in copper smelting to begin development as a major metals manufacturer. But perhaps no single entrepreneur was more valuable to Japan during this time than **Shibusawa Eiichi**. For four decades after 1875, he used his position as head of the Daiichi Bank to serve as a kind of venture capitalist and promoter for hundreds of new enterprises. Joined by men such as Iwasaki, Yasuda, Furukawa, and Ōkura, Shibusawa created a nascent industrial economy that was soon competing with those of France, Germany, and Great Britain.

Private entrepreneurs were also the driving force behind rectifying one last deficiency of the late-Tokugawa economy, the lack of institutions engaging in international trade. Even before the Restoration, the Mitsui enterprise was learning how to purchase commodities on the domestic market and to sell them to foreign buyers in the new treaty ports. After the Restoration, it became obvious that Japan would have to develop expertise in purchasing commodities abroad for import into the country, with or without foreign-controlled treaty-port commerce. At Mitsui, **Masuda Takashi** took the lead in developing this expertise by organizing Mitsui bussan, the oldest comprehensive international trading firm (*sōgo shōsha*) in Japan. Such firms have historically handled domestic sales, imports, and exports while providing information and financing to their customers. Since the 1870s they have played a crucial role in Japan's evolution as an international economic power.

Economic change was pervasive during the first three decades following the Restoration, and economic renovation was widespread. Better transport and communication facilities, an improved banking system, and new institutions for production and trade were among the accomplishments of this era. These innovations increased trade, investment, and production, giving a boost to the heretofore tiny manufacturing and service sectors of the Japanese economy. In the still large agrarian sector, however, in which more than 70 percent of the Japanese workforce still toiled in 1889, the changes were mixed. The more rational land tax system introduced in the early 1870s lowered the real tax burden for many farmers, but the deflationary policies of the 1880s impoverished many tenants. Amid these contradictory tendencies, advanced agricultural practices were diffused more widely and helped greatly to increase overall production, by 1 to 2 percent per year. Therefore, Japan ended this period having achieved significant economic renovation but not yet dramatic economic growth.

SOCIAL LIBERATION

The Meiji Restoration was a political revolution that promoted widespread economic renovation and also brought a measure of social liberation to a populace that had been constrained in many ways during the Tokugawa era. The lifting of formal constraints did not immediately produce a radically different kind of society. Rather, the social changes occurring during the Meiji era were gradual and limited, especially with respect to status, standard of living, demography, family and community life, and gender. Education, however, was the one social arena in which the Meiji era did witness significant changes.

During the Tokugawa period, Japanese society had been divided into four strata for purposes of administration and control. The samurai, or the warrior class in general, occupied the highest stratum of society and enjoyed a wide range of social, political, and legal privileges. As we have seen, most samurai were required to live in castle towns and to serve their military masters in a variety of roles. Immediately below them in the ideal vision of society were the peasants, who were seen as the necessary and valued producers whose labors ensured prosperity. They were required to reside in rural areas and to confine their labors to farming. During the Tokugawa period, in many domains, peasants were told by domain authorities what they could grow and how and where they could sell their output. Although artisans were also valued as producers, they were too few in number to warrant the same esteem that society bestowed on the peasantry. At the bottom of the status hierarchy rested the merchants: in terms of orthodox Confucian values, they were regarded as social parasites living off the productive labor of others.

As we have also seen, changes were taking place well before the Restoration that undermined some of these formal distinctions. For example, many samurai were confronting difficult economic conditions, and a spirit of enterprise among the peasants was undermining constraints on their behavior and stimulating broader market-oriented activity. Additional large-scale artisanal establishments were emerging, often secretly in rural areas, and merchants were carving out a role for themselves that conflicted openly with the one prescribed by social orthodoxy.

A more realistic vision of Japanese society in the late Tokugawa period can be found in the socioeconomic status and material conditions of the existing groups. The shōgun and most of the larger daimyō constituted a thin stratum at the top of society. They and their dependents pursued lives of privilege and some ostentation: their mansions were large and well maintained; they dressed in the finest silk garments; they used lacquer serving ware decorated with gold; and they ate polished white rice, drank the best sake and tea, and enjoyed rare fruits and condiments. These were the people who administered and benefited from an authoritarian military regime devoted primarily to the extraction of resources—in contrast with the promotion of production.

Just below them in the socioeconomic hierarchy was a group consisting of smaller daimyō, high-ranking samurai in large domains, large merchants in the major cities, and rich farmers in the countryside. Surprisingly, in view of the opulence that has surrounded the imperial house since 1868, the emperor would have been an occupant of this socioeconomic stratum as well, because the stipend he received from the shōgun was equivalent to that of a high-ranking samurai. The people in this stratum of society also lived in some comfort. They did not have multiple residences, as did the largest military lords, but they usually lived in one large dwelling with many rooms staffed by domestic servants. They, too, wore fine silk garments, at least on formal occasions, and they probably had several changes of clothing for daily use. They may have eaten polished rice frequently, but they probably stretched it out by mixing it with other grains such as millet or barley. They did not enjoy the same easy access to prized fruits and condiments as the upper group did, but they could afford to indulge in such luxuries on special occasions. This stratum, together with the upper stratum and the dependents of both, probably constituted, at most, 15 percent of the Japanese population.

A family like Tarō's belonged to the middle stratum of society. Peasants residing in small villages made up most of this group, which may have encompassed another 30 to 40 percent of the people. It also included many middle- and lower-ranking samurai households, as well as artisan and merchant families in the cities and castle towns. People in this wide swath of Japanese society led simple, frugal lives in small, one-story, two-room wooden dwellings, uninsulated, unheated, and uncooled. Their homes had little furniture of any kind, and most of them had only one change of clothing—if that. The more widespread use of cotton provided many in this stratum with padded quilts to keep off the cold at night and with cotton garments that were comfortable to wear and easy to clean. Their diets were similar to those of Tarō's family: heavy on cereal grains, such as millet and barley and small amounts of rice, combined with pickled vegetables and tea. Fish and fresh fruits were rarities; meat and dairy products were virtually unknown. Their caloric intake was low, possibly as low as 1,700 calories per day. The peasants' body stature also was small, with most adult males barely five feet tall.

The rest of society lived in virtual poverty. This subgroup consisted of landless tenants in rural Japan, the lowest-ranking samurai, and people in the lower ranks of urban society: clerks, messengers, stable hands, domestics, prostitutes, gamblers, and others. They were lucky to find a small hut in the countryside or a tiny one-room rental in the cities. They scrambled from one day to the next just to put enough food on the table, and they had barely more than the clothes on their backs. Overworked, poorly nourished, and constantly subject to disease, families in this large segment of Japanese society endured high rates of mortality and the constant threat of demise.

Such poverty was one reason that families engaged in various forms of population control during the Tokugawa era. Husbands and wives may have exercised some prepartum controls, using herbal medicines to inhibit pregnancy or relying on the withdrawal method. But postpartum control in the form of infanticide seems to have been the most widely used method for restricting population growth. In this way a family would know the sex of an infant and be able to make decisions on that basis. Families often allowed boys to live while eliminating girls, though under some circumstances, girls were favored over boys. Moreover, it was not just poor families that used infanticide to control family size. Wealthy families used it to achieve an appropriate sex ratio among their offspring or to limit the overall size of a family. Middle-ranking families, too, made these calculations as they decided whether or not to allow an infant to survive.

As a consequence of practices like these, the total population of Japan between the early 1700s and the early 1800s remained almost stable at about 30 million people. The occasional famines, natural disasters, and epidemics resulted in large numbers of deaths in short periods of time. But Japan was free from the scourge of many European-style epidemics because its seclusion policies were so successful in keeping out Europeans—and their diseases. Thus, long-term population stability was the aggregate outcome of millions of family-level decisions made to keep lives and resources in some kind of balance, according to a ruthless calculus that combined considerations of poverty with those of survival and prosperity.

Japan's population in 1850 was spread across a variety of different kinds of communities. The three largest cities—Edo, Kyōto, and Ōsaka—may have housed about 2 million people among them. Each domain had a castle town where the population was dominated by samurai, merchants, artisans, and their dependents. Many smaller cities or large towns had developed around the ports, marketplaces, Buddhist temples, Shinto shrines, and post stations. And thousands of small rural villages dotted the landscape.

Every community in the land underwent divisions and conflicts—they were a product of status distinctions, income inequalities, personality differences, and other causes. But these same divided and conflicted communities also experienced widespread reciprocity, cooperation, and mutual aid. These social traits were necessary to ensure survival in large cities where urban residents had to provide their own sanitation services, road repair, and fire protection. The same traits were fostered in rural villages by forms of cooperative labor exchange, collective support of local festivals, and upkeep of irrigation works and public facilities. Thus, community life was a combination of conflict and cooperation, division and cohesion that usually was balanced by a slow-changing equilibrium.

Within such communities, whether rural or urban, most families were small and nuclear, normally consisting of a mother and father and one or two children. Wealthy families were often larger, with an extra child or two and one or two grandparents as well. This kind of stem family, consisting of members drawn from three generations, was held up as a social ideal, though economic and demographic realities prevented most families from realizing it. Life expectancy hovered around the high thirties to low forties during the late Tokugawa period, so many people failed—as Tarō's grandfather did—to live long enough to see their own grandchildren, even if they married early.

Within most families, males reigned supreme, especially in samurai households. Females were reared to serve males, and they were expected to manage domestic affairs while the husband earned his stipend by serving his lord. In merchant, artisan, and farm households, however, women had greater responsibilities. They dealt with customers, oversaw household staffs, and kept business accounts in urban shops. In rural areas women shared heavy farm chores with their husbands while managing the household and rearing the children. In households like these, out of necessity men and women had to work with a greater sense of partnership, which may have earned women greater respect and given them a bit more power. But pervasive patriarchal norms still operated in this essentially martial society, relegating most women to a clearly subordinate position.

Female inequality was underscored by the way in which educational opportunities were distributed. At the end of the Tokugawa period, as many as half the men may have possessed some measure of literacy, whereas barely 15 percent of women did. Most of the literate women were from the samurai class or the upper reaches of the merchant and wealthy farmer groups, in which they received some formal education. But most women simply were not given any formal education at all, nor were most men. Those men who did acquire formal training came from the upper reaches of society: daimyō and samurai households, wealthy merchant and artisanal homes, and families in the upper ranks of rural society. Samurai often were educated in domain schools established by daimyō in order to train their administrators. Others acquired their learning in "temple schools," private schools often situated in a Buddhist temple where the instructor might be a Buddhist priest, a samurai, or an independent educator. A very small number of select and privileged individuals, usually samurai, were able to acquire some advanced training at private academies in the large cities of Edo, Kyōto, and Ōsaka. Thus, before the Restoration, formal education was a haphazard process, often obtained through privilege and good fortune in a diverse body of institutions that met the educational needs of only a small part of society.

In the wake of the Restoration, three government policies changed some of these social conditions. One policy was the abolition of the old system of four classes in 1872. A second was the pensioning off of the samurai in 1876. And

the third was the creation of a nationwide system of public education beginning in the early 1870s.

Abolishing the old class system opened Japanese society to a wide range of
opportunities and encouraged both geographic and occupational mobility.
Tokugawa society had ascribed status to individuals, especially males, by making one's rank in society and one's occupation hereditary. Sons of samurai had
to be samurai; sons of farmers, farmers; and so on. But after the Meiji Restoration, men and women were free to leave their father's abode and to choose
their occupational calling. At the beginning of the 1870s this release of constraints spurred many people to leave old castle towns and rural villages to find
their way in the bustling environment of the new capital, Tōkyō. Many left
after failing to find a place for themselves. Others caught on briefly only to slip
into obscurity later. But some were lucky to find secure jobs and to rise up the
ladders of status, wealth, and power. It was their drive and enthusiasm that
gave early Meiji society its distinctive verve and optimism.

In addition to liberating people from historical constraints, the Meiji government permitted all households to take surnames. During the Tokugawa
era, families with surnames were confined mainly to the military class and to
privileged families among artisans, merchants, and farmers. A family like
Tarō's did not have a surname before 1872; within the village, they probably
would have been known simply by Tarō's name. How this might have affected
the sense of personal esteem and social identity in lower-ranking families we
will never know, but being allowed a surname after 1872 surely was a psychological boost to many.

Less salutary consequences flowed from the pensioning off of the old samurai class. Their pensions consisted of government-issued bonds, the most generous going to the highest-ranking former samurai and being the equivalent of
about fourteen years of annual income. Many others received far less. Some
samurai took the government's cues and invested wisely and profitably in
banks and other ventures. Others failed to invest wisely, or at all, or they received so little that they exhausted their pensions almost immediately. Such
samurai, who may have numbered in the hundreds of thousands, fell further
into poverty that was only exacerbated by the deflation of the early 1880s.

The most positive long-term benefits of social change during the Meiji era
arose from government policies that created a nationwide system of **public education**. The initial steps in this program were taken under the leadership of
the **Ministry of Education**, a national bureaucracy that thereafter served as
the nerve center of Japan's system of public education. In the 1870s the ministry and its officials experimented with a variety of systems that had different

funding and organizational forms, eventually settling on a nationwide system of compulsory education lasting for at least four years (raised later to six). In this way, a very large share of each cohort aged six and above began to receive basic instruction in reading, writing, arithmetic, and civics.

In the 1880s the government continued to expand the system of public education. It created higher elementary schools that provided eight years of basic instruction. It oversaw the creation of middle schools that provided an additional three to five years of education for children ranging between twelve and nineteen. It developed teacher-training colleges to produce instructors for elementary and middle schools. And it gradually began to introduce public higher schools. These were the elite feeder schools for a handful of national universities such as **Tōkyō Imperial University** and **Kyōto Imperial University**. These schools were purposely structured to train bureaucrats and technicians for service in government posts and the private sector.

A few other higher-level institutions of education emerged during the early Meiji period. They later became universities, too, but they originated as private academies on the model of the small proprietary establishments for advanced training that existed during the Tokugawa period. In fact, one of the most famous of these new private institutions, **Keiō Gijuku University**, began in 1858 as a small academy under the leadership of Fukuzawa Yukichi. Fukuzawa was a public intellectual and cultural mediator who played a major role in interpreting the West to Japan during the Meiji era. Another private academy, which later became **Waseda University**, grew to prominence after the 1880s under the leadership of **Ōkuma Shigenobu**, a former government official turned party politician. Both Fukuzawa and Ōkuma strove to offer a private-sector alternative to the government- financed and -controlled imperial universities. They felt that Japanese society needed leaders who valued dissent and different viewpoints.

These new universities, both public and private, were the seedbeds for a significant new social group: Japan's modern professional class. This class was identified by its high level of education, its relatively secure employment in white-collar administrative work in both the public and the private sectors, and its relatively high incomes and living standard. The members of this class came to staff the offices of the central government and its agencies, high-ranking posts in prefectural and municipal governments, and a variety of managerial positions in the new financial, commercial, and industrial firms in the private sector. They lived in new homes in what were then desirable neighborhoods, especially in Tōkyō. And they enjoyed a standard of living second only to that of the most fortunate former daimyō, the greatest of the old and new merchant houses, and the leaders of the army and navy.

With the creation of a new peerage in 1884, members of these groups—former daimyō, high-status business families, and prestigious military figures—joined the former court aristocracy to create a modern version of a noble class. Between 1884 and its abolition in 1947, this class held a privileged status in Japan under only that of the imperial household. Its members were objects of aspiration to the most ambitious and a symbol of prestige for everyone in Japan. They also held a near monopoly over the seats in the upper house of the bicameral national legislature that was established in 1890, where they served as a conservative restraint on the exercise of popular authority.

Beyond this formal change and the gradual impoverishment and disappearance of the former samurai class, the socioeconomic features of Japanese society did not undergo deep or sweeping changes in the two decades following the Restoration. A few families, such as the Iwasaki, Mitsui, Ōkura, Yasuda, and Shibusawa, grew significantly richer than most in Japan. Some wealthy landlords were able to exploit the deflation of the early 1880s to enhance their landholdings and regional influence, and many poorer peasants were driven even deeper into debt and poverty by the same deflationary conditions. But there were no significant changes in the overall structure of society; these came at a faster pace during the twentieth century.

Nor did significant changes alter former demographic, familial, or gender patterns. The opening of the ports did introduce Japan to European contagious diseases such as typhus and cholera, so death rates rose somewhat during the first two decades after the Restoration. But birthrates seem to have risen, too, so the overall population crept upward toward 40 million by 1889. Families, especially in rural areas, grew slightly larger on average, but little seems to have changed in the basic contours of family, kin, and community relationships. Nor were there notable changes in relations between the sexes. The government did sponsor overseas study for a small group of women during the 1870s and 1880s, an experience that reaped some returns for women more generally, but only later. Wider opportunities for women to be educated also had subtle, cumulative effects on their standing in society, but those changes, too, were decades away.

Given the sweep of economic renovation during the early Meiji period, we might expect visible increases in the general standard of living. Indeed, some groups did benefit from the changes, especially the new professional class, some members of the old military and court aristocracies, and leaders of the new economic combines. The middle groups were able to enjoy the increased comforts provided by cotton quilts and floors with reed mats (*tatami*), along with slight improvements in their diets. But so many poorer families suffered so deeply from the deflation of the 1880s that on average these gains seem to have balanced out.

The early Meiji era witnessed some social changes often provoked by government policies. Many people won social liberation from the constraints of the Tokugawa era, but others, especially the samurai, lost their privileges and livelihoods. Some benefited from the creation of new educational institutions, but many suffered from the Meiji state's economic policies. In general, Japanese society seems to have grown slowly and changed minimally during this period, as if biding time until the torrents of industrialization and urbanization struck.

CULTURAL FERMENT

Cultural changes accelerated during the late Tokugawa and early Meiji, reshaping ideologies, religious practices, popular diversions, and literary developments.

Two broad currents of ideas dominated intellectual debate during the final decades of the Tokugawa period: Confucianism and nativism. Confucian ideas were initially spelled out in ancient Chinese texts that had been available in Japan for centuries, but during the Tokugawa era, these texts had been integrated into a Japanese universe of experience. They were eagerly put to work by the shōgun, their governments, and the scholars in their employ to provide fundamental rationales for Tokugawa authority.

Two features of Confucian thought were especially well suited to their purposes. One dealt with the conception of a benevolent ruler. According to the Confucian view of the polity, political leaders first cultivated their own ethical, moral, and ritual behavior. If they succeeded in achieving their own right conduct, the empire itself would be well governed. In this way, political stability — often achieved through fear and intimidation — became a self-fulfilling rationale for its own continuation. Confucian thought also dealt with the five relationships that ruled both social and political conduct: that between ruler and subjects, parents and children, husbands and wives, older brothers and younger brothers, and friends and friends. Only the last of these five relationships was based on equality; all the others were unequal hierarchical relationships in which the inferior party obeyed the superior. Thus, subjects obeyed rulers, children obeyed parents, wives obeyed husbands, and younger brothers obeyed older brothers. This conception of society was both a prescription for stability and an order for compliance and so provided the philosophic rationales for the governance of shōgun and daimyō.

The second current of thought that appeared during the last decades of the Tokugawa era was nativism, also referred to as *national learning* and *national teaching*. Nativism arose as a deliberate challenge to Confucian thought, because Confucianism was rightly viewed as an alien, non-Japanese body of ideas. Nativist thinkers returned to ancient Japanese texts for their inspiration and ideas. These texts dated back to eighth-century historical and poetic writings that explained in mythical terms the origins of the Japanese people and their earliest history.

Nativism soon developed a politically heretical influence. As nativist thinkers studied the ancient texts highlighting the significance of the imperial line in Japanese history, they began to extol the virtues of imperial rule and to question the legitimacy of the shōgun. When the shōgun dealt ineffectively, in their eyes, with the foreign problem after 1853, the nativists had an ideological excuse ready at hand: they claimed that the shōgun had unjustly usurped the emperor's power. Borrowing the Confucian notion that when the country was badly governed, the ruler had lost his mandate to rule, the nativists began to lay the ideological foundation for the overthrow of the Tokugawa regime. This argument meshed nicely with the practical political objectives of the samurai activists and revolutionaries, so they eagerly adopted it, with the consequences covered in the Political Revolution section.

Ideological heresy cropped up in another way during the late Tokugawa period, but this time within the tangled corpus of Confucian thought. From as early as the medieval era, China had developed an imperial bureaucracy that was recruited through arduous examinations that winnowed out all but the best. This institution and its procedures were based on the Confucian notion that gentlemen-scholars should rule the land in the service of the emperor. Such men should possess martial skills and be able to use them if needed. First and foremost, however, they should be reflective thinkers schooled in the richness of Confucian social and political philosophy and should rely intuitively on such knowledge to govern the realm properly. Central to this notion was the belief that such talent was not inherited; rather, it had to be nurtured.

Thoughtful samurai with a critical intellect had recognized as early as the 1600s that a hereditary system of rule had serious faults. First, it did not ensure that all leaders, whether they were shōgun, daimyō, or high-ranking samurai, would be up to the task. Biological fate would—and indeed did—they claimed, put into positions of authority some men who did not have the abilities to discharge it. Second, recruitment solely by heredity prevented talented individuals born into the lower ranks of society from ever achieving high office.

In the late Tokugawa period, these notions began to have some effect. In some domains the daimyō recognized that it would be to their benefit to appoint men based on merit. Satsuma was one domain in which the merit ideal was put into practice, for example, when men from lower-ranking samurai families were promoted into the highest ranks of the daimyō's administration. Merit thus played a role in bringing to the fore Japan's own version of gentlemen-scholars, the leaders of the Meiji Restoration. Merit continued to play an increasingly greater role as the university system developed and as an examination system for recruitment into the national civil service evolved after the 1890s.

With Japan's opening to the West in the 1850s, the cultural ferment deepened through its exposure to new ideas introduced from Europe and the United States. Some of these ideas concerned political matters and stirred debate over international law, civil codes, forms of government, and liberties and freedoms. Other ideas had a more specifically social content and stimulated discussion of gender relations, family life, opportunities, and social mobility. Still other ideas focused on the individual, introducing new concepts of self and personal psychology.

Exciting as these new ideas were, relatively few Japanese were exposed to them before the twentieth century. In the Meiji era, the discussion of Western ideas was confined largely to coteries of literate, well-educated males only in the largest cities, especially Tōkyō. Indeed, the very presence of Western ideas gave rise to a new kind of specialist in Japanese society, the cultural mediator. They were nearly always men who knew a foreign language or had traveled abroad or both. Their special knowledge entitled them to interpret to a wider Japanese audience the character and essence of the foreign nation, text, or behavior under discussion. Such authorities became a fixture on the Japanese intellectual scene, and variants of this type of cultural mediator—many of them little more than instant experts—still thrive in the Japanese media today.

In the same way that several currents of thought characterized the intellectual life of this period, several intermingling practices marked Japan's religious life. To introduce this concept of religion, however, only invites controversy, first because until after the early 1870s, there was no word in the Japanese language that meant "religion." Even then, the term was coined only to enable the discussion of Western faiths. Religion also is controversial because even today Japanese "religion" differs in some obvious ways from the kind of church-based religion most familiar to Americans. For example, most Japanese religious structures do not have large sanctuaries where observers can gather to worship. Nor do they hold regular services at which a religious authority speaks to them about a body of doctrine or morality. Indeed, some mainstream Japanese "religions" do not even have a body of doctrine to convey or an explicit code of conduct to communicate.

Before the 1870s Japan did have institutions and practices that enabled groups and individuals to interact with deities. One set of institutions, practices, and doctrines was known as Buddhism, first introduced into Japan from India by way of China in the sixth century A.D. Buddhism had a priesthood, physical sites of worship called temples, a written doctrine, a multitude of icons, wide-ranging ritual practices, and parishioners. Buddhist priests were specialists at conducting funerals and commemorations for the dead. Buddhist temples and sects also owned a sizable amount of property managed for financial purposes.

Another set of religious practices became known—but only after 1868—as Shinto. Before then, what is now called Shinto was a diverse body of ritual practices overseen by priests at sites usually called *shrines*. These practices established a relationship between individuals and deities known as *kami*. (The word *kami* can also be pronounced *shin*; thus, *shin-tō*, the "way of the gods.") Shinto practices before the 1870s were concerned primarily with propitiating the gods, that is, making them feel good and well served so that they would arrange good fortune for the supplicant. Thus, ritual practices often consisted of food offerings made by priests to the gods in return for their blessings. Or at an even more local and individual level, a supplicant seeking good health, safety, or good fortune might make small material offerings (coins, a stack of fruit) at simple shrines in the forest. Before 1868, therefore, Shinto was not an institutionalized "church," but more a mood, a set of feelings, and an orientation to the world. Shinto kept human beings and nature in harmony and fostered a sense of community at the local level.

During the early Meiji era, the relationship between Buddhism and Shinto changed dramatically. Buddhism had previously been patronized and protected by the Tokugawa house. During the Restoration, Buddhist priests in different parts of the country continued to side with the Tokugawa, stood on the sidelines, or did not support the Restoration forces. Partly to punish the Buddhist priests and partly to implement the religious implications of the Restoration, its leaders offered their political support to the Shinto priests. The new government also confiscated much of the Buddhists' property. In addition, it turned a blind eye to attacks on Buddhist institutions after 1868 that resulted in the widespread theft of icons and the destruction of temples. Buddhism thus suffered a body blow from which it was slow to recover. Within a decade, Shinto also saw its national, political influence waning, although it continued to thrive locally through its customary ritual practices.

The annual festivals sponsored by many local shrines were a crucial popular diversion between the 1850s and the 1880s. Such festivals were usually celebrated at least twice a year, once in late summer and again around the new year. On these occasions, parishioners decorated shrine grounds, set up booths for selling food and talismans, fortified themselves with ample amounts of sake, and hoisted through the streets portable shrines that purified an area for religious purposes. These events gave people in both rural villages and urban neighborhoods a chance to take off a day or two, to reenergize themselves through intense social interaction, and to nurture a sense of community.

In the cities, popular diversions often took place in designated "pleasure quarters," districts where prostitution was legal. These quarters were the center of a floating world, or *ukiyo*, where people could cast aside their daily cares and lose themselves in the idle pursuit of pleasure. The most famous of these districts was the Yoshiwara in Edo, but Kyōto, Ōsaka, and other cities had similar areas. Here, samurai on the prowl rubbed shoulders with merchants on the town, all in pursuit of the most fashionable courtesans and the best entertainment. Garish houses of assignation were side by side with restaurants, bars, trinket shops, and pawn brokers, thereby satisfying a wide range of consumer desires and enticing the unwary into a fateful love affair, a destructive drinking binge, or a ruinous financial arrangement. In districts like these the shōgunate tried—but with only modest success—to suppress the boisterous, hedonistic inclinations of plebian city dwellers, not to mention often uncontrollable samurai.

During the early Tokugawa period, the pleasure districts spawned new forms of artistic and literary endeavors. The *ukiyo-e*, or illustrations of the floating world, were woodblock prints. Often produced in pastels such as light blues and yellows, these prints depicted the denizens of the floating world, especially the popular courtesans and kabuki actors or scenes of the floating world itself. *Ukiyo-e* later had a profound impact on the Impressionist painters of France, but in the 1850s, 1860s, and 1870s, they were an inexpensive form of popular art that urban dwellers could buy to brighten a dark apartment wall.

Woodblock prints were also used to illustrate the new form of popular literature inspired by and set in the pleasure districts. The man who made such commoner literature famous was Ihara Saikaku (1642–1693). Born and reared in Ōsaka—the most intensely commercial city during the Tokugawa period—

Saikaku developed a form of prose literature that relied heavily on dialogue and descriptive scene setting to convey a sense of the behavior and mores of the *chōnin* population, as this brief exchange illustrates:

"Finally he was asked the reason for using thick chopsticks at the New Year.

'That is so that when they become soiled they can be scraped white again, and in this way one pair will last the whole year.'

'As a general rule,' concluded Fuji-ichi, 'give the closest attention to even the smallest details.' "[4]

Such homilies, related in a vigorous, lively style, portrayed the habits of commoner Japanese and shaped their values at the same time. Saikaku inspired several successors, but they seldom possessed his creative genius. By the end of the Tokugawa period, this plebian prose descended into a kind of playful but harmless comedic form, lacking attention to plot, characterization, or psychological depth.

Even after the Restoration, this style of prose literature continued to exercise a hold over both writers and readers. But within a decade, younger Japanese began to learn Western languages, read European literature, and translate foreign books. They soon discovered that foreign novelists, especially Russian and English, explored a far wider range of issues than did the prose writers of the Tokugawa and early Meiji. One of the first Japanese writers who tried to synthesize European and Japanese literary styles and social concerns was **Futabatei Shimei**. Strongly influenced by Russian novelists, Futabatei combined the dialogue and descriptive passages of Tokugawa prose with the individualistic and introspective features of Russian writing, in order to uncover the relationships between the individual and a changing society that remained hostile to personal freedom. Another writer explored similar relationships even more effectively by depicting the world of children living in the Tōkyō pleasure quarter. Although **Higuchi Ichiyō** (1872–1896) lived only a short time, she left behind a few short stories and a novella that show a poignant understanding of the tensions and frustrations of social life in the early Meiji period.

Preserving its autonomy after the 1850s forced Japan to take action on several fronts. Ambitious samurai led a political revolution that eventually promoted widespread economic renovation. Both government policies and economic alterations prompted social change, but it was restricted and minimal in comparison with what was yet to come. Cultural ferment fostered heretical ideas that contributed to the Restoration and led to new debates over religious practice and social values. All these events set Japanese society gently bubbling in anticipation of the changes soon to rise to the surface.

NOTES TO CHAPTER I

1. Conrad Totman, *Early Modern Japan* (Berkeley and Los Angeles: University of California Press, 1993), p. 540.
2. Items in the Historical Narrative that appear in boldface are explained at greater length in part II.
3. Susan B. Hanley, *Everyday Things in Premodern Japan: The Hidden Legacy of Material Culture* (Berkeley and Los Angeles: University of California Press, 1997), pp. 197–198.
4. From Ihara Saikaku's *The Eternal Storehouse* of 1688, excerpted in Donald Keene, comp. and ed., *Anthology of Japanese Literature: From the Earliest Era to the Mid-Nineteenth Century* (New York: Grove Press, 1955), p. 361.

CHAPTER TWO

Integrating the Nation, 1890–1931

During the period between 1890 and 1931, Japan faced a recurring challenge: How could it achieve political unity over a fractious society undergoing rapid change in an unruly international environment? Economic spurts that gave rise to a cycle of booms and busts contributed to the uneven changes of this era. Such cycles spurred far more social turmoil than before, by promoting geographic and occupational mobility, the growth of cities and suburbs, the emergence of new social groups and values, and more widespread distress and dissent. Social turmoil also encouraged, and was encouraged by, cultural divisions that gave rise to new ideas, religious organizations, diversions, and literary practices. Amid widespread political contention, old power holders and new competitors struggled to impose unity on the nation.

To appreciate the significance of this period in the larger context of Japan's modern history, it is useful to envision Japan as a society subjected to two contradictory sets of forces. One set fostered centralization; the other, dispersion. The centralizing tendencies took different forms in different arenas of Japanese society. In the economic arena, centralization was manifested in a consolidation of resources in the hands of the national government and a few large, private business enterprises. In the social arena, centralization led to population concentration in the largest cities, especially Tōkyō and Ōsaka. Centralization in the cultural arena took the form of attachments to an amorphous cultural orthodoxy. And in the political arena, centralization appeared as attempts to create an ever stronger, and increasingly more authoritarian, state.

Political integration was not fully realized, however, because the tendencies toward dispersion worked against it. Sometimes dispersion was caused by people who opposed centralization. At other times dispersion was the result of changes that were overwhelming and unmanageable; they drew people along whether they wanted to go or not. In the economic arena, dispersion fostered a diffusion of resources that balanced and mitigated some of the effects of concentration. Socially, dispersion led to the appearance of new social groups, as well as more widespread forms of dissent. Culturally, intellectuals, religious leaders, fun seekers, and writers deliberately contested the suffocating effects of orthodoxy. And politically, broader participation led to higher levels of conflict that impeded compliance with state demands.

The constant tension between centralizing and dispersing tendencies made this four-decade period one of the most dynamic in Japan's modern history. Society pulsated with a sense of creativity, vibrancy, and opportunity. However, proponents of the dynamic new modes of economic, social, cultural, and political change ultimately failed to prevail. Relying heavily on inertial forces embedded deep in society, conservative and military figures who were determined to achieve integration under orthodoxy persisted at their efforts. They seldom gave ground, and they often retrieved ground once lost. By 1931, the proponents of this conservative, aggressive outlook were on the brink of triumph.

ECONOMIC SPURTS

Japan's economy experienced some growth and crucial development between 1890 and 1931. Ranging from a low of almost zero to a high of nearly 8 percent, the average rate of growth was about 3 percent a year. This period coincided with Japan's modern industrial revolution, so it is noteworthy that Japan's annual growth rates during this time were approximately double those of Great Britain during the first industrial revolution between 1780 and 1830. In key sectors of the Japanese economy, growth rates were low and change was sporadic, especially in the agricultural sector and the artisanal and commercial sector. The greatest changes took place in the new manufacturing, commercial, and service sectors, which witnessed high growth rates and extensive organizational development. The national government continued to experiment with its various roles in the economy, and international trade became a more important endeavor. Ultimately, the success of the economy hinged on the expansion of a viable domestic market. Its failure to develop appreciably was a principal reason for the sluggish performance of the economy as a whole during this period.

Cycles of boom and bust, usually associated with war, strongly shaped economic outcomes. The Sino-Japanese War in 1894–1895 caused a modest economic spurt that petered out quickly. It was followed by about a decade of gradual decline until the Russo-Japanese War of 1904–1905 caused another upward spurt. The economy then descended into a second decline until World War I stimulated a boom that led to rapid economic development. That boom, too, was followed by a long bust, and a devastating earthquake in the Tōkyō area in 1923 prolonged the downturn. Throughout the 1920s, therefore, the Japanese economy remained in the doldrums.

The boom-and-bust cycles affected economic sectors differently. Caused by wars, the booms generated demand for military supplies and services. New firms in manufacturing, commerce, and transportation thus benefited from the growth spurts. Agriculture and indigenous manufacturing and commerce reaped fewer gains from the upward spurts. However, the postwar downturns affected the entire economy, new and old manufacturing, and agriculture as well. To understand the processes of economic change during this period, it is useful to begin with sketches of the agrarian sector and indigenous manufacturing and commerce, before turning to a discussion of new economic organizations and the roles of government and trade.

Agriculture remained the bedrock of the Japanese economy during this era, with agricultural workers forming the largest single segment of the labor force. Numbering about 17 million in 1890, they made up about 70 percent of all workers. In the next four decades, the number of farm workers declined. The sharpest drops occurred with the beginning of the World War I boom, when many jobs in manufacturing and commerce lured younger sons and daughters and poor tenants off the farm and into the cities. By 1931, the number of farm workers had fallen to about 14 million. Because so many of the new jobs in the economy had been created outside agriculture, these 14 million were now only 46 percent of the national total. Despite this drop, Japan was still a nation of farmers.

The value of agricultural output in the economy as a whole declined more rapidly than the agricultural labor force, although the absence of reliable figures prevents estimates for the first decades of this era. When reliable figures began to appear after the turn of the twentieth century, agricultural output constituted about a third of the total, more in some years and less in others, until about 1919. Owing to a severe depression in agricultural commodity prices during the 1920s and also to the collapse of world silk prices in 1929, agriculture's share of the domestic product dropped to about 16 percent in 1931.

This relatively poor showing by so many workers was caused by the significant productivity gap between agriculture and other economic sectors. One worker in a well-equipped new factory could produce far more highly valued goods than could even the most diligent farm worker, because farm workers still toiled in labor-intensive fashion, using centuries-old tools and techniques. They prepared the soil for planting with hoes and shovels, or, at best, with animal-drawn plows. They planted their fields by hand, bent over in mud up to the knees, and they weeded their crops by hand also. When they harvested their crops, they relied on hand-held scythes and even more back-breaking effort, and when they sold their crops, they had to push their carts to the nearest markets.

Because Japanese agriculture was still not mechanized during this period, there were no mechanical transplanters or harvesters, no motor-driven plows, and no trucks. But even if such devices had been available, most farmers could not have afforded to buy them. The one mechanical device that farmers did purchase during this period was small electrical motors, which they used to run threshing machines and to move water through irrigation systems. Such motors did save much labor time and effort, making some farm tasks easier and a little more efficient.

A few other changes enabled farmers to work more productively and efficiently. The greater use of fertilizers, such as synthetic chemicals and imported bean cakes, enhanced productivity on the farm. Many farm families also entered the sericulture industry, to grow silk worms, raise mulberry leaves, and produce raw silk. The growth of the sericulture industry raised the income of many farm households, as did the introduction of some animal husbandry, such as the raising of chickens and pigs. Additional land was brought under cultivation, and the output of rice and other grains increased. Consequently, total agricultural output grew during this period, although at low annual rates of barely 1 to 2 percent. Such growth made it possible for the domestic agricultural sector to supply 90 percent or more of Japan's basic food needs during this era.

The indigenous manufacturing (artisanal) and commercial sector formed another large segment of the economy during this period. Exactly how large it was is impossible to say, owing to the quality of statistical evidence. This sector consisted of small establishments operated by families using simple equipment and manual labor. Such establishments made and sold a wide range of goods used for food, clothing, and shelter, and until about 1920 they supplied most of the domestic demand for such goods. Japanese consumers continued to eat what they had for centuries, so imports did not challenge small firms that made and sold condiments, beverages, and other processed foods. Most people also continued to wear Japanese-style undergarments, pants, shirts, blouses, outerwear, and footwear, and as a result, domestic firms enjoyed a near monopoly on the supply of yarns, fabrics, and clothing. And most homes were built in the Japanese style, using reed floor mats, sliding paper doors, wooden siding, and domestically made roofing materials. As late as 1931, the artisanal and commercial firms that made and sold these household necessities may have employed as much as 40 percent of Japan's labor force. Moreover, this sector may have produced as much as half the value of all manufactured goods. Like the agricultural sector, this sector, too, was large and indispensable. It grew slowly and sporadically, just enough to satisfy—at a relatively low level of consumption—the needs of the expanding population.

The most rapid economic growth took place in new firms created during the Meiji era (1868–1912) and after. These firms were in the commercial, financial, transportation, communication, mining, and manufacturing sectors. Around the turn of the century, they were joined by new firms in the utilities industry, providing electricity to companies and households for the first time. In these sectors, the annual rates of growth were high, often four or more times higher than in agriculture, with some sectors expanding six to fifteen times during the next three decades.

Two features of these sectors are important. First, they started from a small to nonexistent base in 1890. Consequently, the high rates of growth exaggerate the real size of these industries in comparison with agriculture and the artisanal sector. Second, even after four decades of rapid development, these new firms and enterprises were still only a small segment of the total economy in 1931. Even the new manufacturing firms themselves were still small. Only about a dozen manufacturing concerns had more than ten thousand workers in 1930, and most of them were spinning firms employing young women at very low wages. The new firms thus employed a small share of the labor force, perhaps 15 percent in 1931, although they contributed a larger share of total domestic output, around 30 percent.

Among these new enterprises were the *zaibatsu*, a term that originated in the 1910s to refer to the expanding private enterprises under the control of such families as the Mitsui, Iwasaki (**Mitsubishi enterprise**), Sumitomo, and Yasuda. During the 1910s these enterprises assumed the organizational form that prevailed until their dissolution in the late 1940s. At the core of each *zaibatsu* was a family-owned and -controlled holding company that served as its managerial and financial center, providing strategic leadership and financing for the individual firms that carried the *zaibatsu* name. Individual firms under the control of a holding company differed by function among *zaibatsu* and also in the timing of their appearance. At Mitsui, the oldest and most important firms were the Mitsui Bank, the trading firm (Mitsui bussan), and the coal-mining operations, all established in the late nineteenth century. In the twentieth century, Mitsui expanded into shipbuilding and chemical manufacturing and also affiliated with papermakers and textile firms. At Mitsubishi, the most important older businesses were shipbuilding, coal mining, real estate, trade, and banking. In the twentieth century, Mitsubishi also created new firms in steelmaking, electrical manufacturing, and aircraft manufacturing and affiliated with several insurance companies. For strategic purposes, it concentrated more on the heavy industrial sector than Mitsui did. Sumitomo had always been a metals processor, and it continued to concentrate on metals manufacturing during this period, beginning to diversify on a large scale only in the 1920s. Yasuda differed from the other three *zaibatsu* by concentrating almost exclusively on banking and insurance. It did not own and operate a variety of firms as the other *zaibatsu* did, although it did invest in many firms across many industries.

Zaibatsu were thus financial conglomerates that owned and operated firms in a variety of sectors. They were not vertically integrated to control production of a single commodity, such as oil, from its discovery and mining through refining to retail marketing. Rather, they were concerns linked through an interactive synergy. *Zaibatsu* banks financed manufacturing firms that stored their output in *zaibatsu* warehouses, shipped their goods on *zaibatsu* carriers, and sold their products through *zaibatsu* trading firms. This synergy was one characteristic feature of Mitsui, Mitsubishi, and Sumitomo, and one explanation for the evolution of these rather distinctive groupings. Another reason for their evolution rests on financial considerations. During the 1910s and 1920s, many new firms in Japan relied on the stock market for financing, leading to a great deal of irresponsible speculation. This undercut the firms' stability by making them easy targets of speculators and frequent victims of bankruptcy. By creating their own mechanisms for financing older firms and underwriting the costs of new ones, the *zaibatsu* holding companies insulated themselves against such speculation and constructed a sounder financial environment in which to operate.

As rationally managed business organizations, the *zaibatsu* set the standard for other firms to follow. They were among the first Japanese firms to hire college-educated, professional managers to oversee individual firms and eventually to take leadership positions at their holding companies. **Nakamigawa Hikojirō** and **Dan Takuma** at Mitsui were two of the first men to be hired for this purpose. They both entered Mitsui around 1890 and went on to play key roles in later decades. Men like these set other standards, too, by encouraging more businesslike methods of operation, securing autonomy from government control, and relying less on government favoritism. The more profit-oriented approach instilled by this new breed of professional manager lay the groundwork for the growth and development of the *zaibatsu* in the 1910s and 1920s.

It was during this period that the *zaibatsu* established their predominant position in the Japanese economy, primarily because of their financial and commercial capabilities. *Zaibatsu* trust and commercial banks, insurance firms, shipping lines, and trading companies dominated their segments of the economy. Some *zaibatsu* manufacturing firms were important as well, especially the Mitsubishi shipbuilding firm, and the *zaibatsu* coal mining firms were large and prosperous. However, the industrial renown of Japan's *zaibatsu* really stems from the wartime era between 1932 and 1945, whose foundations were laid during the 1910s and 1920s. It was during this time that the *zaibatsu* defined their mature organizational form and developed the financial and managerial resources needed to expand even faster after 1932.

If the consolidation of the *zaibatsu* represented a tendency toward the centralization of economic resources, the development of other industrial sectors served as a force that dispersed the resources more broadly. The front-runner among Japanese industries between the 1880s and the early 1930s was the textile sector. It was dominated by large spinning firms producing cotton and woolen yarns, and it also included weaving establishments and silk spinners. One of the leaders in the industry was **Kanegafuchi Spinning**. Led for many years by an energetic, imaginative, and public-spirited executive named **Mutō Sanji**, Kanegafuchi was known for its innovative labor policies. In 1930 five other textile firms were among the twenty-five largest corporations in Japan. Centered in the Ōsaka region, Japan's textile industry had limited ties to the *zaibatsu*, raised its funds through private investors, and prided itself on its autonomy and risk taking.

The shipbuilding industry also flourished during this period, its peak coinciding with the boom of World War I. Although both Mitsubishi and Mitsui were represented in this industry, private firms such as **Kawasaki**, Uraga, and Harima also were important participants. Whereas the textile industry employed almost exclusively unmarried women under the age of twenty-five, shipbuilding attracted an increasingly more skilled labor force of adult, married males. It was therefore a seedbed for the development of Japan's blue-collar, urban-based working class, and also for labor activism after the 1910s.

Two other new industries appeared during this era that played a major role in the Japanese economy for decades to come: equipment making and electrical manufacturing. These industries developed not only because private-sector entrepreneurs wanted to make profits. They also arose for reasons of national pride, military security, and economic welfare. Japan relied heavily on the importation of factory machinery in the Meiji era and on the importation of technology into the 1920s. This reliance left the country vulnerable during times of war, kept import costs high, and relegated Japanese engineers to a second-class status. More than anything else, it was the pride of Japanese engineers in their work that encouraged them to produce substitutes for costly imports and ensure Japan's industrial self-reliance.

Toyoda Sakichi was a major figure in this movement to develop indigenous expertise in the field of industrial equipment. He was an inveterate tinkerer who spent his life improving spinning and weaving equipment. By the 1930s, products from the Toyoda Automatic Loom Company were good enough to replace those once imported from the Platt Brothers firm of England. Odaira Namihei was a college-trained engineer whose inventiveness and drive underlay the emergence of Hitachi, a maker of a wide range of electrical goods and appliances that was incorporated in 1920. Matsushita Kōnosuke was another inventor and entrepreneur who established a small firm in 1918 to make electrical components in the Ōsaka area. Firms like these were small establishments that had only weak ties, if any, to the *zaibatsu*, but they grew rapidly during the 1910s and 1920s and played an even greater role in the Japanese economy after 1931.

In addition to developing indigenous technology to replace imports, some Japanese firms used new technologies to improve and expand output, and they grew quickly in the process, especially in the 1920s. Many artisanal firms adopted large-scale, factory-based techniques and became mass producers for the growing urban consumer market. Food processors making sake and soy sauce were among the artisanal establishments that grew in size and scope to join the circle of new manufacturers. Entirely new firms that canned vegetables and made nonalcoholic beverages joined them as the food-processing industry entered a new era.

One of the most innovative developments during this period involved firms that began as private railways carrying passengers into new suburbs on the periphery of cities like Ōsaka and Tōkyō. Kobayashi Ichizō is often credited as the visionary who first appreciated the opportunities brought by suburban development. Working for a private railway (now called Hankyū) in the Ōsaka area, Kobayashi got the idea of building department stores at the head of his line. Attracting an almost captive audience that had to walk through the store in order to get on or off trains, these new *depaato* (department [stores]) profited from the larger incomes of the new urban groups and boosted the fortunes of the railway. Similar firms quickly introduced these practices in the Tōkyō area. In addition, they often added a construction firm to subdivide plots in the suburbs and build new homes on them, thereby increasing the number of riders on their trains and customers in their stores.

The private sector was thus subject to the forces of centralization, which consolidated resources among the *zaibatsu*, and dispersion, which spread the available resources among a variety of industries. The government's role in economic affairs during this period represented another form of centralization, that is, keeping the state a major agent in the economy. This happened in part because the government continued and expanded the obligations it had assumed during the early Meiji period and in part because it assumed a critical new obligation in the late 1890s.

Following the Matsukata deflation, the Japanese state continued to charter banks and to supervise and regulate the financial sector. During this time, it also created another state bank, the Industrial Bank of Japan, to provide funding for new manufacturing enterprises. The state also continued to operate and expand the postal system and the telegraph system and, at the beginning of the twentieth century, introduced a state-owned and -operated telephone system. A postal savings system that was operated through local post offices attracted deposits from households and small businesses. The state then invested these funds in infrastructure, such as roads and harbors, thereby benefiting the depositors and the nation as a whole. In 1906 the government nationalized a large share of the main intercity rail lines in the country, and for the next eighty years the national rail system carried the bulk of the nation's land transport. Finally, the government continued to operate army arsenals and naval shipyards, expanding the latter to include sites at Kure, Sasebo, and Maizuru, as well as Yokosuka.

In the 1890s the state began the construction and operation of a government-owned steel mill at Yahata on northern Kyūshū, after the legislature finally approved its financing. In this case, too, minimizing imports and providing for national security were major considerations. Because Japan was importing larger quantities of steel, its import bills and trade deficits were rising. Moreover, it was dangerous for an emerging military power not to have a domestic steel industry. The Yahata Iron and Steel Company finally opened in 1901. In the early years, cost overruns were common and losses constant, but the firm eventually began to turn a profit in the 1910s and benefited from an enormous windfall during the World War I boom. By then, Yahata was producing most of Japan's iron and steel products. Even so, in 1913 all of Japan's steel output was just 1 percent of the United States' steel output, offering further testimony to the still small scale of the new industrial sector in Japan as late as the 1910s.

Despite being small, Japan's manufacturing output did have some effect on the composition and destination of its exports during this period. At the end of the nineteenth century, befitting its status as still an agricultural nation, Japan was essentially a commodities exporter, mainly of silk, tea, and coal, until

World War I. Then, with the retreat of European suppliers owing to the war, Japan was able to sell more manufactured goods on Asian markets, especially textile products. When the war ended, Japan lost the markets it had briefly served, but it still continued to export substantial quantities of raw silk and textile products. Asia bought most of Japan's exports during this time, followed by North America and Europe. Sales abroad of Japanese products were essential to pay for the imports—especially cotton, iron ore, and machinery—required to sustain Japan's growing industrial sector. Even though both exports and imports expanded during this period, Japan still accounted for less than 3 percent of the world's trade around 1930. Germany's share was four times greater, and the United States' was more than five times greater.

Although the years between 1890 and 1931 were crucial to Japan's development as an industrial and trading power, they were more transitional than definitive. The massive agricultural sector and the still large artisanal and commercial sector grew only slowly, hindering the emergence of a larger, more buoyant consumer market. Banks, insurance companies, trading firms, and some new industrial sectors, however, did grow rapidly. Shipbuilding, textiles, chemicals, equipment making, utilities, and electrical manufacturing all expanded. These patterns of economic development left the *zaibatsu* and the government in positions of economic dominance by 1931 and ensured their centrality in economic affairs during the calamitous fourteen years to follow.

SOCIAL TURMOIL

As more people in Japan's growing population moved from rural areas to cities and metropolitan regions, social turmoil was the result. New family structures and community styles evolved in urban areas that offered greater freedom and autonomy, at least among privileged groups in society. They became the social and cultural trendsetters of the era. Although many other groups had neither the wealth nor the leisure to partake of society's new opportunities, as more of them received more education, they came to recognize the heavy cost of inequality. Accordingly, some began to organize and to express their dissatisfaction with the status quo, though with limited effect in most cases.

The Japanese population grew from about 40 million in 1890 to about 65 million in 1931, although mortality rates remained virtually unchanged at about twenty to twenty-two deaths per one thousand persons a year. The population rose because the number of live births each year increased from about twenty-eight per thousand in the early 1890s to about thirty-three per thousand in the early 1930s. More live births were the result of improved medical care for more families, the reduction of serious childhood and epidemic diseases, better sanitary conditions, and more material resources available in a slowly expanding economy.

During this period, more of Japan's growing national population were drawn to the largest and most important metropolitan regions. One of these was centered in Tōkyō and included an urban belt that extended along the western shore of Tōkyō Bay where the port of Yokohama and the industrial city of Kawasaki were located. A second metropolitan region spread out from the commercial, financial, and manufacturing city of Ōsaka at the head of the Inland Sea to include the old capital of Kyōto and the new port city of Kobe. A third region began to appear around Nagoya at the head of Ise Bay in central Japan, and a fourth developed on northern Kyūshū around the government steel mill at Yahata and its nearby port.

These regions grew quickly, especially after World War I. In 1890 they may have accounted for barely 10 percent of Japan's population, but by 1930 they were home to almost one-fourth of Japan's people. Nearly 11 million people lived in the six largest cities of Tōkyō, Ōsaka, Kyōto, Nagoya, Kobe, and Yokohama alone.

In addition to these large cities, small cities with populations between 50,000 and 200,000 also grew quickly during this period. In fact, in the 1920s, these smaller cities grew even more rapidly than did the largest ones, adding more than 4 million people. The smaller cities were scattered throughout the country, though most were located in a long thin belt along the southern shore of Honshū. This belt started just north of Tōkyō and stretched along the old Tōkaidō road to Ōsaka and then westward to Hiroshima. Some of these small cities were former castle towns now serving as prefectural capitals. Others were sites of naval shipyards; a few were commercial ports; and many were textile towns and industrial communities where firms such as Hitachi, Toyota, and Matsushita were building their first factories.

The concentration of so many new, mobile residents in urban areas had widespread social implications and, as we will see later, cultural and political implications. From a social perspective, urban concentration affected birthrates, family structure, and community life.

During the latter part of this four-decade period, average birthrates in urban areas began to drop below those in rural villages. The differences were small at first, but over time they widened and assumed greater importance. It is difficult to know exactly why urban birthrates declined, because the demographic data are poor and we know little about family decision making during this period. Nonetheless, there are plausible reasons that people residing in cities had fewer children than their rural counterparts did.

First, many urban areas had pronounced sexual imbalances among their young people. Cities dominated by spinning mills had a surplus of unmarried young women, whereas cities with shipyards and steel mills had an overpopulation of young, single males. Because nearly all births took place in wedlock (including high levels of common-law marriage), those cities with skewed sex ratios had lower per capita birthrates. Second, the economic pressures of urban living dissuaded city families from having large numbers of children. Whereas in the country, children could help around the farm from an early age, in the city, they could not be easily employed as money earners and had to be supported with cash income. Moreover, the cost and availability of housing worked against large families in cities: there were simply physical and psychological limits to how many children a family could rear in a one-room tenement.

As a consequence of these considerations and others we may never fully understand, the average size of urban families decreased. Whereas a typical farm family might have had three children during the 1920s, an urban family was far more likely to have only one or two. Moreover, three-generation stem families were much less common in the cities. Eldest sons staying home to inherit the farm usually remained in the family home with the parents. Younger sons who left the farm were usually freed from the burden of living with and caring for their parents and were thus able to establish a small, nuclear family in the city to which they had migrated. Consequently, the families of many new urban residents usually numbered three or four, whereas rural families were far more likely to have five or six members.

The younger men and women forming small urban families thereby won a measure of psychological freedom and social autonomy. They did not have to care for aging parents, as their older brothers did in the villages. Unlike their rural counterparts who had to rely heavily on mutual assistance, city dwellers did not have to cooperate nearly so much with their neighbors, so they could avoid many of the entanglements common to village life. Initially, in fact, few urban newcomers even knew most of their neighbors. This release from mutual assistance freed the new urbanites to choose their friends, both at home and at work. They could also use their free time, make their political allegiances, and develop their outlook on life without the pressures to conform that were so intrusive in small villages. The new type of community life that appeared in urban areas during the 1910s and 1920s reflected, drew on, and reinforced this kind of freedom and autonomy. Moreover, the social dissent and the cultural experimentation characteristic of the 1920s grew directly out of these new modes of interaction at the individual, neighborhood, and community levels.

Among the many new social groups that emerged in the cities and metropolitan regions of Japan after 1890, the new professional class (first mentioned in chapter 1) best personified these social changes. Headed by men with high educational levels, white-collar occupations, and fairly secure, salaried employment, the new professional families took advantage of the freedom and autonomy of urban living to become social and cultural trendsetters. They settled in the fashionable neighborhoods on the edge of the downtown districts or in the fast- growing suburbs along private rail lines. The wives in these families shopped for upmarket goods and foreign imports in the new *depaato* managed by the rail companies. Husbands and wives alike purchased the diverse array of newspapers and new magazines that appeared during the 1920s. Furthermore, the men in these families often voted for the more progressive political parties. These were the people with the knowledge, wealth, and leisure to exploit the dynamism and opportunity that society offered.

Numerous other new social groups enjoyed none of these advantages, however. Textile workers were usually women in their teens and early twenties who had left school after four to six years of education to take jobs that paid very low wages yet required them to work twelve-hour days six days a week with few annual holidays. An almost equal number of young, poorly educated women worked as domestic servants at even lower wages, under close supervision, and with virtually no holidays. The young males who were forming an urban, blue-collar working class enjoyed only slightly greater advantages. They often had only six years of education, but if they were fortunate enough to obtain a job in a large shipyard or a major steel firm, they were paid much more than textile workers or domestics. However, until World War I, their wages would barely support a family of four. During this period, millions of other young men found work in small retail and wholesale firms. They were essentially apprentices who often lived with the proprietor and his family, taking their meals with them, and earning only a nominal wage.

When we combine these new social groups with the rural populace to form the full view of Japan's socioeconomic structure, we can understand why the economic performance during this era was so sluggish. To put it simply, the early decades of Japan's urbanization and industrialization enriched rather few people, perhaps 15 to 20 percent of the populace at most. Poor or nonexistent evidence makes precise claims impossible, but the available materials suggest that most people experienced only a slight increase, if anything, in their real standard of living between 1890 and 1931.

Some of the largest socioeconomic groups saw the smallest gains. Tenants in rural Japan who rented the land they worked had among the lowest cash incomes in the country, most of which they had to spend on food, clothing, and shelter. Then, although the general welfare of rural tenants had improved slightly by the early 1920s, the agricultural depression that struck in the late 1920s drove many tenants into poverty and debt. The same depression had a severe effect on many farm families that both rented and owned land. Although they may have had slightly higher cash incomes than the tenants, they also found themselves sinking into debt and poverty. These two groups may have made up nearly one-third of the Japanese population in 1931.

Urban groups making up an equivalent share of the population also were impoverished. The poorest urban residents lived below the poverty line, even in a society whose living standards were already low. They squeezed into rooms nine feet square, ate discarded food, and dressed in rags. Situated just above them were families in which the husband worked sporadically, the wife compensated with in-home work (such as carving toothpicks or packing matchboxes), and even the children hustled for cash. These families barely survived from one day to the next. Factory workers, both male and female, were perhaps slightly better off, because they often had lodging (even if it was very crowded) and food (however little) provided by their employers. Their cash incomes, however, were extremely low and often unavailable, because the companies held their wages until the workers' contracts expired or paid their wages in advance to the workers' parents. Domestic workers and apprentices in small firms could usually count on food and lodging, but their cash earnings also were very low.

Consequently, well over half the Japanese population received low cash incomes that they often spent immediately on necessities. It is not surprising, therefore, that two industries dominated the manufacturing sector in Japan into the 1920s: food processing and textiles, the goods that consumers had to buy. Vast numbers of people exhausted their resources on these essentials, however, so there was little or no demand for even the smallest consumer durables, such as electric fans or radios, much less refrigerators or automobiles. The very low purchasing power of most families was thus a heavy brake on more rapid economic growth.

Some groups, however, were able to buy what they needed plus some discretionary items. In rural Japan, farmers who owned land of adequate size, worked hard, and avoided debt could afford to buy necessities and also occasional luxuries while setting some money aside. In urban Japan, the professional classes, some proprietors of small retail shops and wholesale houses, and some small factory owners were in this group. It was a kind of "middle class," but only because it was in the middle between a mass of poor households and a very small number of extremely wealthy families.

The wealthiest families in Japan during this period were landlords in the countryside and entrepreneurs in the cities. The largest landlords owned hundreds of acres or more and made money from their land in the form of rents. They also invested in many ancillary activities, such as banking, sake brewing, and stock ownership, and they were actually the managers of diversified portfolios, invested partly in agriculture and partly in other sectors. Although they had enough material resources to live very well if they wished, most of them preferred to maintain the appearance of frugality. The families that profited from the *zaibatsu* consolidation during this era were probably the richest in the land, next to the imperial household itself. Such families were rather ostentatious, living in huge mansions, maintaining large staffs, driving imported automobiles, traveling abroad, educating their sons in Europe, and flaunting their wealth at public, aristocratic gatherings.

These disparities in wealth were caused by the unevenly distributed returns in the growing economy. The highest growth rates were not in agriculture or in the artisanal and commercial sector, in which most people were employed in menial jobs. Rather, the highest rates of growth and the highest returns were in some of the new industrial enterprises and in commercial and financial institutions, especially the international trading firms and the commercial banks. The profits from these endeavors flowed into the hands of the owners, who reinvested them, spent them, or saved them. Although this behavior was beneficial in that it stimulated continued growth in areas that attracted investment, it did little to improve the material welfare of most Japanese, which slowed Japan's ability to "enrich the nation" between 1890 and 1931.

During this time, the educational system developed a closer relationship to the economy, by both serving its needs and being served by its returns. Schools served the economy's needs by providing workers with various levels of credentials and skills. The foundation of the system was six years of elementary school, and by the turn of the twentieth century, nearly every school-age child in Japan was acquiring a basic competence in reading, writing, and arithmetic. At that point, almost three-fourths of them entered the labor force, taking jobs in factories and small shops and on the farm.

The remainder pursued learning at higher levels. Middle schools nearly doubled in number and tripled in size during this era, serving the needs of students who wanted more learning, a higher degree, and better job prospects. Middle-school graduates usually entered the labor force as clerical and administrative personnel in public- and private-sector organizations. Two other higher-level options became more widespread and inviting during this period. Normal schools were one option. They prepared teachers for the public school system and served as a channel of upward social mobility for students from disadvantaged backgrounds. Higher technical schools were the other option, producing many of the technicians and engineers who contributed to the growth of such firms as Hitachi, Toyota, and Matsushita.

Higher schools, and the colleges and universities for which they served as feeder schools, were at the top of the educational hierarchy. Attracting the sons of the professional class and other privileged socioeconomic groups, higher schools, colleges, and universities, and their student bodies grew substantially during this period. The number of students in attendance tripled between 1910 and 1930 alone, although there were still fewer than 200,000. Until the University Law was passed in 1918, there were only a handful of official, nationally supported, imperial universities. But by 1930 there were forty-six universities, most of them small, private institutions with enrollments of fewer than one thousand. Because their graduates in any year still comprised less than 1 percent of their age cohort, a university-level education remained a prized accomplishment. Even so, owing to the sluggish economy in the 1920s, there were not enough jobs at home to absorb all the nation's university graduates, so many were forced to take positions with Japanese firms in the country's colonies of Korea, Taiwan, and Manchuria.

Most educational institutions above the elementary level were for males, but during this period women's schools at the middle and higher levels appeared for the first time. Nevertheless, all-girl middle schools were finishing schools for prospective wives, not training centers for able employees. Their curricula stressed home economics, flower arranging, and other domestic skills at the expense of subjects such as law, engineering, and politics. But a few institutions emerged to train women at the college level as well, such as the predecessor of **Tsuda Women's College** in Tōkyō. These institutions trained a small group of women who were literate, educated, and capable of writing about and reflecting on larger issues concerning women's place in Japanese society.

These small numbers of literate and educated women had only a modest impact, however, on changing the position of women in Japanese society during this time. The established norms were too deeply entrenched to be quickly altered. Moreover, beginning in the 1890s, the Japanese state began instituting new norms for women that in many ways only reinforced the prevailing ideals. The essence of the new state vision was embraced in the phrase *ryōsai kenbo*, meaning "good wife and wise mother," a prescription for female conduct that blended visions of Victorian family roles with images of the proper samurai wife. Good wives and wise mothers were devoted to managing the home, serving the needs of the husband, and rearing the children.

Although some women found that their situation meshed nicely with the good wife, wise mother ideal, most did not. The ideal conformed with the conditions in urban professional homes. Husbands in such families earned incomes that enabled their wives to stay at home, manage domestic affairs, and care for the children. But for most women, the ideal was a chimera. Farm wives spent long hours in the fields or at supplementary jobs and still had to find time to cook, clean, and care for both children and elderly parents. The wives of shopkeepers and artisans were also deeply involved in the work of their husbands' establishments. And just to make ends meet, wives of factory laborers often had to supplement husbands' salaries with piecework or paid jobs. Most women thus went about their work largely oblivious to the demands of this state-voiced ideal.

A few women, however, were courageous enough to contest society's vision of women's roles and to disagree with orthodox views. They were the pioneers of a **women's movement** in modern Japan. Some of them joined groups such as the Blue Stocking Society. Formed in 1911 under the leadership of Hiratsuka Raichō and others, the society promoted women's liberation through a journal and diverse public activities. Other women formed organizations to press for women's suffrage. Ichikawa Fusae was a leader in this effort from as early as 1918. Still others articulated the cause of women by writing articles in newspapers and magazines and speaking in public about equal opportunity, male-female equality, better welfare provision, and more attention to women's needs.

Women were not the only dissenters in this era. The **Hibiya riots** in 1905 were a popular protest against the terms of surrender in the Russo-Japanese War, resulting in widespread destruction, personal injuries, and a few deaths. This was the first sign of a more dissident urban populace willing to confront the state. The **rice riots** of 1918 were another indication of popular discontent. Sparked by high rice prices, these riots involved thousands of people—fisherwomen, coal miners, industrial workers, and common citizens—throughout the nation, and their efforts did eventually force the government to adopt new policies to reduce the cost of rice.

Out of incidents like these grew larger, more unified efforts to advance the interests of social groups that were becoming more politically self-conscious. Beginning in the 1910s, a **labor movement** was formed that articulated the social, economic, and political demands of industrial workers, especially male heads of household living in metropolitan areas and working in large-scale, heavy industries. At about the same time, a **tenant movement** began in the countryside, drawing attention to the social and economic distress of the poor peasantry. It resulted in a slight improvement in general conditions for some of them. The **buraku liberation movement** also began in the late 1910s, which highlighted the social and economic plight of a minority group that, owing to its ties with special occupations, had long suffered discrimination.

Organized movements like these were vivid symbols of the differences emerging in Japanese society. Population growth was accompanied by urban concentration, but the people that gathered in the growing cities and metropolitan regions were increasingly more diverse. They included desperately poor families, disadvantaged textile hands and domestic servants, blue-collar industrial laborers struggling at the edge of survival, and millions in the commercial sector who were barely making ends meet. These were the new social groups that provided much of the impetus for the labor movement and *buraku* liberation and, to a lesser degree, the women's movement. The concentration of population in the cities thus spread dissent among social groups, injecting a fractious force into the body politic.

CULTURAL DIVISIONS

Social diversity both reflected and reinforced cultural divisions, so that dispersion and centralization were also features of cultural life in the four decades after 1890. The state was a powerful, persistent force in promoting centralization, using a variety of institutions to nurture an attachment to an orthodoxy that emphasized imperialism, patriotism, and nationalism. Standing against the state was an array of intellectuals, political activists, youth, fun seekers, religious believers, writers, and others who both wittingly and unwittingly contested the thrust of the orthodoxy. Despite the appeal of dissenting ideas and behavior, the state succeeded in winning over the great mass of the Japanese people.

The ideas making up the cultural orthodoxy were an amorphous mix. Some drew on Confucian thought, others on nativist thought, and still others on Western thinking, first introduced in the nineteenth century.

One of the principal claims was that the nation was like a family whose head was the emperor, a kind of god/father. According to nativist thinking, the emperor's divinity was based on his direct succession from an unbroken line of imperial sovereigns that stretched back to the mythical origins of the Japanese people. His powers were thus uncontestable, for to challenge them was to question the very essence of the nation. The emperor was a putative father because he was the head of the figurative family of the Japanese people. In this capacity, he deserved the unquestioning loyalty and devotion that a father in the household also did, according to Confucian norms.

Another set of orthodox claims invoked the metaphor of the village. In highly idealized terms, villages were regarded as cohesive communities in which people engaged happily in cooperation and mutual aid. Village members recognized the value of such interaction and appreciated how it both improved their livelihood as individuals in families and as families in the community. The nation was thus regarded as a village writ large. As in the village, the subjects of the nation-state should be pleased to engage in cooperation and reciprocity, because it was in everyone's interest to do so.

In a society envisioned in terms of such metaphors, a common lexicon of values was strongly endorsed, of which two were patriotism and nationalism. Japanese subjects should by nature, if not out of self-interest and communal interest, support the state and its policies. Imperialism was another value that came to be strongly endorsed by state agents and institutions, in two ways. Imperialism was first and foremost an ideological construct that underlay support for a distinctive system of monarchy. Japanese subjects should obey the emperor and his servants because all subjects were Japanese and thereby linked to the emperor through birth and blood. The other facet of imperialism was colonial expansion. Asian wars beginning in 1894 had led to a gradual expansion of Japanese authority in Taiwan, Korea, and China. Because these events took place under the auspices of the emperor's state and reflected his imperial will, Japanese subjects had a natural obligation to support, if not actually celebrate them. On these issues, German notions of state power also came into play.

Other values treated as important elements in the orthodoxy were harmony, loyalty, and sincerity, which were an invitation to political compliance. Japanese subjects should cooperate harmoniously out of a sincere loyalty to the emperor and the nation.

The various strands of this orthodox ideology were communicated through a wide variety of state organs and institutions, including the public elementary school system. The Imperial Rescript on Education (see the Appendix), originally issued in 1890 and surviving until 1945, was filled with the rhetoric of imperialism, patriotism, and nationalism. In some schools it was read aloud or repeated from memory each day. Elementary schools also introduced morals courses in which the secular and political thrust of the preceding ideas was drilled into the minds of young children.

Newly formed **state-guided organizations** offered other ways in which these ideas could be communicated to target audiences. First among such organizations was the **Patriotic Women's League**, established in 1901. It organized women to support war efforts and provided a venue in nearly every community for instilling the values of patriotism, nationalism, and imperialism. Also dating from 1901, the **Imperial Reservists' Association** promoted the same values. Its members consisted of former military conscripts scattered in towns and villages across the country. The **Imperial Agricultural Society** operated to ensure the compliance of landlords. Established in 1925, the **Greater Japan Alliance of Youth Organizations** was designed to appeal to young males between about fifteen and twenty-five.

Yet another manner in which agents of the state sought to cement allegiance to the emperor and the nation was through repeated stagings of imperial tours, pageants, and visitations. The Meiji emperor undertook more than one hundred tours, and even the sickly Taishō emperor made a number of tours and public appearances in the 1910s. Riding a white horse and decked out in European-style military garb, the emperors struck a majestic pose as they moved through these carefully choreographed events. In a society without television, these visitations offered common subjects an opportunity to see the sovereign and bask in his aura. Although some people did regard these events as staged and cynical, most subjects responded as the state's agents hoped they would, with a sense of awe and adulation.

Another institution was mobilized to reinforce the imperial and patriotic values of the orthodoxy: Shinto shrines. After the turn of the twentieth century, the national government began to support a hierarchy of Shinto shrines and administrators who would assist the state in promoting its goals. Shinto shrines were designated as sites of worship to celebrate Japanese soldiers who had died in battle. They were thus used to reinforce the imperial ideology, emperor worship, and colonial expansion.

Through these numerous institutional venues, the state and its supporters created a continuing attachment to orthodox values among most members of Japanese society. Shrewdly utilizing the elementary schools, the state inculcated these ideas in nearly everyone over the age of six, beginning at the turn of the century and continuing to the end of the Pacific War. Youth organizations then reinforced these ideas in young men, and the reservists' associations continued the effort among older men. The women's leagues brought most adult women into the net, and the agricultural societies ensured that influential adult males were absorbed. In this way, the amorphous ideas of a centralizing state orthodoxy penetrated the largest social groups in Japan, especially in rural areas.

Orthodox values were durable and pervasive, and their proponents were relentless in reinforcing them, leaving very little space in which to advocate alternatives. Nonetheless, alternatives did arise, offering a counterpoint to the orthodoxy by advancing different perspectives, using different venues, and appealing to different social groups.

The orthodox ideas congealed around an organic view of society. They were socially encompassing in their reach and largely unconcerned with individuals, social subgroups, or minorities as such. Indeed, the Confucian-influenced ideas quietly effaced individualism at the outset by situating "man" in a captive web of relationships—with friends, brothers, spouses, parents, and rulers. Social cohesion—not one's personal psyche—was the central concern of orthodox theory. The alternative ideas advocated after the turn of the twentieth century emphasized just the opposite.

One set of alternative ideas derived from European thinking about individuals and natural rights. In contrast with orthodox views, these ideas recognized the dignity of the individual as an autonomous, critical subject capable of determining his own destiny. During the Meiji era, one such strain of thought was fed by the ideas of Samuel Smiles (1812–1904), a Scottish author. Smiles wrote a manual for individual success entitled *Self Help*; it was translated into Japanese in 1870 and became a great hit among young Japanese. By the turn of the twentieth century, individualism was being debated as a virtue in its own right, especially by young men worried about arbitrary state power and military conduct. In the 1920s, therefore, individualism became a clarion call for many excited by prospects for political democracy.

Another set of alternative ideas concentrated on matters of class and were inspired by both Marxist and socialist writings. These ideas were introduced at the turn of the century in the form of a Christian socialism associated with settlement-house activities patterned on American examples. Marxist ideas flowed into Japan in the wake of the Russian Revolution of 1917, finding a receptive audience among students, intellectuals, political activists, some workers and tenants, and a few women. In all cases, these ideas injected a note of acrimony into intellectual debate and political action, because their class analysis was premised on the existence of adversarial relationships between the disadvantaged and the powerful, an assumption contradicting the orthodox claim that society should be a politically compliant, harmonious body.

These alternative ideas were communicated, debated, acted on, and rejected in numerous venues. Where both individualism and Marxism were concerned, the nation's elite higher schools and universities played a critical role, as their intellectual climate differed greatly from that in the elementary schools where teachers inculcated the orthodoxy. Teachers in higher schools and universities were freer to use texts on liberalism, Marxism, and socialism with their bright, privileged charges. During the 1920s, in fact, some of the men who were to govern Japan during the chauvinistic years of the 1930s actually flirted, as students, with many radical thinkers and ideas.

Other venues through which alternative ideas and values circulated were the daily newspapers' editorial pages, cultural sections, and special correspondents discussing a variety of social and political issues. Journals and magazines ranging from serious pamphlets published by a socialist political sect to weeklies and biweeklies put out by fast-growing publishing houses catering to a mass market were forums for such issues as well. These same houses also turned out hundreds of texts translated from European languages, enabling students, faculty, and interested laypersons to read about liberalism and socialism. After the turn of the century, many Japanese writers, male and female, began addressing alternative ideas—and lifestyles—in their novels, novellas, and short stories, which also found a gradually larger audience, especially in the 1920s.

The least formal venues for exposure to, discussion of, and action on alternative ideas and values were the cafés, coffee houses, entertainment districts, and movie theaters. American films found their way to Japan in the 1910s and attracted a sizable audience during the 1920s. They provided a vision—however fanciful and implausible—of different lifestyles. Japan had long had its pleasure quarters for the display of heretical ideas and lifestyles even during the Tokugawa period. In the twentieth century, new types of establishments, such as cafés and coffee houses, appeared. They combined the lure of female companionship with the appeal of self-indulgence, and they became a magnet for anguished college students and distraught intellectuals.

The social groups that reveled in these new ideas were as varied as the ideas and the venues themselves. One important group among which ideas about rights, individualism, and class flourished was "youth," meaning essentially young men in their late teens and twenties. Owing to the social changes that began in Japan in the 1880s, the very concept of youth underwent transformation. Previously, in an agrarian society without a formal education system, children had grown almost imperceptibly into adults, without passing through a formally identified period of youth. During the 1880s, however, a clearer distinction was made between the years spent in elementary school and what followed. But for most children, what followed was still entry into the labor market, and for them, there was no significant pause between the dependent years of schooling and the more independent years of work.

There was, of course, an extended moment when young men were no longer students and not yet responsible—that is, married—adults. In rural villages, youth associations were organized to harness the energies and channel the enthusiasms of such young males. The conservative former bureaucrats and military officers who dominated the leadership of the national headquarters of these associations tried to make the transition from childhood to adulthood as seamless as possible, by using their organizations to distract village youth with lectures on farming and practice in military drill.

Young males in the cities faced more numerous choices, especially if they were students pursuing higher degrees. They often lived away from their families and outside the labor market for a decade or so while in their teens and early twenties, creating a clear-cut period when they were freed from family supervision and job obligations. Able, therefore, to spend a great deal of time reflecting on the meaning of youth, and even larger issues, many of them did just that. By the turn of the century, the cities thus witnessed the emergence of a kind of youth culture that has persisted and blossomed down to the present day.

This youth culture had a serious aspect, especially at the turn of the century. Indeed, the two most important writers of the Meiji era, **Mori Ōgai** and **Natsume Sōseki**, extensively described the dilemmas of youth in their writing. As a culturally conservative military officer, Ōgai portrayed youthful literary subjects who pondered the balance between freedom and obligation. More playful and irreverent, Sōseki used comedic depictions of blundering youths to illustrate their problems with life, but he also was capable of exploring the depths of youthful despair and its lifelong costs, as he did in his masterpiece, *Kokoro*. Works by Japanese authors like these, along with Russian novels, German philosophy, and English political theory, provoked reflection, discussion, angst, and action among students and intellectuals throughout this period.

Youth culture had its wanton, hedonistic aspect as well. Drunken revels, escapades with café waitresses, and dissipating travels at home and abroad were all part of this facet of youth culture and the individualism in which it was partly rooted. College boys and other young fun seekers were not the only participants in this pattern of conduct; so were self-styled intellectuals and city dwellers down on their luck. **Nagai Kafū** depicted this side of urban life in his short stories and novellas, and **Akutagawa Ryūnosuke** gave it a bizarre, fantastical twist in his work.

The *mobo-moga* phenomenon of the 1920s was another part of the youth scene. *Mobo* were "modern boys," and *moga* were "modern girls." The latter were more intriguing—and more controversial. Modern girls were creatures of Tōkyō, and within Tōkyō, the Ginza area, a downtown district that was the city's hot spot during the 1920s where people went to see and be seen. Dressed in manly apparel (Western-style pants, as opposed to Japanese-style kimono), sporting short, masculine haircuts, and smoking long cigarettes, modern girls liked to *Gin-bura*, or "hang out," and stroll along the Ginza. They were nonconformists who tweaked the noses of sedate society and, in the eyes of older men, threatened the nation with their sexually seditious behavior. As a leading student of the subject put it: "The Modern Girl stood as the vital symbol of overwhelming 'modern' or non-Japanese change instigated by both women and men during an era of economic crisis and social unrest. She stood for change at a time when state authority was attempting to reestablish authority and stability."[1]

There is some doubt about the very existence of the modern girl. Some have portrayed her as little more than a figment of the conservative male imagination. Moreover, even by the 1920s, few young women in Japan had the money, leisure, and audacity to engage in this kind of conduct. Nonetheless, enough images of such women did appear in newspapers and magazines to lend credibility to their existence. In his novel *Naomi*, **Tanizaki Jun'ichirō** offers a vivid portrayal of one highly individualistic young woman of the 1920s.

Modern girls strolling the Ginza were not the only women in the 1910s and 1920s who found alternative ideas appealing. **Yosano Akiko**, a well-known poet and translator of classical Japanese literature, was also a prolific writer whose columns on women and their rights attracted a large audience. **Hayashi Fumiko** published a literary version of her life history as a child of the lower class struggling to find a place in a volatile society. Her *Vagabond's Diary* became an immediate best-seller. Other women were moved by the ideas of Ichikawa Fusae to consider their limited political rights and lack of equality. In these ways and more, many women were challenged to reflect on the assumptions about women's roles implicit in the orthodox view of Japanese society.

Workers, tenants, and *burakumin* embraced ideas about class, class conflict, and political organization because they offered solutions to the distress and inequality that so many of them suffered. Frequently drawing on the assistance of college-educated specialists in law, administration, and politics, these groups organized unions to promote their interests. Workers confronted managers; tenants petitioned landlords; and *burakumin* broadcast their plight. Both their actions and their ideas challenged the orthodox premises, and these people often faced strong resistance and sometimes virulent reprisals. Nonetheless, they won just enough battles to achieve a measure of credibility that sustained their organizations through the 1920s.

Finally, during this period a large number of "new" religions cropped up throughout Japan. They were new because they arose independently of the established religions of Buddhism and Shinto, usually around the leadership of a single, charismatic individual. These leaders often came from disadvantaged backgrounds and suffered great difficulties in life, but they had had a vision or an experience that turned them to religion. Many of them attracted their flocks in the role of healers, as they seldom had a deep or well-articulated body of doctrine to communicate; self-help and faith were the staples of their teaching. Nonetheless, they drew large followings and provided a psychic balm for other individuals from the lower ranks of society who were enduring personal, physical, social, or economic distress.

Alternative ideas thus attracted social support from diverse groups on the margins of mainstream society. Youth, especially unemployed urban youth, were temporary sojourners in a role that disappeared once they took a job and married. Women were still regarded as subordinate to men in every respect, despite the efforts of some to alter this view. Industrial workers, rural tenants, and *burakumin* also were marginal members of society, easily replaced in a precarious economy with high unemployment. The adherents of "new religions" usually were outsiders as well. In addition, these groups were sharply divided among themselves and seldom able to cooperate in advancing their ideas and agendas.

In contrast, the orthodoxy drew its supporters from the heart of society. They included most adult men, many adult women, a majority of the nation's youth, and virtually all its children. The state thus constructed social support for orthodoxy from the ground up, beginning with schools and families, moving to communities, and ending with the nation. It controlled orthodox adherence from the top down, through a variety of state institutions and agencies. Despite their merits and some enthusiastic supporters, alternative ideas circulated mostly on the edges of Japanese society, challenging but not moving the orthodoxy. Only a devastating defeat in war would dislodge it.

POLITICAL CONTENTION

Economic spurts led to social turmoil and cultural divisions creating political contention in the four decades after 1890. While assuming ever more symbolic importance, the throne in fact lost real power during this period. The genrō who controlled the state at the outset of this era had first become in-fluential in the 1870s. They clung to power for the next forty years until a new generation of leaders finally ascended the stage in the late 1910s. The new leaders, however, found it difficult to centralize power in their hands. Changes in bureaucratic conduct, political party influence, interest-group activities, and legislative behavior all were dispersing power beyond a small ruling circle, dividing, if not actually weakening, the state's authority. While these contradictory tendencies played out on the domestic scene, a militant expansionism grew in Japan's Asian empire, with ominous implications for the future.

Three of Japan's four modern emperors were on the throne during this short period. The **Meiji emperor** was still a vital force in national affairs when he convened the first meeting of the national legislature, the Diet, in 1890. In the next two decades, however, the emperor retreated from the demanding public schedule he had followed previously; government leaders pressed him into the background; and diabetes diminished his energies. His death in 1912 brought an immense outpouring of popular sympathy and also led to the con-troversial suicides of the army general **Nogi Maresuke** and his wife, who killed themselves out of loyalty to a deceased master.

This injection of Tokugawa-period samurai values into the Westernizing at-mosphere of the 1910s was a jarring event, and it provided the central theme for Natsume Sōseki's *Kokoro*, one of the most penetrating and powerful novels written in twentieth-century Japan. Sōseki conveyed the import of these deaths through the voice of the protagonist in *Kokoro*, who wrote in his own suicide note to a young friend that

> at the height of the summer, Emperor Meiji passed away. I felt as though the spirit of the Meiji era had begun with the Emperor and had ended with him. I was overcome with the feeling that I and the others, who had been brought up in that era, were now left behind to live as anachronisms.[2]

The death of the Meiji Emperor thus caused a strong feeling of closure but a weak sense of renewal.

This had something to do with Mutsuhito's eldest son, Yoshihito, who suc-ceeded him as the **Taishō emperor**. Hampered by modest natural abilities, the effects of meningitis suffered in childhood, and strokes later in life, Yoshihito could not properly discharge his duties, and court advisers quickly pushed him into the background. They finally dislodged him in 1921 by making his eldest son, Hirohito, the regent. When Yoshihito died in 1926, Hirohito ascended the throne as the **Shōwa emperor**.

By this time, it was becoming customary for the sovereign to regard himself as a constitutional monarch, on the English model. Government officials still kept the emperor informed, and they consulted him on state affairs. They also did everything they could to win his approval for policies they advanced. But the emperor seems to have listened and asked questions far more than he offered advice or gave orders. Such conduct clouded the real intentions of the imperial will and left government leaders to interpret the emperor's words according to their own interests. Rather than acting as ruling sovereigns with their own views and policies, therefore, the emperors during this era rose above the fray of political battle, giving up real power in return for the infallibility associated with their largely symbolic position.

The real contests for power took place among the men who could exercise influence through formal and informal channels. In formal terms, these were the prime ministers, cabinet ministers, and leaders of the army and navy. In informal terms, the small circle of influential men was the Meiji oligarchy, or *genrō*. Members of the second generation of Restoration leaders, the *genrō*, included such figures as **Itō Hirobumi, Yamagata Aritomo, Matsukata Masayoshi, Katsura Tarō,** and **Saionji Kinmochi.** These five men, and three others who had played roles in the Restoration as samurai from three leading domains, monopolized the prime ministership from 1890 through 1918. All of them had served as bureaucrats, cabinet ministers, and/or military officers since the 1870s, so they had long, and often varied, service in the government. After they left formal office, they continued to exercise power by relying on their stature, experience, and contacts. In the case of the *genrō*, they could further bolster their claims to power because the emperor authorized them to serve as his advisers. In this role, they selected and approved the men who became cabinet ministers and prime ministers.

Until well into the 1910s, therefore, a small circle of Restoration veterans dominated the formal and informal positions of influence in the Japanese state. Almost all of them were former samurai from the domains of Satsuma and Chōshū, and they shared many life experiences. They did differ in some respects, though. Yamagata detested political parties; Itō embraced them. Katsura, an army general, espoused war; Saionji, an aristocrat's son, preferred diplomacy. But however diverse and competitive they were, this cohort of leaders was usually able to keep the ship of state on a reasonably steady course. They could negotiate their disputes in order to pursue policies that they all, more or less, supported.

Such amity and shared interests were less common among their successors, in part because of the changes taking place in Japan itself after 1890. The contention among government leaders in the years after 1918 is also associated with the leaders' attributes themselves. In the thirteen years between 1918 and 1931, nine different men held the prime ministership. Two of them were career military officers. Two started careers as businessmen: **Hara Kei** was a journalist before he entered the Ministry of Foreign Affairs, and **Katō Takaaki** worked for the Mitsubishi *zaibatsu* before becoming a diplomat. **Takahashi Korekiyo** spent many years as a Ministry of Finance official and government bank officer. Three other prime ministers began their careers as bureaucrats, too. Hara, Katō, and Takahashi, along with the three former bureaucrats, then became political party leaders later in life. Finally, **Inukai Tsuyoshi** spent his entire adult career as an elected politician. Both literally and figuratively, therefore, these men represented a wide range of interests, owing to their career paths, allegiances, and personalities.

In addition, these leaders operated under constraints that their predecessors had not faced. The oligarchs obtained their formal positions because they and their revolutionary predecessors had seized power by force. The new leaders, however, were still co-opted by the *genrō*, because there was no formal procedure specified in the constitution for the selection of prime ministers. But unlike most of the *genrō*, new leaders after 1918 were often political party heads. Therefore, besides winning allies and supporters among a small circle of oligarchs, they were also constrained by an electorate whose votes determined whether or not leaders could govern with a parliamentary majority. Finally, they had to know how to deal with a corps of skilled bureaucrats who were becoming increasingly difficult to coordinate and control.

It was during this era that Japan's national civil service, or **bureaucracy**, assumed many of the features for which it is still well known today. The foundation for change was laid gradually in the 1890s and early 1900s when the government instituted a civil service examination system whose purpose was to recruit men according to the principle of merit, carefully defined. Generally, these were university graduates who had specialized in law and public administration. In practice, however, from the 1890s to the present, most of the men recruited into the highest ranks of the exam-based civil service have been graduates of the legal divisions of the prestigious national universities in Tōkyō and Kyōto. They have been the smart, well-educated, and competitively selected individuals overseeing the day-to-day administrative affairs of the Japanese state.

Bureaucratic power expanded after 1890 with the growth of government services and resources. The greater number of schools demanded a larger Ministry of Education. More banks, financial firms, and tax payers required a larger Ministry of Finance. More industrial firms led to the creation of the Ministry of Commerce and Industry. The increasing complexity of political, economic, and social affairs also led to the growth of bureaucratic power. Colonial interests required ministerial oversight. New technologies such as the radio led to new bureaucratic regulations and personnel. The nationalization of many of the railways in 1906 made the Communications Ministry larger. Finally, bureaucratic power increased because government leaders had to rely on the bureaucrats' technical assistance to identify issues, set agendas, develop legislation, and implement laws. The bureaucracy thus became an indispensable element in the conduct of the nation's political affairs.

While gaining power overall, the bureaucracy also experienced greater internal division. The recruitment and promotion programs used in the civil service contributed to some of these divisions. Each ministry usually administered its own specialized exam. Successful applicants entered a ministry after graduating from university and usually spent their entire careers in the civil service. Although some people were given short-term appointments to other ministries, most bureaucrats remained in just one. As a result, they developed strong attachments to that ministry, its policies, and its objectives, which led to a strong sense of turf consciousness, or identity with one's own ministry at the expense of others. This turf consciousness in turn produced many interministerial conflicts that ensured the bureaucracy could not, and would not, act as a monolithic force in national politics.

Further dispersing the once centralized power of the state during this era was the expansion of the voting public. When the first Diet election was held in 1890, barely 1 percent of the Japanese people could vote, as the ballot was restricted to men aged twenty-five and older who were long-term residents in their communities and significant taxpayers. The following decades were marked by movements by workers, tenants, and women to expand the franchise. In 1919, responding in small measure to these movements, the government loosened some voting restrictions, and the electorate increased to about 5 percent of the total population. Following even more concerted political action, in 1926 the Diet passed a universal manhood suffrage law that enfranchised nearly all males over the age of twenty-five, thereby enabling about 20 percent of the population to vote in national elections for the lower house.

This expanding electorate invigorated political parties to mobilize support for elected representatives in the Diet. Political parties had first appeared in the 1870s and 1880s during the heyday of the **Freedom and People's Rights Movement**. In the absence of a national legislature, many of these parties lasted only a short time. Those whose successors still operate in Japan today originated at the turn of the twentieth century. The first of these was the **Seiyūkai**, which Itō Hirobumi used to pursue his political ambitions as a *genrō*. Drawing support from a large base of landlords and their tenants in the countryside, and the businessmen and their employees in the cities, the Seiyūkai pursued conservative policies at home and expansionist policies abroad. The party's principal opponent first appeared in 1913. It reorganized under the banner of the **Kenseikai** in 1916 and became the **Minseitō** in 1927. Although it, too, pursued expansionist policies abroad on some occasions, the Minseitō took a somewhat more progressive line on domestic affairs, because it drew more support from the emerging middle groups in the cities than did the Seiyūkai. **Socialist parties** also appeared for the first time at about the turn of the century, but they did not become a force in electoral politics until after the passage of the universal manhood suffrage act in 1926.

When the electorate was still limited between 1890 and 1919, political parties were essentially small, elite organs whose members were primarily elected legislators in the national parliament and prefectural assemblies. They mobilized their supporters through hierarchical networks of allegiance. For example, a Diet member from a particular district made direct contact with a few influential landlords and businessmen in his constituency. These persons in turn each mobilized some other voters on the basis of personal, business, or political obligations. Pork-barrel politics cemented the ties among voters, influentials, and representatives.

When the electorate expanded, first in 1919 and then in 1926, political parties came to rely on interest-group alliances as a further device to mobilize support. The Seiyūkai, which held office for a majority of this period, was a kind of government party that deftly employed its ties to state-administered organizations, such as the Imperial Agricultural Society and the Imperial Reservists' Association. It also cultivated ties to new interest associations that spoke on behalf of the business community, such as the **Japan Industrial Club**, formed in 1917. The dissident movements that arose among workers, women, and *burakumin* often joined forces with socialist parties to promote their interests. During the 1910s and 1920s, interest groups and political parties thus combined to create broader venues through which some, but by no means all, of the Japanese people could express their political demands.

It is important to note here one form of collective action that Japan did not take during the 1920s, because its absence played a crucial role in shaping the evolution of Japanese politics in the 1930s. As combatants in World War I, both Germany and Italy had to reincorporate large numbers of demobilized soldiers into poorly performing economies after 1919. Psychologically fragile, politically frustrated, and often unemployed, many of these former soldiers in both Germany and Italy turned to violent action through paramilitary organizations. Hitler and Mussolini exploited just such groups to lay the foundation for their authoritarian regimes. Because Japanese military forces did not engage on a large scale in World War I, Japan did not have to deal with the problems of reintegrating numerous former soldiers into its poorly performing economy. Nor did violent, paramilitary groups emerge in large numbers during the 1920s. Thus, no counterpart to a Hitler or Mussolini appeared in Japan, no fascists or storm troopers emerged, and popular politics centered on the Diet.

Parliamentary politics began in the 1890s with disputes over budgetary matters. The *genrō* sought to control the budget so they could pursue the national policies they preferred. However, the Meiji constitution gave some control over annual budgets to the lower house of the Diet, and legislators took advantage of this provision almost immediately. Thus began a long-standing tug-of-war between legislators and the government over national expenditures. The legislators, representing a growing portion of the public, began to encroach on some of the previously unlimited powers of the *genrō*.

But the elected representatives themselves remained elites representing the interests of a limited segment of the population, and therefore, budgetary battles usually dealt with incremental changes in the support of education, the infrastructure, or the military. Fundamental shifts in government outlays, to improve welfare provision or to redistribute income, for example, were minor issues on the parliamentary agenda during this era. Debates over the scope of suffrage were frequent, however, especially after the 1910s, and they did lead to significant change in 1926—at least by the standards of early-twentieth-century politics.

Parliament also engaged in some foreign policy matters, although they remained in Japan—as in most countries—a preserve of elite decision making. In the early years of this period, the unequal treaties and tariff autonomy remained the top foreign policy concerns, as they had been since the 1850s, although the government was finally able to resolve these issues. In 1894 it negotiated the cessation of the unequal treaties, to take effect in 1899. The government was also able to regain control of tariffs in 1911. In the meantime, Japan concluded a treaty of alliance with Great Britain in 1902 and renewed it in 1905. In 1907 it had also achieved a détente with France and Russia. By the second decade of the twentieth century, if not before, Japan had thus begun to associate with the major diplomatic powers of Europe on a basis of apparent equality.

Another dimension of Japan's foreign relations during this time had even more significant implications: continental expansion. Beginning in 1894 and continuing into the 1940s, Japan pursued imperial objectives on the Asian continent. It defeated China in the Sino-Japanese War of 1894–1895 and demanded a large indemnity as well as control over the island of Taiwan and the Liaodong Peninsula (in Manchuria), although France, Britain, and Russia stepped in to prevent Japan from taking control of the peninsula. This persuaded Japan to act more cautiously toward the major European powers in the future, but the intervention did not prevent Japan from taking control of two important cities on the peninsula and from incorporating Taiwan into its overseas empire in Asia.

Korea was the next object of Japan's imperial designs. Worrying about Russian influence in the area, Japan worked diligently after 1895 to persuade the European powers that it had a natural right to supervise Korean affairs. Indeed, the Russo-Japanese War of 1904–1905 was fought to assert this claim. As a result of the negotiated Japanese victory in this conflict, Japan defended its assertion of special rights in Korea and also gained control of the southern half of the island of Sakhalin. In addition, it won possession of the South Manchurian Railway, thereby gaining a legitimate toehold in the northeastern provinces of China (also known as Manchuria). A few years later, Japan assumed effective control of Korea, which functioned as a Japanese colony from 1910 until 1945.

China persisted as a target of Japanese influence. Its control of Taiwan emboldened Japan to think of Fukien Province, across the straits from Taiwan, as a natural area for the expansion of Japanese influence. Japan also sought access to Chinese raw materials, and the Twenty-One Demands addressed to China in 1915 were aimed in part at taking control of China's coal and iron ore. Japan won another toehold in China in 1914. Obligated by treaty to enter World War I on the side of Great Britain, Japan took control of former German concessions on the Shandong Peninsula. But Manchuria loomed the largest in the Japanese imagination. Many Japanese observers saw its rich agricultural and mineral resources as a valuable asset in Japan's grand design for economic development. Consequently, private, public, and military groups maneuvered constantly in the Manchurian region after 1906 to expand Japan's influence.

The reasons for Japan's designs on an Asian empire are numerous. First, Japan was mimicking the West to some degree. If the major powers could scramble for empire, then Japan could, too. Beyond this, some believed that Japan had an obligation to assist its Asian neighbors to preserve autonomy and promote economic development in the face of "Western" encroachment. As Korea and China found it more difficult to achieve these objectives, however, some in Japan grew impatient. They began to adopt a more patronizing attitude toward China and Korea, arrogating to Japan a superior position that granted it the right to act on behalf of lesser Asian nations. From that point on, it was only a short step until people began arguing that Japan actually had to seize direct control over Korea, and at least parts of China, out of diplomatic, economic, and military necessity.

One group in Japan backed an expansionist approach to Asia from the 1890s onward: the Japanese army. More than any institution in Japan, the army was always involved when an incident in Asia led to expanded Japanese authority. This was true in 1894–1895, in 1904–1905, in 1910, and in 1918–1922, when an army expeditionary force in Siberia tried to impose Japanese influence north of Manchuria. The foremost student of the Japanese army in the 1920s has written that by then, the army presented "a strange and contradictory picture — a mixture of pride, arrogance, and hubris on the one hand, and the haunting fear of impending calamity on the other."[3] Throughout the 1920s, the Japanese occupation forces in Manchuria, the Kantō army, provoked incidents that were excuses for the extension of Japanese authority. The assassination of the Manchurian warlord Zhang Zoulin in 1928, which occurred when an army general was prime minister, was one of the most crucial of these. All these events were indications of the army's zealous support of the country's militant expansion and direct control of the Asian continent. Finally, in late September 1931, the Japanese army provoked an incident in Mukden that led to the colonization of Manchuria, unleashed the army's expansionist frenzy, and set Japan on the course toward war.

NOTES TO CHAPTER 2

1. Miriam Silverberg, "The Modern Girl as Militant," in *Recreating Japanese Women, 1600–1945*, ed. Gail Lee Bernstein (Berkeley and Los Angeles: University of California Press, 1991), p. 263.
2. Natsume Sōseki, *Kokoro*, trans. Edwin McClellan (New York: Regnery Gateway, 1957), p. 245.
3. Leonard A. Humphreys, *The Way of the Heavenly Sword: The Japanese Army in the 1920's* (Stanford, Calif.: Stanford University Press, 1995), pp. 180–181.

CHAPTER THREE

Fighting for Development, 1932–1973

The four midcentury decades spanned one of the most eventful periods in Japan's modern history. They began with economic depression and imperial conquests and were followed by war, devastation, defeat, and foreign occupation. These events were gradually repaired during a postwar revival that took nearly a decade to complete, at which point Japan entered a period of stunning economic growth. Discontinuities are thus a central feature of this period, although we should not dwell on them at the expense of continuities.

A somewhat grim analogy with family life helps explain the complexities of this era. Imagine a family in which the father, a strong patriarch, is an abusive alcoholic suffering a brain tumor. He has long been a demanding personality with destructive habits, so the tumor only worsens conditions. His behavior deforms the world around him and threatens his wife and children. After an extended illness that is damaging to everyone, he finally dies.

His death is a relief to surviving family members. The enormous stress has been lifted, and they are able to live in a far safer environment. They have lost the force at the center of their lives but found new strength in themselves. They have also rediscovered friends, relatives, and neighbors and regained a foothold in the community.

The family's readjustment is hampered, however, by an unexpected event. The physician and therapists who had been treating the father now have moved into the family home, to oversee the recoveries of his wife and children. The new occupants take over the best rooms in the house, demand the best food, and expect people to bow to their every wish. Obviously, this turn of events complicates and postpones the family's readjustment, but once the caregivers have moved out, the family recovers quickly.

In this analogy, the sick, abusive father is the Japanese military, and his behavior parallels that of the military; it was also irrational, deforming, and destructive. The wife and children are Japanese society which was brutalized by forces that were a part of it but beyond its control. The physician and therapists are the Allied occupying authorities who "moved in with" the Japanese in late 1945 and stayed for nearly seven years.

In this analogy, the period of illness and abuse coincides with the years of war between 1932 and 1945. The father's death is the rupture that divides the wartime and postwar periods, causing agony but also providing relief. The Occupation is a period of difficult readjustment, when the caregivers facilitate the reascent, rebirth, and regeneration of Japanese economic, social, and cultural life, respectively.

In addition to these cataclysms, one concern permeated the entire period: How could Japan achieve economic development? Before and during the war, this aim was pursued with the use of military force. After the war, it was driven by necessity, because survival demanded economic recovery. By the 1950s, national purpose motivated the fight for development, and by 1973 Japan finally produced achievements that surprised almost everyone.

POLITICAL AGGRESSION AND RETREAT

A coalition of military leaders and bureaucrats persuaded Japan to conquer Asia and wage war against the United States. The war, however, was a nearly suicidal undertaking, as some of them realized from the beginning. It went poorly from the outset, caused enormous losses at home and abroad, and resulted in a humiliating defeat. After the war, the Allied occupiers entered Japan and initiated sweeping reforms that drastically altered laws and institutions, although many political personalities and patterns of behavior nonetheless endured. Following the Occupation, a new coalition of national leaders emerged, consisting of former and incumbent bureaucrats working in cooperation with corporate executives from the private sector. Operating in a more pluralistic political environment, these leaders easily persuaded the nation to retreat from foreign entanglements and to focus on economic growth as its highest priority.

The keynote for the first third of this era was struck in early 1932, when the Japanese military established a puppet government in Manchuria. This event created an imperialist euphoria in Japan, and it also certified the unruly, aggressive conduct of the Japanese army in Asia. Throughout the 1920s, Japan's Kantō army had provoked incidents that could be used to expand Japanese authority in China. But such incidents often betrayed disorder within the army, especially the problem of insubordination by lower-ranking officers. Their conduct was, in turn, a reflection of deeper divisions within the army itself.

This internal conflict was apparent among officers tied to at least three different groups. One group was the old Chōshū clique, rapidly losing its power following the deaths of its former leaders, **Yamagata Aritomo** and **Katsura Tarō**. A second clique consisted of officers loosely allied around men from the old Saga domain, one of whom was **Araki Sadao**. This group was sometimes referred to as the Imperial Way faction. It stressed support for the emperor and a somewhat blind and irrational belief in the superiority of the Japanese fighting man armed with rifle and bayonet. The third group, sometimes known as the Control faction, consisted of fast-rising younger officers trained at the army academy and the army war college. They had seen action in Europe during and after World War I, and they advocated total war planning, that is, military preparedness based on an industrially well developed economy. **Nagata Tetsuzan** was a leading figure in this group.

Despite their differences, all these groups shared a desire to expand Japanese influence in Asia, and for purposes of strategic planning, they all recognized Russia as the principal enemy. The navy, in contrast, saw the United States as its most likely opponent and pursued a different set of objectives. The navy wanted more battleships and destroyers in order to protect sea-lanes that would give Japan access to raw materials in Southeast Asia and the South Pacific. During the 1920s, these differences—within the army and between the army and the navy—were played out in budget battles and political strife. That strife grew during the 1930s as both services competed to obtain more funding. Always more unruly and venturesome, the army increasingly took actions that forced the government, and the navy, to support it after the fact. As early as 1933, the army's conduct resulted in ever larger outlays for military spending.

In these actions, the army found allies in two critical places. Some were in the ranks of the civil bureaucracy. Called *reform bureaucrats* at the time, these men were often bright graduates of the best universities who had assumed key positions at the Ministry of Commerce and Industry. They favored centralized national planning as a solution to Japan's economic ills, and they were willing to collaborate with the military in order to achieve their policy objectives. In the early 1930s, some members of this group, such as **Kishi Nobusuke**, established personal and professional ties with aspiring army leaders, such as **Tōjō Hideki**, while on bureaucratic assignment in Manchuria. They shared an interest in industrializing Manchuria to aid the expansion of Japanese military influence. These shared interests blossomed during the 1940s when Kishi served as a cabinet minister under Tōjō.

The army's other ally during the 1930s consisted of various direct-action groups. They were sometimes formed from extremist civilian organizations, but often they were small cliques of active-duty military men, usually low-ranking officers in the army. No clearly defined political agenda united these groups. Rather, they found common ground in their support for the emperor, aversion to the political parties, suspicion of the *zaibatsu*, and frustration over the course of events.

On three critical occasions during the 1930s, groups like these engineered the removal of influential party politicians, government leaders, and military figures. The first occasion was in 1931, when terrorists assassinated the party leader **Inukai Tsuyoshi**. His death ensured the advent of a series of cabinets led by army generals and navy admirals and dominated by military figures. The second incident occurred in 1935, when an assassin killed Nagata Tetsuzan. Nagata had been trying to slow the military's expansion in China, and his death removed a strong opponent of the Imperial Way faction. The third crucial incident came in 1936, when army officers assassinated the minister of finance, **Takahashi Korekiyo**, who had been trying to brake the increase in military expenditures. His death removed another influential opponent of rapid military expansion.

These incidents had an intimidating effect on parliamentary politics. Legislators grew less willing to challenge military requests and to oppose military policies. Political parties were accused of being corrupt, vacillating, and ineffective by both the public and extremist groups. The parties on the left were hounded and driven underground by the government. When civilians were chosen to form cabinets, they often favored military policies anyway or were too weak to oppose them. This was especially true of **Konoe Fumimaro**, an aristocrat who was prime minister on two critical occasions. In addition, except to order the punishment of coup leaders in 1936, the **Shōwa emperor** apparently took no action to prevent the military from having its way. The leading authority on the Shōwa emperor calls this "Shōwa's tragedy" and notes that although "the emperor had opposed war—at least until November 1941—he absolutized those principles [of limited monarchy] to the point where he ruled out the kind of dramatic imperial intervention which might have caused the government to think twice before plunging into the maelstrom of total war."[1]

In 1937, when the Japanese army in Manchuria forced its way into north China, there were few political figures left in Japan who could effectively oppose its action. From then on, the government began to mobilize the nation for war, using **neighborhood associations** to build support from the ground up. In 1940 it created the **Greater Japan Patriotic Industrial League** to bring workers behind the war effort. In the same year, the government forced the political parties to disband and support the new **Imperial Reserve Assistance Association**. Konoe intended the association to be a Japanese variant of Germany's National Socialist Party, but it never functioned with the same unity or effect. When the Tōjō cabinet approved the attack on the U.S. naval base at Pearl Harbor in late 1941, Japan was united in its resolve—at least on paper—to fight a quick, successful war.

Unfortunately, neither its plans nor events worked out as expected. Japan did not possess, or have access to, the raw materials needed to fight an economic power far stronger than itself. Initially, it advanced quickly but then stalled. Long supply lines, poor coordination, and inadequate transport forced armies in the field to adopt desperate and self-destructive solutions. By late 1942, the Allied forces were beginning a successful counterattack, reaching the home islands with air raids in 1944. Following months of devastating bombing that leveled many Japanese cities and killed hundreds of thousands, the United States dropped atomic bombs on Hiroshima and Nagasaki in early August 1945. These nuclear bombs finally persuaded the emperor to announce surrender on August 15.

The Allies lost no time in entering Japan. Advance troops and the Supreme Commander of the Allied Powers, General Douglas MacArthur, arrived in December 1945. He and his subordinate officers, most of them Americans, set about immediately to reform Japan from top to bottom. These reforms reached into economic, social, and cultural institutions, and they had an especially deep influence on political institutions.

Some of the earliest Occupation reforms dealt with the military and wartime leaders. The army and navy were disbanded, and the Ministries of the Army and Navy were abolished. Some military officers were tried, and a few of them were convicted and sentenced to death by the International Military Tribunal for the Far East. (Numerous others were tried, convicted, and killed on site in various Asian theaters of war.) Almost all members of the wartime Diet were purged, or removed from office, along with officers of the **Imperial Reservists' Association** and the Imperial Reserve Assistance Association. In addition, these two **state-guided organizations**, and others like them, were abolished. More than three thousand high-ranking business leaders were purged. Although a few hundred high-level bureaucrats were also purged, most of the bureaucracy remained intact. The Allies had opted to rule indirectly, through the organs of the Japanese state, rather than directly, as they did in Germany, so it was necessary to retain most of the civilian administrators of the national government.

The most pervasive political reforms were implemented by means of a new constitution in 1947 (see under Documents in the Appendix). Drafted almost entirely by a small group of Americans and essentially imposed on the Japanese, the postwar constitution was intentionally designed to address the defects of the Meiji constitution, especially in regard to the emperor, the Diet, the executive branch, the military, local government, and the citizenry.

The postwar constitution calls for the emperor to be merely a "symbol of the state," and since 1947 the emperor has had no formal governing powers. He does have a number of state duties, such as convening the Diet, but he is no longer the theoretical center of the Japanese state in any sense. In the forty-four years that remained to him after defeat, Hirohito dutifully honored his constitutional role, as has his son and successor, the **Heisei emperor**.

Like the Meiji constitution, the postwar constitution calls for a legislature with an upper and lower house. Owing to the abolition of the prewar peerage, members of both the upper house and the lower house are drawn from all walks of life. The legislature, or Diet, is the country's supreme lawmaking body and so does not have the weaknesses of the prewar Diet, which was merely advisory and could always be overruled by imperial edicts. Rather, the postwar Diet has far more authority and thus gives political parties a much stronger lease on life.

The postwar constitution requires that the prime minister be selected from sitting members of the Diet. This provision, too, resolves the problem with the Meiji constitution that it had no provision for selecting a prime minister. This lack of provision enabled the powerful, informal *genrō* to quash popular, public influence on the executive and to preserve clique government. Since 1947, however, the Japanese public has played at least an indirect role in the selection of the prime minister, and the constitution requires that at least half his cabinet also be elected representatives. In practice, most postwar cabinets have consisted almost entirely of elected politicians.

The most crucial change in the postwar constitution involves the role of the military. Article 9 (see under Documents in the Appendix) denies Japan the right to maintain a military force and the "right of belligerency of the state," but since 1954 Japan has had a legally established military known as the Self-Defense Forces, which operate under the auspices of the cabinet-level **Self-Defense Agency**. These forces number only about 250,000, but they have been consistently ranked among the top ten in the world with respect to their quality. Numerous court cases have tested their constitutionality. Occasionally, some lower courts have ruled against them, but they have always survived on appeal. Throughout the postwar era, some political groups also have sought to revise the constitution in order to legalize the use of Japanese troops abroad but, so far, to no avail.

The postwar constitution also dramatically changed the mode of local governance in Japan. Previously, prefectures, cities, towns, and villages had operated as arms of the national government. But under the 1947 constitution, they have enjoyed far more autonomy, electing their own executives and assemblies. Although the state has restricted local autonomy in many ways, the 1947 constitution created a new arena of elective politics that has made local governments far more attentive to the demands of the citizenry.

A principal achievement of the new constitution has been to create a body of citizens—in contrast with subjects—and to give them the formal powers they need to exercise their will. The prewar constitution vested all powers in the emperor, but the postwar constitution vests sovereignty in the people. It gives women the right to vote, and it lowers the voting age to twenty. Neither the voters nor their representatives have always exercised popular sovereignty in a wholly democratic manner, but the legal potential for more democratic politics has been available since 1947.

During the Occupation, Japan, its leaders, and its people had to pursue political practice under surreal conditions. They had a democratic constitution, but the occupying authorities still exerted a strong influence. Eventually, however, the Allies tired of the costs of occupation, and they began to discuss treaties to end it. In 1951 Japan, the United States, and other powers signed a treaty of peace in San Francisco, and the occupiers left the following year. American military troops remained to meet the obligations of a security treaty also signed in 1951, making the United States primarily responsible for Japan's defense, under an American nuclear umbrella and at minimal direct cost to Japan.

During and after the Occupation, party politics rose to the fore. The prewar parties, which had been disbanded by 1940, were revived as soon as the war ended. A liberal party and a democratic party took up where the prewar **Seiyūkai** and **Minseitō** had left off, and in 1955 they joined to create the **Liberal Democratic Party** (LDP), which has formed almost every government since then. The **Japan Socialist Party** (JSP) emerged after the war to pursue the programs of its prewar predecessors, as did the **Japan Communist Party**. For the first fifteen years after the war, these two parties of the political left competed vigorously against their conservative foes. Although they eventually attracted about a third of the voters into their fold, they never won a majority so as to form their own government.

In the 1960s two centrist parties were added. The **Democratic Socialist Party** appeared in late 1959 when right-wing dissidents in the JSP broke off to form their own party. In 1967 the **Clean Government Party** (Kōmeitō) ran candidates in a lower house election for the first time. This unusual party drew its support from members of an evangelical Buddhist sect. These new parties reflected the growing segmentation of Japanese society, and they led to more diverse political policies and practices.

Throughout this period, the conservative parties won majorities or struck alliances that enabled them to form nearly every government. Between 1947 and 1954, **Yoshida Shigeru** dominated Japanese politics as the leader of the Liberal Party. A former diplomat, he concurrently headed the **Ministry of Foreign Affairs**, which allowed him to control Japan's relations with its American occupier and to pursue policies that served Japan's interests. Yoshida argued that Japan should assume a low posture in foreign affairs and take advantage of American military protection to pursue economic development. As much as any single individual, he was responsible for articulating the rationale for Japan's political retreat in the early postwar years.

Yoshida recruited into his party a large number of talented, former bureaucrats. In their "descent from heaven" (**amakudari**), they made elective politics their landing spot. They did not succeed him immediately. Such figures as **Ishibashi Tanzan** and others served brief terms in office during the mid-1950s. Beginning in 1957 and continuing until 1972, Yoshida's bureaucratic successors presided over the prime ministership and most key cabinet positions. Kishi Nobusuke, prime minister between 1957 and 1960, was a relic of the prewar era. He had been a "reform bureaucrat," an ally of Tōjō Hideki, and a wartime cabinet minister. **Ikeda Hayato**, a former finance ministry official, followed Kishi with a four-year term in office. **Satō Eisaku**, Kishi's brother and a former high-level official of the Transport Ministry, served a seven-year term until 1972. All these men brought to elective political life the haughty demeanor of powerful bureaucrats and a preference for technocratic (top-down, directive) governance. But they also shared a commitment to national goals, had broad contacts among their contemporaries and subordinates, and knew how to get things done.

Some of their most helpful contacts were businessmen and former bureaucrats in the private sector. One former bureaucrat close to Kishi was **Uemura Kōgorō**, Kishi's prewar associate in the Ministry of Commerce and Industry. Purged after the war, Uemura had played an informal role in helping revive the Japanese economy, and in 1952 he became the executive director of Japan's major big business organization, **Keidanren**. When the president of Keidanren, a well-connected businessman named **Ishizaka Taizō**, resigned in 1968, Uemura assumed the presidency himself for the next six years. Therefore, this former bureaucrat, who shared the outlooks, objectives, and styles of government leaders, was in a critical position to coordinate private-sector interests with government policies during the years of high-speed growth. He also raised enormous sums of money to fund LDP candidates.

Two other interest groups that played an integral role in the policy process of this era were **Nikkeiren** and Nōkyō. Nikkeiren was a business association like Keidanren, although it had a more narrow and specific purpose: to coordinate management's views of and policies toward labor. In this role, Nikkeiren countered the political influence of the union movement and promoted good relations between workers and managers. Nōkyō was the national organization of agricultural cooperatives which carried out a variety of essential marketing, purchasing, and financing activities in rural areas. It also served as a vehicle for mobilizing the farm vote behind the Liberal Democratic Party.

In addition to LDP officials and private-sector influentials, incumbent bureaucrats were a third group of national leaders who provided the political vision and capability to advance economic development after the war. Some were in the **Ministry of Finance**, where they drew up budgets, supervised the financial system, determined interest rates, and allocated capital in a way that satisfied central government policies. Others were in the **Ministry of International Trade and Industry** (MITI). The MITI controlled the allocation of foreign exchange within the Japanese economy as well as the right to license foreign technology to Japanese users. Another cabinet-level body that assisted in Japan's rapid growth was the **Economic Planning Agency**, formed in 1955. It gathered and disseminated information on the economy and drew up plans to guide development.

One of these plans—the emblematic policy of the high-growth era—was the Income-Doubling Plan (see Documents in the Appendix). Drawn up in the late 1950s at the behest of Ikeda Hayato, this plan called for dramatic increases in investment, output, trade, and incomes. Much to the surprise of its supporters, not to mention its skeptics, the plan achieved many of its goals in advance of projections. The political benefits of these successes redounded to Ikeda and the LDP, and they laid the foundation for a long period of conservative rule. Such success also forced other nations to begin taking seriously Japan's emergence as a world power.

Nonetheless, still chastened by defeat in war, a humiliating occupation, and a backlog of domestic needs, Japan kept the low diplomatic profile that Yoshida had advocated. It restricted defense expenditures to less than 1 percent of the gross national product. It avoided diplomatic crises. It sought amicable relations with as many nations as it could manage, for example, by restoring commercial ties with the People's Republic of China in 1962 and diplomatic relations in 1972. Because of its political retreat after the war, Japan was able to concentrate on the postwar era's national obsession: growth.

ECONOMIC DEFORMATION AND REASCENT

Civilian bureaucrats and military officers alike tried to plan rationally for the conduct of economic affairs during the war years, but events nearly always ruined their designs. Everyone was struggling to survive in an environment that was both hostile and volatile. Old industries went into eclipse while *zaibatsu* enterprises and other military producers thrived. Their growth carried Japan through a second phase of industrial revolution, this one based on heavy industry. By the end of the war, however, Japan's economy had been destroyed by the effort to sustain a losing endeavor. Widespread destruction, isolation from world markets, and Occupation policies further retarded its recovery. Once it had recovered in the mid-1950s, however, the economy reascended during a two-decade period of rapid growth that brought Japan abreast of the advanced industrial nations.

In 1932 Japan's economy was still struggling with a deep-seated depression. Agricultural and other commodity prices were still well below earlier levels. Unemployment rates were high, and underemployment was widespread, especially in agriculture and the commercial sector. Consumption levels were low, and household debt was rising. People seemed to be working harder, and they were in some cases actually producing more than before, but many did not benefit materially from their efforts.

These conditions changed quickly with the conquest of Manchuria and the evolution of a quasi-wartime economy. Political pressures, driven by both the takeover and the military, forced the government to develop reflationary policies. Also called *pump priming*, these policies relied on government bonds to finance the increased economic activity. Because most increases in government outlays went to the military, a large share of the new financing supported firms that produced military goods. Accordingly, the Japanese economy moved quickly out of depression, propelled by a boom in heavy industry.

Some observers have detected in Japan between 1932 and 1945 a government-directed industrial policy. They contend that bright bureaucrats in two ministries (Finance, and Commerce and Industry), acting with the advice of economists and other intellectuals, identified needs, set targets, allocated resources, and directed the private sector to pursue policies of growth. There is some truth to this assertion, because some bureaucrats did try to do these things, at least on paper. But this broad claim exaggerates the influence of civilian bureaucrats and also ignores the significance of other actors and their behavior, as well as the context of change in the domestic political economy.

Other significant actors in Japan between 1932 and 1945 included the military and private-sector business leaders. Since the late 1920s, well-placed army officers had been advocating rational, long-term, strategic planning for total war, and by the 1930s men such as **Nagata Tetsuzan** were putting such plans into action. Thus, military planning under the exigencies of war was just as influential in shaping economic policies as was civilian planning at the Finance and other ministries. Moreover, military plans often differed from those of civilian bureaucrats, so conflicts between bureaucrats and the military were endemic between 1932 and 1945. Although planners expected private-sector businessmen to respond docilely to government directives, they proved remarkably resistant to state intervention in corporate affairs. Business leaders did eventually cooperate with the war effort, but they also retained more autonomy than civilian and military planners had expected, and their firms profited immensely.

Much of the economic conduct during the war was actually ad hoc. Although there were some central plans and efforts to control wages, supplies, labor assignments, and production quotas, many companies and most families had to make do as best they could. For example, families who could not obtain necessities through the government-controlled rationing system turned to black markets for their needs. Firms that required more workers did not hesitate to bid up wages and lure them away from competitors. Thus, a kind of catch-as-catch-can response best exemplifies what happened in the Japanese economy in the late 1930s and early 1940s, as everyone had to adapt continuously to the demands of survival and production amid global war.

Between 1932 and 1945, the key economic elements were agriculture, the artisanal and commercial sector, the manufacturing enterprises producing for the military, and other manufacturing firms. The agricultural sector went through three brief shifts during this short period. In 1932 many farmers still were struggling with low prices, high costs, and rising debt. Technology remained static, so the prevailing modes of production did not change until the effects of the industrial boom were felt. When urban employment and incomes rose, consumer demand also increased, stimulating better conditions in agriculture. The late 1930s were thus years of improvement for many farm families, who were able to pay off some of their debts and raise their standard of living. But when the war expanded, more adult males were drawn out of agriculture, and the smaller labor force led to a reduction in cultivated land (of about 10 percent) and a drop in output. By 1944, mothers and children fleeing bombed cities began overwhelming farm villages. At the end of the war, Japan's agricultural sector faced a depressing combination of technological stagnation, overpopulation, and underproduction.

The artisanal and commercial sector experienced a fate similar to that of agriculture. In the early 1930s it was overemployed and underproductive, but the industrial boom allowed it to prosper during the mid-1930s. However, when the government began rationing commodities (such as food and fuel) in the late 1930s, both artisanal and commercial establishments began to feel the pinch. Declining incomes, urban flight, and the bombing campaigns all left this sector of the economy devastated by 1945.

As long as the war lasted, military producers profited. These included steel-makers, shipbuilders, aircraft manufacturers, metals producers, and firms making electrical and communications equipment. Some firms and industries grew at stupendous rates between 1933 and 1942, producing a dramatic shift in the Japanese economy away from a reliance on agriculture and light industry (especially textiles) toward domination by the heavy industrial and chemical sector, a change that persisted long after the war ended.

Zaibatsu enterprises exploited the opportunities that war offered, expanding rapidly and making extraordinary profits. The **Mitsui enterprise** continued as a major financial provider and coal supplier and created under its own name a number of firms in shipbuilding, precision metals and machinery, and chemicals. It also invested in other firms making electrical and communications equipment. One of these was **Toshiba**, an electrical manufacturer formed in 1939 in a merger between two firms in the Tōkyō area. Toshiba became a mainstay in the Mitsui combine and accounted for more than half its annual profits during the last years of the war.

Even more than Mitsui, the **Mitsubishi** and **Sumitomo enterprises** served the military's production needs. In 1934 Mitsubishi consolidated its shipbuilding, aircraft-manufacturing, and equipment-making businesses in a single firm, Mitsubishi Heavy Industries. This firm provided naval vessels and military aircraft in massive numbers during the war, and it returned enormous profits, in fact, the highest of any single *zaibatsu* firm. Other Mitsubishi firms profited during the war by selling coal, providing financing, and making chemicals. Sumitomo concentrated, as it always had, on metals making and made huge profits. It also began manufacturing electrical equipment, by investing in such firms as Nippon Electric Company (NEC).

As large as the *zaibatsu* firms and enterprises became, they could not meet the demand for military production on their own. Therefore, older firms grew and new firms emerged to supplement their efforts. **Kawasaki Heavy Industries** expanded in this period to build more ships and aircraft. Other old-line shipbuilders, such as Uraga Dock and Harima Industries, also prospered during the war. Whereas Sumitomo remained a steelmaker, Mitsui and Mitsubishi largely abandoned steel production in 1934. In that year, the former Yahata Iron and Steel Company combined with Fuji Steel and a number of smaller firms to create the Japan Steel Corporation (see **New Japan Steel**). By the end of the war, it was producing more than half of Japan's steel output, more than four times as much as the second-place firm, Japan Steel Tube.

New firms were more common in such industries as aluminum, aircraft manufacturing, and electrical goods manufacturing, most of which were established in the 1910s and 1920s. Shōwa denkō became an important firm in the aluminum industry. Located in the Tōkyō area, it was a family-controlled concern sometimes referred to as one of the "new" *zaibatsu*. Tachikawa and Nakajima were two major aircraft makers, along with Mitsubishi. Remnants of the Nakajima firm survive as Fuji Heavy Industries, which makes Subaru autos. In addition to Toshiba, **Matsushita Electrical Industries** also grew rapidly to meet wartime demands following its incorporation in the Ōsaka area in 1935. Yet another enterprise that played a role in the war effort was Riken, a conglomerate that was the brainchild of a scientist at Tōkyō Imperial University named **Ōkōchi Masatoshi**. His venture is less well known for its postwar successor, Ricoh, and better known for his emphasis on low-cost, mass-production techniques for high-quality goods.

Japan's auto industry dates back to the turn of the twentieth century, although foreign firms such as General Motors made most of the cars produced in Japan then. In an effort to encourage domestic production, the Diet passed a law in 1936 that made foreign manufacture nearly impossible and offered incentives to domestic automakers. One Japanese firm had formed two years earlier and was in a position to take advantage of the new law. Part of another "new" *zaibatsu* organized by a clever entrepreneur named **Aikawa Yoshisuke**, **Nissan Auto** built its factories in the Tōkyō area and had ties to the Yasuda *zaibatsu*. In the same year that Nissan incorporated, the Toyoda Automatic Loom Corporation in Kariya (near Nagoya in central Japan) created a division to develop a Japanese-built auto. That division was spun off in 1937 as a new corporation called **Toyota Motors**. Both Nissan and Toyota had been created to make cars, but when the war intervened, they were forced to make trucks instead. It was only in the 1950s that they turned to automaking on a large scale.

The emergence of so many new firms in these often newer industries had a significant effect on the small- and medium-size enterprises. Many of the new firms, and some of the old ones, made large-scale, complicated products such as ships, aircraft, and trucks that contained many components requiring skillful manufacturing. Rather than make all components under the umbrella of a single firm, such manufacturers preferred to concentrate on the final assembly and to rely on subcontractors to supply components on demand. Therefore, as these branches of heavy industry expanded after 1933, so did the small- and medium-size firms that provided their components. This is a distinctive characteristic of Japan's mass-production industries that still persists. Among a relatively small number of large, well-financed producers, there exists an elaborate network of numerous, small-scale, precariously financed suppliers.

As the war proceeded, older industries that were not producing for the military declined in importance. The textile industry suffered especially. Cotton imports were reduced. Textile machinery was scrapped. Textile workers were reassigned. Output dropped, and profits shrank. Other industries that were not producing for the war effort also found it difficult to obtain raw materials, hire workers, and sell to consumers. Consequently, the lumber and furniture industries, publishing, food processing, and papermaking all went into retreat.

By the end of the war, Japan's economy was drastically altered. Most of the available resources were being channeled to a hopeless struggle to sustain the military. The nation concentrated an irrational effort on aircraft manufacture, shipbuilding, arms making, and steel and chemical production. Nearly every able-bodied worker was mobilized to work in military plants, including schoolchildren, young women, and Korean forced laborers. At the same time, the civilian economy was in shambles, and the Japanese people were making do with less food, poorer clothing, and worse shelter than they had for decades.

The Allied bombing campaign forced this desperate economy to its knees. The air raids that began in 1944 destroyed half the built-up areas of Japan's seventy largest cities. Many residential and commercial areas were razed in attacks that targeted military and production facilities, with the latter especially hard hit. Nearly all the country's aircraft plants and many of its shipbuilding docks were destroyed. Its steel, chemical, and munitions industries were heavily damaged, though not completely destroyed. At the war's end, less than 50 percent of Japan's production facilities were still standing.

These were not the only economic dilemmas the country faced when Allied troops arrived in late 1945. Most of Japan's merchant marine lay at the bottom of the Pacific Ocean, so the country had almost no commercial shipping. The yen was nearly worthless, making it impossible for Japan to buy imports or to make exports. Cities lay in ruins, and transportation facilities were hanging on by a thread. The people were underfed and underemployed, and black markets were thriving.

Amid these depressing conditions, Allied occupiers undertook two major economic reforms, one directed at agriculture, the other at big business. An ambitious land reform was initiated in 1946. The Allies viewed rural Japan as consisting of two classes of farmers, exploiting landlords and poor tenants, and so they set out to erase such inequality. They quickly discovered a more complex reality, however. Although there were a few unfair landlords, most landowners held small farms and often worked the land themselves. There were poor tenants, too, but not as many as imagined, about a third of the farm population. In addition, many farmers were both owners and tenants, and they made up nearly 40 percent of all farm households.

Faced with these discoveries, the Occupiers wisely relied on the assistance of Japanese bureaucrats and farmers to carry out the spirit of the reform program. They established in each village a council whose members reflected the distribution of landlords, tenants, and others in the community. The council purchased land from owners and redistributed it to tenants, on what proved to be very favorable terms. Within a few years, about 90 percent of the agricultural land had passed into the hands of owner-cultivators, and tenancy had all but been eliminated from rural Japan.

The second economic reform was the dissolution of the *zaibatsu*. Strongly influenced by New Deal views of the evils of economic concentration, the Allies were determined to reduce the economic might of the *zaibatsu*. They began by seizing the assets of the holding companies and the *zaibatsu* families and then sold those shares on the public market to small investors. They abolished the holding companies and removed *zaibatsu* family members and wartime executives from management positions. They also broke up individual firms, especially the international trading companies and industrial giants such as Mitsubishi Heavy Industries. (Most of those firms reconsolidated after the Occupation, between 1952 and 1954.) The Allies also created a Fair Trade Commission to guard against monopolies and to prevent interlocking directorships.

Zaibatsu dissolution also called for a reduction in the influence of the *zaibatsu* banks. Before the banks were reformed, however, the Occupation's policies shifted. Both cold war politics and the rise of the Communist Party in China pushed the United States to make Japan the workshop of Asia and to restore its economy. Therefore, the *zaibatsu* banks were never broken up but began immediately to serve as an important, but by no means the sole, source of capital for firms that were part of their *zaibatsu* lineage. In this way, the old *zaibatsu* banks assumed after the war the roles of the prewar holding companies, providing funding and investment advice to the firms affiliated with them. This new pattern of alliance came to be known as the **keiretsu**.

By the time the Allied authorities left Japan in 1952, reconstruction was nearing completion, and the economy was returning to the levels it had reached around 1936. Japan was still an essentially agrarian nation in which per capita incomes were low and the standard of living was far behind that of the United States and Great Britain. Therefore, few observers, either in Japan or abroad, imagined what the next two decades would bring.

Despite relatively poor conditions, Japan had a number of assets beneficial to development. Many young and underemployed workers were eager to find jobs, even at low wages. Many executives had experience gained during the war with managing firms under difficult conditions. Resurgent corporations in both light and heavy industry were numerous and accomplished at their tasks. The nation's banking system had proved to be strong and resilient, and the international trading companies were uniquely qualified to facilitate global commerce.

The first steps toward reviving the Japanese economy had been taken in the late 1940s. The initial policies emerged out of a consensus that incorporated the views of a broad cross section of leaders, including government bureaucrats, university economists, public intellectuals, business executives, trade association officials, and elected politicians. The consensus was rooted in a practical vision of what was necessary and feasible. Leaders identified several sectors on which to concentrate scarce resources: steelmaking, coal mining, electrical power, chemical production, and shipbuilding.

These were the sectors in which Japan had existing capacity, and they were interrelated in promising ways. Steel was needed for reconstruction purposes and for building ships, which in turn would help restore international trade. Coal and electrical power would be needed for energy and heating, and chemical production would provide synthetic fertilizers to enhance farm output. These industries had revived to a critical point by 1950, when they received an unexpected boost from the Korean War. Indeed, that war's demands provided the stimulus needed to return much of the economy to a solid footing.

During the period of high-speed growth between about 1955 and 1973, Japan acted under a balanced partnership between the public and private sectors. The national government provided the infrastructure (in the form of transportation and communication facilities), channeled investment capital to large-scale producers at favorable rates, and drew up plans for the national allocation of economic resources. The public sector underwrote most of the costs of educating the high-quality labor force essential to growth. The government also ensured, especially through a program of price supports for rice, that farmers were not driven into poverty by the urban-based industrialization that took place after 1955. In addition, the national budgets in this era were not burdened by large defense expenditures or costly outlays for welfare. There-fore, the central government was able to exploit the country's limited resources to maximum advantage.

The private sector contributed by responding to the government's plans, in-centives, and resources and by providing the kind of diligence, creativity, and entrepreneurship that had been in evidence since well before the Meiji era. However devastating the war had been to the Japanese economy, many man-agers, enterprises, and firms persisted across the wartime/postwar divide to pro-vide the human and organizational resources needed for its development.

These survivors included a wide variety of firms. Some were descendants of the *zaibatsu*, now operating through *keiretsu* alliances. The former *zaibatsu* enterprises were especially strong in banking, international trade, electrical manufacturing, and some fields of heavy industry (especially shipbuilding at Mitsubishi). They were not well represented, however, in the steel industry, in which an industry giant, **New Japan Steel**, was formed by the merger of Fuji and Japan Steel in 1970, under the leadership of **Nagano Shigeo**. Older, non-*zaibatsu* firms such as Kawasaki Steel and Japan Steel Tube were other major firms in the steel industry. The former *zaibatsu* also were not active in the rapidly expanding auto industry; only Mitsubishi was an entrant. Nissan and Toyota vied for dominance, facing a serious challenge from Honda, an upstart firm created after the war by the technical innovator **Honda Sōichirō**. The tex-tile industry staged a brief comeback in the immediate postwar period, but it faded under challenges from lower-cost producers abroad. Some of the old firms survived, however, by reorganizing to become synthetic fiber producers or by entering entirely new fields, such as cosmetics at Kanebo (the successor of **Kanegafuchi Spinning**).

Some new firms sprang up after the war and grew rapidly to become among the best known in Japan. These included enterprises such as Sharp and Casio, which specialize in consumer electronics, and Kyocera, a ceramics maker. Among such firms, **Sony** is probably the most famous. Descended from a wartime firm that made radar for the Japanese navy, Sony grew under the imaginative leadership of **Morita Akio** to symbolize Japan's technical creativ-ity, productive capability, and marketing expertise.

These firms are familiar because they export their products to the United States and elsewhere. Exports were important to the Japanese economy dur-ing this period of high-speed growth. Sales abroad earned the foreign curren-cy that enabled Japan to purchase the imports needed to manufacture its finished goods and, increasingly, to feed its people. But foreign trade, although essential, never formed as large a share of Japan's gross national product (GNP) during this era as many think. Exports and imports both hovered at about 10 percent of GNP, a far lower percentage than in Germany and other European trading nations. Nonetheless, both the world demand for Japanese products and ready access to raw materials helped speed the pace of growth after 1955.

Despite the importance of trade, Japan produced largely for itself during this period, which is why the economy grew as it did. Simply put, domestic consumers were the most important force behind the rapid growth in the 1950s, 1960s, and early 1970s. The domestic market had restrained growth during the 1920s and 1930s because consumers were often poorly paid or unemployed and unable to purchase the products that Japanese firms were capable of making. After 1955, in contrast, most of the job-seeking populace was nearly always employed, and most people were paid wages and salaries that rose annually in real terms. This purchasing power drove demand; demand stimulated investment; investment created more jobs; more and better-paid jobs increased incomes and savings; and savings spurred further investment. This virtuous cycle lay behind the real growth rates of 10 percent per annum between 1955 and 1973.

When the Japanese people found themselves better off, they began to spend a little more freely, spurring growth in the service sector. Banks grew to capture savings and to finance new homes. Insurance companies gained more policyholders. Cafés, bars, and restaurants attracted millions of new customers. Travel firms expanded to cater to the footloose and curious, and retail outlets and department stores attracted a new breed of shopper. One flamboyant entrepreneur who exploited these changes was **Tsutsumi Yasujirō**. He laid the foundation for a burgeoning family enterprise with a private railway serving rural towns northwest of downtown Tōkyō. His heirs have expanded an empire that includes the Seibu and Parco department stores, the Seiyū marketplaces, the Prince Hotel chain, the Lions professional baseball team, and the Seibu Railway.

No segment of the Japanese economy remained unchanged during this era, least of all agriculture. It was during this period that a mechanical revolution finally came to rural Japan. Trucks, threshing machines, motorized plows, and mechanized rice transplanters all revolutionized farm labor. By releasing farmers from arduous manual work, mechanization enabled husbands and wives in farm families to supplement their incomes with full- or part-time jobs in schools, municipal offices, retail shops, or construction firms. These jobs paid wages and salaries that, when combined with earnings from farming, enabled farm families to enjoy incomes on a par with their urban counterparts. Higher farm incomes also sustained the growth of a consumer society. And even though they spent less time in the fields, farmers still increased the overall output of the agricultural sector and met domestic demand for most staples of the daily diet.

The economic conditions Japan enjoyed in 1973 thus differed dramatically from the ones that had obtained in 1932. War had slowed the Japanese economy and levied a heavy cost in many ways. But it still provided valuable experience for managers, firms, and enterprises, government officials, and the Japanese people as a whole. They absorbed, adopted, and adapted lessons from that experience as they dealt with problems of occupation, reconstruction, and growth after the war. Operating as they always had during the modern era, the leaders of the Japanese economy and the workers in the Japanese labor force invested pragmatism, ingenuity, and a great deal of hard work to achieve the objective of economic development. One century after the Meiji Restoration, they could justifiably claim that they had finally "enriched the nation."

SOCIAL CHAOS AND REBIRTH

Japan sank into social chaos between 1932 and 1945. But until conditions became much worse in the late 1930s, the early changes associated with the boom in heavy industry still were positive. They created millions of new jobs, raised the standard of living, and sped the growth of cities and suburbs.

Most of the new jobs were in the heavy industrial sector and in the small- and medium-size enterprises affiliated with it. Thus, steelmakers, military arsenals, ship builders, electrical equipment makers, and aircraft manufacturers hired the most workers, usually males in their teens and older. These firms drew their workers from the jobless and underemployed in urban areas, from the heads of farm households willing to move to the cities, and from the ranks of young school leavers.

Such men often made more money. People who had previously had no jobs, or poor jobs, now found themselves with steady work and a reliable paycheck. Some of the widespread urban poverty of the 1920s thus began to diminish after 1933. Moreover, urban consumers' increased purchasing power stimulated the demand for agricultural output, and farm incomes began to rise as well.

With better job opportunities, Japan's population map was substantially redrawn. The metropolitan regions around Tōkyō and Ōsaka, which had swelled so quickly between 1915 and 1930, grew even more rapidly during the

1930s. The western shore of Tōkyō Bay, stretching from downtown Tōkyō through Kawasaki and Yokohama to Yokosuka, became a major industrial zone, as did the belt in west-central Japan that stretched from Ōsaka westward through Kobe to Himeji. In addition, smaller cities got bigger during this time as their coal fields, steel mills, naval shipyards, electrical firms, and other enterprises expanded to satisfy the military's demands. Rural villages, however, began to stabilize or decline in the face of these changes, as younger sons and daughters and sometimes whole families left to seek their fortune in the cities.

The benefits of this economic boom were short lived. War demands after 1937 led to wider constraints on economic activity, for firms and individuals alike. Production was aimed at maximizing the output of ships and aircraft, which reshaped employment opportunities at first and then perverted them. When able-bodied males were no longer available to staff production lines, firms turned to young women out of work as textile hands and household servants. In the last years of war, aircraft plants even employed university students, schoolchildren, and Korean forced laborers.

Restraints also appeared in the form of rationing and austerity measures. Some essentials, such as sugar and fuels, were rationed before 1940, with far more commodities coming under government control and distribution after 1940. The dismantling of the textile industry made clothing more precious. Home repair and construction became difficult and expensive, so the quality of housing declined. As the home islands were cut off from iron and steel imports, people were expected to contribute metal items for the war effort. Personal mementos, bridge railings, and temple bells all disappeared under these orders. In an already dreary atmosphere, the government and its state-guided organizations harped on the need for economy and self-restraint in expenditure. Large funerals, gaudy weddings, and showy festivals all but disappeared.

Rural villages had easier access to food during the war years than did the cities, but they, too, faced hardships. Near the end of the war, some villages had almost no adult males in residence, as they had either been drafted into the military or hired away by factories. Women of all ages were forced to spend more time working on the farm in order to compensate for the loss of male workers. Even so, they could not sustain earlier levels of production, and they found it difficult to maintain all the plots that their families had once cultivated. Households everywhere lived in fear of two notices from the village office: a draft order taking away another son or a telegram announcing the death of a father, brother, son, or uncle.

Severe food shortages began in the early 1940s, caused by declining farm output at home, restrictions on imports from abroad, and crumbling systems of transport and distribution. Luxuries disappeared, as did the occasional ex-travagance, such as a special fish or exotic fruit. Then even essentials became difficult to obtain, especially in the metropolitan areas. People were forced to reduce their consumption of rice, and they seldom ate meat or other proteins. Many prided themselves on surviving on the *hinomaru bento* (the rising-sun-flag lunch box): a reddish, pickled plum on a thin slab of white rice.

Suffering was already widespread when the Allied bombing campaign began. Starting in mid-1944, American planes made hundreds of air strikes and dropped thousands of tons of bombs on Japan's largest cities. Even before the bombing began, some fathers had sent their wives and children back to family homes in the countryside. Nearly 4 million people fled the Tōkyō area in the last years of war; another 3 million fled the Ōsaka area. By the end of the war, more than half the populations of the largest cities had gone to the countryside.

In late 1945, most of Japan's largest cities were flattened. For long stretches, only smoldering ruins were visible, with a twisted steel frame or a stone ware-house standing here and there above the destruction serving as a mute re-minder of a once-thriving society. Rail systems, roads, transport facilities, wholesale markets, and distribution points were destroyed, badly damaged, or inoperable. These difficulties, coupled with the diminished farm output, left everyone scrambling for food just to survive. Most people were getting by on barely fourteen hundred calories a day, consisting almost entirely of carbohy-drates, but almost no protein, and few vitamins and minerals. Thousands of families' homes had been destroyed. Millions of homeless mothers and chil-dren were living with families, relatives, and friends scattered around the country, and several million Japanese army, navy, and civilian personnel were spread across Asia from Manchuria to Indonesia.

Rebirth after the war began in the most literal way. Finally reunited in a peaceful environment, husbands and wives had children in record numbers. The birthrate returned to that of the early 1920s, and for several years almost 2.7 million infants were born annually. However, the upward spike ended quickly. In 1950, the number of births dropped from about thirty-four per thou-sand to about twenty-eight per thousand, a rate that fell steadily thereafter. With the successful treatment of tuberculosis in the first decade after the war, mortality rates fell steadily, too, dropping almost by half. This combination of vital rates increased the population from about 72 million at the end of the war to about 110 million in 1973.

While husbands and wives were having more children, the Allied occu-piers were giving birth to a new system of education. Troubled by the role the schools had played in the military atmosphere of wartime Japan, Allied authorities wanted to democratize and Americanize them. They therefore paid little heed to the varied, flexible prewar system and quickly reorganized the schools along American lines. After six years of elementary training, communities were expected to provide three years of compulsory middle school, followed by three years of high school. Students who wanted more education could then go to two-year community colleges or four-year colleges and universities, public or private.

This organizational reform created both problems and opportunities. Japan had buildings and personnel for elementary instruction and, for the most part, middle-school instruction, too. But in the 1940s, it did not have enough high schools and colleges with qualified teachers to meet the Occupation's demands for higher-level education. Accordingly, for a decade or more, many new high schools, colleges, and universities functioned at substandard levels. These deficiencies were gradually rectified during the 1960s, so that by the end of this period Japan had an adequate system of public education, training most students through the high-school level and providing postsecondary education for nearly 40 percent.

The schools played a crucial role in training and placing workers in the rapidly changing labor force. In the early postwar period, middle-school graduates immediately found jobs in factories and shops and on the farm. Those completing high school could expect work that was both easier and higher paid, in the service sector, in government offices, and in the private sector. College graduates obtained the best positions, as corporate managers and government bureaucrats.

Japan's rapid economic growth after 1955 reconfigured job opportunities in both urban and rural areas. Fewer hands were needed in agriculture, so several million workers were able to quit farming to take jobs in the towns and cities. Expanding manufacturing firms developed an insatiable appetite for production workers during the 1960s. And as cities and incomes grew, the service sector attracted more workers. By 1973, the distribution of the Japanese labor force approximated that of other advanced industrial nations. Agriculture had shrunk to 12 percent of all workers. Manufacturing and construction employed 34 percent of the labor force, and the service sector occupied the remaining 54 percent.

The shift away from agriculture promoted a resurgence in urbanization. Urban flight during the last years of the war had drastically reduced the populations of large cities such as Tōkyō, Ōsaka, and Yokohama. Indeed, conditions were so difficult after the war that some cities had to prevent people from returning until 1949 or so. Once a basic level of reconstruction had been reached, however, people began pouring back into the large cities. The geographical pattern of urban settlement was by now a familiar one. Tōkyō and Ōsaka were the main magnets, followed by key regional cities such as Nagoya and Kita Kyūshū. Rural industrial cities with major industries, such as Hitachi and Toyota, also grew rapidly. In addition, the number and size of suburbs exploded to absorb the people spilling out from the centers of the oldest, largest cities. By the end of this period, the majority of Japanese resided in urban areas.

The ideal urban household was a nuclear family with two children. The father was a *sarariiman*, "salary man," or a white-collar, salaried worker. He usually had a college education and worked in the managerial ranks of a corporation or in the administrative offices of a public entity. His job was a secure one that provided not only a regular salary but also twice-annual bonuses, a variety of benefits (such as family allowances, commuting subsidies, and health care), and even the use of a company-owned vacation retreat.

His domestic counterpart was the *kyōiku mama*, or education mama. She took care of the children and household while her husband spent long hours six, and even seven, days a week at his place of work. The wife was expected to respond to all his needs and to manage the family budget, care for the home, and rear the children. She was expected to ensure the success of the family in the next generation by loving, coddling, nudging, and threatening the children, especially the sons, to do well at school. Good grades would ensure admission to the best high schools and the most prestigious universities. Graduation from a prestigious university would in turn ensure success in one's work life. Achieving these goals redounded to the benefit of the household, but not achieving them marked a mother's failure.

Out of these occupational, educational, and personal dynamics arose the somewhat stereotypical, but nonetheless apt, image of the postwar Japanese family. The father was not just a distant figure. In many households, he was an absent figure. He was away from home during most daylight hours, had little to do with raising the children, and did almost no housework or home repair. His job was his life. This produced fathers who were focused, repressed, and depleted. Mothers were expected to be devoted, diligent, and cheerful. But most middle-class, urban families were beset with anxieties about educational success and upward mobility, leaving them somewhat cheerless and neurotic. A leading authority on the Japanese family put it this way: "Most mothers do not consciously plan to make their children more anxious. But, being anxious about their children's success and desirous of motivating the child to cooperate, mothers create these anxieties almost instinctively."[2]

Not all women were able to marry salary men and stay out of the workforce to deal exclusively with family matters. Throughout this period, many young girls had to leave school after nine or twelve years to take a job in an office, a factory, or a shop. Some of them worked all their lives, even if they married, because their husbands were too poorly paid or unreliable to provide for the family. Most women worked initially for a period of about six years and then left the labor force when they married, to raise a family. They often returned in their late thirties in part-time jobs to supplement their husband's income and enable the family to save for a new home, pay for school tuition, or simply have some extra money. Almost no women entered prestigious jobs in major corporations or public bureaucracies at the national or prefectural level. Thus, power remained dominated by men, and women were relegated to the domestic sphere and the fringes of the public sphere. Although under the postwar constitution, they enjoyed far more rights than ever before, with few exceptions, they were hesitant to exploit them in a society in which long-standing sexual roles persisted essentially unchanged.

In other ways, though, women's lives did improve. The postwar industrial boom was built in part on the mass production of household appliances that made work in the home easier for women. These included sewing machines, electric rice cookers, refrigerators, vacuum cleaners, and water heaters. Modest as these devices may seem now, they eased the burden of housework considerably. Some women used the time freed by these devices to join community groups, lobby for better neighborhood services, or just pursue hobbies for their own pleasure.

The larger real incomes made these kinds of household purchases possible. Japanese consumers during this era are often caricatured as lemming-like conformists, all going out at the same time to purchase the same hot item. In fact, most families were extremely cautious about their spending. As incomes rose in the 1950s and the 1960s, families first improved their diets from the abysmal lows to which they had sunk in the 1940s. They next bought new clothing and began to repair their homes, expenditures they had deferred out of necessity during the early postwar years. Only after they had attended to these needs did they begin to purchase such new items as sewing machines, which had a very practical purpose: they could be used to economize on clothing costs. Other purchases, such as refrigerators and rice cookers, also were practical, as they reduced the time a wife spent on household tasks. So what appears conformist on the surface was actually prudent behavior.

Japanese households were careful in their savings habits, too. As real incomes grew, families set more aside each year, usually in bank and postal savings accounts. In fact, the portion of income saved on average by Japanese families rose slightly each year between the early 1950s and the early 1970s until it exceeded 20 percent in 1973. This savings rate was, in any given year, three to five times higher than the savings rate of an average American household. High savings rates were not only a symbol of financial security for individual families. They also contributed immensely to Japan's economic growth, because household savings accounts multiplied millions of times over provided low-cost capital for growing enterprises.

These years were not without conflict, however. The **labor movement** enjoyed a brief period of popularity just after the war. Workers organized to win higher wages, better working conditions, and a voice in corporate decision making. Then, fearing a loss of power in the face of a strengthening adversary, management staged a counterattack against unions beginning around 1950. Companies fired men who were alleged communists, and they recognized docile second unions to replace the early postwar bodies. By the late 1950s, workers in many private firms had joined labor in a cooperative embrace that ensured labor peace. One exception was the coal industry, in which workers fought an epochal strike against the managers of Mitsui's Miike Mines. When they admitted defeat in 1960, the private-sector labor movement abandoned confrontation for cooperation, almost across the board.

The **student movement** also injected a note of discord into this otherwise complacent era. University students had begun organizing after the war to promote peace and to oppose rearmament, in a movement that assumed critical importance in the late 1950s. When the security treaty between Japan and the United States came up for renewal, students joined with the socialist parties and organized labor to oppose it. They wanted Japan to avoid alignments with the powers fighting the cold war, but they had little success and the movement descended into internal bickering for the next decade. The Vietnam War stirred a final burst of student activism in the late 1960s. Students were still advocating international peace, but this time they also were promoting reforms of university governance. They occupied buildings on major campuses and brought instruction to a halt. After dithering for months, the government finally dealt ruthlessly with the student activists, and collective student protest virtually disappeared after the early 1970s.

CULTURAL REGRESSION AND REGENERATION

Cultural regression marked the years between 1932 and 1945. The drumbeat of orthodoxy became almost deafening, to the exclusion of everything else. As the military became more intrusive, the government harped ever more strongly on the values of orthodoxy, using the schools to emphasize the importance of the emperor, nationalism, and patriotism. General Araki Sadao was even appointed minister of education, giving him a national forum in which to advance the views of the Imperial Way faction. State-guided organizations reiterated the orthodoxy in many forms and sites, to deepen and broaden attachments to the nation. The government mobilized shrines and priests of the Shinto religion to reinforce the imperial message in every village and many neighborhoods. And most writers and intellectuals supported the war effort, by traveling to battlefields to boost the troops' morale and by writing favorably about the national cause.

At the same time that the state strengthened the impact of orthodox ideas, it did everything it could to stifle alternatives. Communists, socialists, and union activists were favored targets. Using regular police forces and special thought police as well, the government conducted intrusive surveillance campaigns, made widespread arrests, and induced confessions and conversions. Those who failed to cooperate were jailed for the duration of the war. With these efforts, by about 1933, the government eliminated the political influence of groups on the far left, and in a few more years, the moderate socialist parties in parliament also knuckled under to support the war effort.

Having quashed the left wing, the government turned in the mid-1930s to a different and somewhat surprising target: the new religions. Chapter 2 noted that a burst of organizing among new religions had begun in the late 1920s. This trend continued into the early 1930s, aided by the chaotic social and economic conditions of the late depression years. More new religious groups formed; they may have numbered more than one thousand by the early 1930s. In addition, some new religions began attracting far more adherents than before. Ōmotokyō, originally founded in the mid-1800s, was one of these. It claimed a membership of several million, raised substantial sums of money, maintained a large headquarters near Kyōto, and had a forceful, energetic leader.

Although the new religions often had a Shintoist orientation and usually adhered to government policies, they came under attack nevertheless. Government officials justifying their actions cited a variety of reasons. They asserted that the new religions were disorderly bodies promoting superstition, sexual adventurism, and general disorder. They resented the unscientific faith-healing practices common to many new religions, and they abhorred fund-raising scams that bilked poor parishioners during a period of austerity. Government officials also saw the mere existence of such large groups as a threat to government control over Japanese society.

Whatever their reasons, government officials vigorously suppressed both the new religionists and, later, Christians. Ōmotokyō bore the brunt of the government's attack. Special police battalions occupied its headquarters in late 1935. They seized its funds and used them to support the military. They destroyed the headquarters building and ensured that it would not be rebuilt. And they jailed the leaders of the organization. This raid was an intimidating example to other religious groups, and most of them fell into line accordingly. Religious bodies did not, therefore, serve as a base of opposition to the war after 1935.

Intellectuals and academics also attracted the ire of the government and its special police forces. A Marxist economist at Tōkyō Imperial University lost his position in the early 1930s for works the government found seditious. A few years later the government and right-wing critics hounded Minobe Tatsukichi out of his position on the law faculty at Tōkyō for daring to suggest that the emperor was merely one "organ" of the state. Many power holders felt this was heresy and moved to silence him.

These efforts to quash alternative views always silenced their targets and also intimidated others who were not direct targets. Many intellectuals and potential critics of government policies thus began to fear for their jobs, their reputations, their families, and perhaps even their lives. As a consequence, there was much self-censorship among Japanese intellectuals during the war. **Nagai Kafū** and some other authors simply stopped writing, apparently assuming that their silence would be construed as opposition. Some, such as **Tanizaki Jun'ichirō**, continued writing but found that even politically innocuous works could fall victim to the censors, as did his saga of family life, *The Makioka Sisters*.

Another response by writers was to revert to a politically neutral aestheticism. The most common form of this writing was the I-novel, a literary subgenre that had emerged around the turn of the twentieth century. The Japanese I-novel focused on the whims, experiences, and psychology of one individual, the author. An obsessive contemplation of the author's life, the I-novel offered a dispiriting vision of the human condition. But because it lacked political relevance and social context, the I-novel provided an ideal mental retreat for writers who could not, or would not, describe the real dilemmas Japan faced in the 1930s. **Shiga Naoya** and, to a lesser extent, **Kawabata Yasunari** produced works during this era that reveal the condition of the writer during a period of pronounced cultural regression. Neither writers nor intellectuals formed a resistance movement in wartime Japan, nor was there any underground movement that authorized a legitimate body of postwar leaders.

Not every writer cowered before the authority of government and censors.

Uno Chiyo managed to publish in 1935 a story about a hapless artist, three young women, and their outrageous affairs. Echoing Tanizaki's *Naomi*, which depicted the Tōkyō-Yokohama "scene" of the early 1920s, Uno's *Confessions of Love* was one of the last works before the war to portray the racy urban set and its romantic adventures. In due course, however, she, too, joined a league of patriotic writers supporting the war effort.

During the war the government frowned on racy behavior. Although some of the "modern boys and modern girls" (see chapter 2) survived, they stopped strolling on the Ginza and instead found quiet back alleys where they could get away from the prying eyes of police and prudes. Under the austerity campaigns and the pressures of impending war, the once-thriving entertainment districts of the big cities fell on hard times, and the good life came under attack. Furthermore, by the late 1930s, few people had the time, money, or inclination to pursue it. People were by then forced to spend their free time sending a brother off to war or receiving a body from the battlefield. Or they were participating in campaigns to collect metal for the war effort or growing vegetables on vacant urban plots just to survive. Events after 1932 brought repression, both political and personal, in their wake, creating an atmosphere of cultural regression.

The first steps toward cultural regeneration took place when the Allied occupiers forced them on the Japanese people. As they had in the political, economic, and social spheres, the Allies left few stones unturned in the cultural arena. They abolished the state-guided organizations that had served as the vehicles for cultural orthodoxy. Youth groups, women's groups, reservists' associations, and other national bodies disappeared and were no longer available to mobilize the populace behind an orthodox viewpoint. Allied authorities ensured that ideas once propagated through the schools were eliminated from the curriculum. Thus, students no longer heard the 1890 Imperial Rescript on Education each morning, and they no longer had to take the morals courses that had cultivated habits of patriotism and nationalism. The Allies also broke up the Shinto hierarchy and abolished the bureaucratic organ that had tied the Shinto religion to the state. All these changes essentially destroyed the institutional context in which cultural orthodoxy had thrived. Orthodoxy thus withered, and its supporters slipped quietly off stage — but only for the next decade.

In place of orthodoxy, the Allies strove to cultivate an atmosphere of democracy and freedom, with the 1947 constitution as its main instrument. It guaranteed the Japanese people a variety of freedoms that they had possessed only contingently under the Meiji constitution. In fact, the postwar constitution's chapter 3, "Rights and Duties of the People," is its longest. Many of these rights are purely political, but they create the legal, intellectual, and cultural environment in which broader freedoms can be pursued. Among these is the freedom of religion, which is "guaranteed to all." The constitution prevents the state from privileging any religion, from engaging in religious education, and from compelling religious action or organization. The constitution also grants freedom of speech and assembly while ensuring academic freedom, and it provides explicit protection against unlawful search and seizure and censorship. The potential for the free and uninhibited exchange of ideas has thus been legally ensured since 1947.

The immediate postwar era also produced debates over issues with novel implications. One topic that attracted widespread discussion was *shutaisei*, a term variously translated as "subjectivity," "subjecthood," or "autonomy." *Shutaisei* means to take action at one's own volition and discretion, so it denotes the ability to act as a free subject enjoying freedom from restraint. The exponents of this concept used it to advocate democratic action. Depending on their political position, they felt that individuals, organizations, and/or classes in Japan needed to develop their own way of thinking, deciding, and acting if Japan were to realize the opportunities offered by the postwar reforms.

Another theme addressed in early postwar debates was peace. The cessation of war and reductions in military spending were seen as necessary in order to prevent the recurrence of another Hiroshima. From the outset, this viewpoint had an implicitly anti-American thrust, because its advocates opposed military alliances with the United States. Peace was embraced most ardently by groups on the political left: students, unions, women's organizations, the antinuclear movement, and the socialist and communist parties. These were the groups that opposed renewal of the U.S.-Japan Security Treaty in 1959–1960, and some of them were still active during the protests on university campuses in the late 1960s.

Both *shutaisei* and peace faded as issues during the 1960s. As Japan recovered and economic resurgence took hold, these ideas remained under discussion, but they had to share the field of debate with other issues. Among these were some old ideas dressed in new clothing. As early as the mid-1950s and with increasing vigor in the 1960s, neonationalists reintroduced into the intellectual debate some elements from the prewar cultural orthodoxy. They were striving to explain, to both Japanese at home and foreigners abroad, why Japan was proving to be so successful economically. They found their explanations in Japanese essentialism: the importance of families and villages and the values of harmony and cooperation. Thus, after a decade of discreet silence, the exponents of cultural orthodoxy gradually returned to the ideological stage, spruced up to comply with the more affluent and pluralistic atmosphere of the postwar period.

One issue that largely escaped thorough public debate was the war. Some thinkers—especially on the left and in the center—were contrite and remorseful about the war. They felt—rightly so—that intellectuals had not done enough to oppose it, and they acknowledged the costs of Japanese aggression. But rather than dwell on the war and Japan's responsibilities, they preferred to look forward and to explore the opportunities that peace and reform offered. In the circumstances obtaining after 1945, their perspective seems justified, as it was a psychologically healthy and politically pragmatic way to deal with conditions at the time.

By largely turning their backs on the war, however, Japanese intellectuals missed an opportunity, first, to confront the complex issues that the war had raised and, second, to persuade the Japanese people and their leaders to do so, too. There are many reasons that Japan did not engage in public debate about their responsibilities for the war, in the often candid, public manner that many postwar Germans and their leaders have done.

First, for many Japanese, the war had been so horrible that suppressing their memories of it offered the only way for them to move on with their lives. Millions of survivors either grieved for their personal losses or regretted their wartime conduct. Therefore, although Japan's postwar leaders have been criticized for failing to address the nation's responsibility for the war and for silencing the debate among the people, the opposite may be true. That is, postwar leaders may have maintained silence out of respect for the suffering of the Japanese people.

A second reason for the public reticence arises from historical circumstances. Legitimate state organizations were responsible for taking Japan to war, not a fringe group under the malign influence of a charismatic dictator. Core institutions—the national bureaucracy, the army, and the navy—caused Japanese aggression, and they did so in the face of little opposition. Germany and Italy could confront war guilt more directly after the war because they could marginalize Hitler and the Nazi Party or Mussolini and his Fascists. It was much easier for them psychologically, morally, and politically to label the war, even the Holocaust, as an aberration. War was less an aberration in Japan because it had emerged from the heart of society and had enjoyed society's support. Having failed to articulate their opposition from the start, Japanese intellectuals were in a weak position to condemn war after the fact.

Finally, the dropping of the atomic bombs on Hiroshima and Nagasaki cauterized Japan against a sense of war guilt. The A-bomb experience enabled Japanese to see themselves as the only victims of an awful weapon of destruction. Although the A-bombs did provoke some in Japan to initiate movements for peace and nuclear disarmament, they seem to have freed most Japanese from the inclination to reflect on their own war guilt and responsibility.

The more open intellectual and cultural atmosphere of the postwar era had surprisingly little effect on the established religions. Shinto shrines and priests reverted to what they had done for centuries. They served their parishioners at the local level, through ritual activities that appeased the gods and nurtured a sense of community. With economic growth, Shinto's inherently secular traits won more adherents in the business community. Developers hired priests to confer blessings and seek the goodwill of the gods for new subdivisions, and corporate executives did the same for new factories.

Buddhist temples and their priests, most of them situated in rural areas, continued to specialize in matters of death. Priests conducted funerals, maintained cemeteries, and commemorated the dead. They also found themselves enveloped by commercial forces. Companies sent young recruits to Buddhist sites to experience the rigors of Zen meditation and the austerities of religious life. Executives felt such experiences equipped young workers for the demands of the business world. These old and new pursuits kept temples and shrines functioning, sometimes at enhanced levels. So perhaps for this very reason, the older religious orders paid little or no attention to deeper religious issues and doctrines and played no viable role in the intellectual debates.

As before the war, the new religions provided most of the dynamism in the religious arena. The kinds of social and economic conditions that encouraged a surge of new religious activity in the late 1920s and early 1930s recurred again in the 1940s. Many new religions grew rapidly as they addressed these conditions. One especially successful body was the Sōka Gakkai (Value-creating society). An offshoot of the Nichiren sect of Buddhism, the Sōka Gakkai took into its fold many who were dislocated by the war and its aftermath. Its adherents were often lower-class or lower-middle-class men and especially women who worked in the commercial sector in urban areas. Having joined the society, they became active evangelizers, widely known for their bold approach to prospective converts standing unwittingly on rail platforms or street corners. A number of other groups, such as Gedatsukai, Mahikari, and Risshō kōseikai, also flourished in the 1950s and after. Attracting anywhere from 10 to 30 percent of the entire population, the new religions of the early postwar era provided a social haven and practical benefits to individuals whose lives had been torn asunder by war or rapid social and economic change.

Writers exploited the new cultural freedoms enthusiastically. In the early postwar years, the social costs of war (though not its political significance) attracted the attention of the major novelists. **Dazai Osamu** wrote movingly about family losses and the disappearance of a way of life. **Yasuoka Shōtarō** depicted the deep emotional and social consequences of war. In his major novella, the protagonist, a man scoured of his morals by the war and bereft of any sense of filial piety, reflects as follows on his mother's death: "What did he need to atone for in the first place, and why? The very concept of repaying one's mother was absurd—wasn't a son already making reparation enough just by being a son? A mother atoned by bearing a son; the son atoned by being his mother's child."[3]

Addressing another wartime legacy, **Ibuse Masuji** immortalized the fate of A-bomb survivors in his *Black Rain*. Older writers such as Tanizaki and Kawabata wrote realistic novels about Japanese family life and other works that probed the sexual fantasies of aging males.

A younger cohort of writers expanded the purview of Japanese novelists even more in the 1950s and 1960s. **Endō Shūsaku** was one of the first Japanese university students to study abroad after the war. His sojourn in France and his interest in Catholicism inspired him to portray the lives of Jesuits in sixteenth-century Japan and saintly figures in the contemporary world. **Abe Kōbō**, a physician by training, stimulated wide interest in his surreal worlds and science-fiction fantasies. **Mishima Yukio** became one of the most controversial writers of the postwar era in 1970 when he committed suicide under bizarre circumstances at the headquarters of the Self-Defense Forces. Before his death, he wrote short stories, novellas, novels, and plays on an array of topics, periods, and characters.

Female writers contributed in significant ways to the growing breadth and intrinsic interest of Japanese literature. **Sata Ineko** portrayed the personal and political dilemmas of women caught up in chauvinistic organizations. **Setouchi Harumi** used her unconventional life experiences to address the possibilities for sexual liberation. Repressed and exploited by her famous writer father, **Kōda Aya** wrote stories that exposed to subtle scrutiny obedient women and their complicated feelings. And **Enchi Fumiko** published brilliant, chilling novels that condemned the behavior of men and unveiled the hatred of women wronged.

Reading was just one diversion for a populace growing more affluent and better able to take advantage of cultural opportunities. In addition to novels, novellas, and short stories, large numbers of Japanese read newspapers, scandal sheets, popular weeklies, and serious monthly publications. Consumers snapped up television sets at phenomenal rates when they became available in the mid-1950s, and many families became devoted viewers of TV dramas, game shows, and news programs. Dining out became a bit more common, as did travel. Fathers had a little more spending money to pay for a night or two out each week with their friends, over beer and snacks on the way home. Spectator sports, including everything from baseball to sumo, attracted larger audiences. And many Japanese participated in sports, especially baseball, swimming, and bowling. Time was still at a premium in a society obsessed with the demands of growth, but popular culture was beginning to exert a growing influence on this wealthier, urban society.

NOTES TO CHAPTER 3

1. Stephen S. Large, *Emperors of the Rising Sun: Three Biographies* (Tokyo: Kodansha, 1997), p. 170.
2. Ezra F. Vogel, *Japan's New Middle Class: The Salary Man and His Family in a Tokyo Suburb*, 2d ed. (Berkeley and Los Angeles: University of California Press, 1971), p. 252.
3. Yasuoka Shōtarō, *A View by the Sea*, trans. Karen Wigen (New York: Columbia University Press, 1984), p. 195.

CHAPTER FOUR

Adapting to Affluence, 1974–Present

After striving for more than a century to achieve affluence, Japan found that it brought more problems than satisfactions. Society segmented into groups and subgroups. Politics fragmented as political parties, interest groups, and the people vied for power. Economic convulsions shook the country and brought its growth to a halt. And cultural distractions drew attention away from serious issues. In the face of these changes, what kind of society should Japan become? was a question asked frequently after 1974. The question provoked many responses but no easy answers. Japan thus is approaching the new millennium with uncertainty and distress.

SOCIAL SEGMENTATION

In the social arena, segmentation affected communities, families, and individuals; youth, women, and the elderly. Segmentation promoted a widespread sense of detachment, both real and imagined, that frayed the social fabric and undercut cohesion. Arising from unprecedented levels of self-regard and self-indulgence, detachment also shaped Japan's political, economic, and cultural life.

Communities were especially prone to segmentation. Urbanization persisted after the 1950s and 1960s, and cities continued to expand. At the end of the twentieth century, 20 percent of the nation lived in cities with a population of more than a million, and 80 percent resided in urban areas. Suburbs on the edge of old city centers, and then commuter suburbs well beyond, were the communities that grew most rapidly, often swelling from small market towns of 50,000 to massive bedtowns of 350,000 in a decade or two.

When tens of thousands of new residents moved into a city each year, the community lost its cohesiveness. Long-time residents, clustered in commercial districts or in old village settlements, retained a sense of community among themselves, but they intentionally kept away from newcomers and strove to retain their hold on local power. One form of segmentation thus divided newcomers from old-timers.

Among newcomers, there were many forms of segmentation. Some newcomers were young singles in their late teens and twenties. Renting cheap apartments and commuting outside to work, they had no intention of settling in the community, developed few if any attachments to it, and invested nothing in it. Other newcomers were young married couples with children, also renting apartments. The husbands in such families commuted outside the city to work while their wives stayed at home to manage the house and rear the children. The wives sometimes participated in community affairs. However, knowing that they might be moving in a short time to another community, they were hesitant to make community attachments.

Some suburban newcomers consisted of families whose head of household was in his forties or fifties moving into their own homes. Intending to stay for the long term, they did have an incentive to participate in community affairs. But owing to their newness in the community, their lack of long-standing social ties, and their own family and work obligations, such couples often spent a decade or more before they built social attachments in their new place of residence.

Detachment and mobility were thus two widespread social characteristics of this urban society. Owing to economic change and other forces, workers and families found themselves moving frequently. In the Tōkyō area, for example, about one in six persons moved each year. Such high rates of mobility impeded social attachments in a person's local community. High mobility rates also encouraged the widespread detachment that divided one family from the next, and many families from their communities.

Behind the detachment and isolation was another set of social considerations having to do primarily with status. Japanese have always been sensitive to differences of status among families. In rural villages, landlords enjoyed privileges that tenants did not. In cities, well-established, old-line families had advantages that newcomers did not. In cities today, populated by apparently similar white-collar, middle-class families, occupational and lifestyle differences divide residents from one another. For example, in one home the head of household might be a forty-five-year-old with a degree from a minor college who works as a manager at a small machine tool firm. This family's networks would be local or, at best, regional. They would probably take vacations in Japan, eat Japanese-style food, and watch game shows and Japanese melodramas on television. The home next door might be occupied by a head of household who is the same age but a graduate of Tōkyō University employed as a manager at Mitsui bussan. Frequently assigned overseas, this family would have cosmopolitan networks, vacation in Europe, dine at French restaurants, and listen to classical music.

These men and their wives might be cordial to one another when meeting on the street, but they all would tread carefully to avoid attachments and dependency. The differences in occupation (caused by the prestige of degrees and employers) and in lifestyles (caused by incomes and personal preferences) would operate in subtle but well-understood ways to keep these families apart. In this way, status differences also segmented communities.

In addition to communities, families experienced segmentation. The stereotype of the nuclear family—father, mother, and two children—is very familiar. So it may come as a surprise that such families constitute barely a third of all households in the late 1990s. The next most numerous household type, about 19 percent of the total, are individuals living alone. Some are widows or widowers, but many are men and women in their twenties and thirties who have never married, some living alone by choice. An equal percentage of family units consist of just a husband and wife, and another 13 percent are stem families embracing three generations under one roof. Thus, Japanese families are actually segmented into four broad types.

Individual families are further segmented by pressures imposed on husbands, wives, children, and the elderly. Male employees have always worked long hours in the postwar era, commonly eight to ten hours each day, six days each week. During the 1980s, when the economy was booming and change was rapid, unpaid overtime became even more common and seventy-hour workweeks were not unusual. Even more than the salary men of the high-speed growth era, many husbands in the last fifteen years have been absentee fathers, which has diminished patriarchy in the home and undercut family cohesion.

Since 1974 wives have experienced perhaps more contradictory pressures than any other group in Japan. These pressures arise owing to their personal goals as women and to the responsibilities that society imposes on them for husbands, children, and the elderly. With respect to personal goals, as women have acquired more education and developed higher aspirations for themselves, many have quietly rebelled against social norms and expectations.

First, women have resisted having more children. Between 1974 and the late 1990s, the annual birthrate fell from seventeen per thousand to fewer than ten, and live births fell from more than 2 million annually to barely 1 million. A typical nuclear family is now just as likely to have one child as two. This reduces the intensity and duration of a wife's child-rearing years while enhancing her ability to pursue her own interests. Second, women are resisting social norms by delaying marriage. Recently, instead of bowing to social pressure to marry in their mid-twenties, more women have put off marriage until their late twenties or early thirties. This further reduces the likelihood of having very many children, and it also maximizes a woman's freedom during her younger years, when she can take most advantage of it. And it gives women the opportunity to pursue careers of their own.

Women's choices are in turn having a perceptible effect on children and youth. Families have deliberately chosen to have fewer children, in part to be able to finance their education at prestigious institutions. These require tuition fees for cram schools (*juku*), where students prepare for exams to enter the best high schools and universities. But attendance at cram schools after regular school keeps children away from home between early morning and late evening. Their absence reduces the time they spend with their parents and immerses them in a youth subculture. Parental indulgence has appeared in other ways, too, especially in homes that are well off financially. Children are showered with material goods from the earliest age, and by the time they are in their teens, they are receiving allowances equal to 100 dollars a month or more. Such money allows them to go out, join friends, and have a good time away from their family, further immersing them in youth subcultures and drawing them away from their mothers and fathers.

In the 1990s, teenage girls—abetted by adult males—created a new subculture with strong antifamily qualities. These girls often come from wealthy families and can afford to buy their own pagers or cell phones, which they use to arrange trysts with married men. Such meetings often result in an exchange of sexual favors for an "allowance." This phenomenon indicates not just a segmentation of, or a breakdown in, the attachments within the family unit; it also shows the amorality of an affluent society, shared by youth and adults alike.

Whereas children and their conduct often drive families apart, the needs of the elderly sometimes draw them together. Life expectancy has increased steadily in postwar Japan as better diets, housing, and health care have become available. When the war ended, life expectancies at birth for men and women were in the low fifties. By the late 1990s, though, they are nearing eighty for men and exceeding eighty for women. The number of the elderly (people over sixty-five) in the population thus has risen dramatically, from about 4 million in 1950 to more than 20 million in the late 1990s. With the retirement age in the late fifties, most men and women face the prospect of two decades of life without steady work or a regular income.

In a fractious political environment lacking consensus on many issues, the elderly problem has become a political football. Some people feel the elderly should be supported with public funds; others oppose this view. Out of the conflict has emerged a compromise that provides substantial public support for health care and some income maintenance. However, the burdens of caregiving and housing fall on the private sector, that is, individual families. This national policy on the elderly essentially forces them on their children and so brings them back together with their families. Thus, an unusually large share of the elderly (estimated at 60 percent or more) live with or near a child, who is often—but not always—a son.

Although this son is the nominal link with the elderly, it is usually a daughter-in-law who shoulders the burden of caregiving. Consequently, Japan's provisional solution to the problem of the elderly has been a setback for women trying to expand their freedom. When they reach their forties, just as they are contemplating the option of a new career or a satisfying avocation, many women now find themselves obliged to curtail their own activities in order to care for an elderly parent-in-law. If the elderly person is bedridden, as many of them are, they impose heavy physical and psychological demands on the caregiver. The problems of the elderly have thus made families come together, but they seldom bring families together. Caregiving mothers are overwhelmed by their new duties while husbands stay at their jobs and children take off with friends.

Social segmentation therefore afflicts communities, families, and individuals in a variety of ways. The growing level of detachment has increased personal autonomy in many ways, but it has been bought at the cost of social cohesion and has impeded consensus on political issues.

POLITICAL FRAGMENTATION

Social segmentation has coincided with political fragmentation. Although the **Liberal Democratic Party** (LDP) has continued to form most of Japan's governments, its grip on power has weakened in this unstable and conflictual environment. Parties have fractured, imploded, or realigned. Interest groups have acted more boldly in some cases, more cautiously in others. Even the once impregnable bureaucracy has revealed flaws. One authority on contemporary Japanese politics noted that negotiation has become "the hallmark of Japanese politics during an age of expanded economic citizenship and social fragmentation. Political bargains can be, and are, struck by a wider range of participants engaged on a much broader field of action than ever before."[1] Underlying these changes is an affluent but frustrated people growing as detached from politics as from communities.

Four broad changes underlay the political instability of the years after 1974: persistent urbanization, reorganization of the labor movement, reform of the electoral system for the lower house, and popular disgust with politics. The lack of social community has hindered the ability of politicians to mobilize support during elections. In the past they relied on local influentials and election agents who exploited established networks of social interaction to build electoral bases. In new suburbs settled by young, unattached, and highly mobile residents, those techniques have not worked, however, and few politicians in urban areas have found reliable substitutes. Consequently, voters living in cities and their suburbs have become a highly contested constituency that is both fickle and unreliable.

Reorganization of the labor movement in the 1980s further complicated mobilization of the urban vote. As they have become wealthier, Japanese union members also have become politically more moderate, if not conservative. They increasingly concentrate on pay issues and job security and leave behind concerns with broader political matters. This moderated behavior by the unions themselves has mitigated adversarial relations with the ruling conservative party and led to a desire to play a more active role in the national policy-making process. To achieve these ends, three private-sector labor federations dissolved in 1987 to form Rengō, an umbrella organization that represents the interests of union members nationally. Two years later the largest labor federation, Sōhyō, which had once been the foundation for **Japan Socialist Party** (JSP) support, dissolved and entered Rengō. Labor's reorganization has seriously weakened the ties between organized workers and the JSP and the **Democratic Socialist Party** (DSP). In fact, within a decade, labor reorganization has virtually destroyed these two parties.

Reform of the lower house electoral system took place with the passage of a Diet law in 1994, with the new system operating for the first time in the 1996 election. It replaced a familiar system that had been in existence since 1947 with a radically new one. The new system combined three hundred seats based on small, single-member districts with two hundred seats chosen on the principle of proportional representation. This system required both new candidates and the complete reorganization of the electoral bases, especially in urban areas. Combined with the alienating effects of population mobility and the reorganization of the labor movement, electoral reform has destroyed many political networks and made them even less stable.

In addition, corruption has fed the popular disgust with politics. Although elective politics has had a tinge of corruption since its introduction in the 1890s, corruption became a more pervasive and visible concern after the 1970s. **Tanaka Kakuei**, prime minister between 1972 and 1974, added to this concern with his fund-raising gambits, his wheeling and dealing, and his 1976 indictment for bribe taking. More corruption problems appeared in the late 1980s that tainted nearly every major leader in the LDP and some other parties, too. In the 1990s, even bureaucrats in the historically clean **Ministry of Finance** were arrested for accepting bribes. As if corruption itself were not bad enough, politicians betrayed the public in the 1990s with their shameless, self-interested behavior during party realignments. As a consequence, the people have distanced themselves from all political parties and turned out at ever lower rates to cast their ballots. Abstention has thus become a form of silent opposition signaling popular dismay with politics and politicians.

Despite corruption, unappealing behavior, vacillating leadership, and other problems, the LDP has clung to power, though it has slipped from being a strong majority party to being the largest minority party, capable of attracting only 35 to 45 percent of the vote in national elections. This loss of support forced the LDP to spend about a year out of office in 1993–1994, but it formed or participated in all other governments after 1974. The party has relied on seasoned political professionals such as Tanaka, **Nakasone Yasuhiro**, **Miyazawa Kiichi**, and Hashimoto Ryūtarō to preside over and referee conflicts among its warring factions. The LDP has drawn its support from virtually every social group in the country, including farmers, businessmen, blue-collar workers, and salary men. Although it has had a precarious base in the populous, metropolitan prefectures, it usually is very strong in the provinces, where it captured two-thirds of the small-district seats in the 1996 election. The party generally manages to provide at least some returns for its many naturally competing support groups.

The LDP saw its longest-standing opponent almost disappear during this period: the JSP was severely weakened by labor's reorganization and then failed to cultivate a broader, middle-class, urban constituency beyond the confines of the labor movement. It did try, however. In the 1980s the JSP vehemently opposed the introduction of a regressive consumer tax. When the tax was introduced in 1989, the party conducted a highly successful upper house campaign under the leadership of **Doi Takako**, and it enjoyed a brief resurgence in electoral support. In the 1990s, however, a series of miscues, ill-fought campaigns, and hypocritical coalition ventures disgraced the party and led to internal war. In 1996 it won only fifteen seats and was on the brink of death. The JSP's unfriendly ally on the progressive left, the **Japan Communist Party**, actually strengthened itself by capturing twenty-six seats in 1996.

Two centrist parties, the DSP and the **Clean Government Party**, both disappeared in 1994 when they combined with two **1990s' reform parties** to create the short-lived Shinshintō, which dissolved in 1997. Meanwhile, several other reform parties also formed, realigned, reformed, or dissolved as well. These parties tried to develop a base in urban areas so as to challenge the LDP on its weakest ground, but they were consistently unsuccessful, being beset with personal animosities, factional quarrels, policy differences, financial weaknesses, and organizational shortcomings. They also failed to distinguish themselves clearly from the LDP on policies and programs. The inherent weaknesses of these parties thus left the LDP in office largely by default.

The reform parties did enact one political change: they brought more women into elective politics. The number of female candidates for the lower house rose from twenty-five in 1973 to seventy in 1996. However, the six victors in 1973 increased to only fourteen in 1996. Holding more than 95 percent of the Diet seats, men have continued to dominate the national legislature, as well as the bureaucracy.

Government policies, voter disgust, corruption, electoral reform laws, and constant party realignments troubled many interest groups that once supported the LDP. In rural areas, farmers grew suspicious of the party. Some of them considered forming a separate party, and many expressed widespread aversion to the LDP and its governance. Nonetheless, lacking viable alternatives, they continued to support the party, although slightly less faithfully than before. Big business groups found themselves caught in the web of LDP corruption and tried to pull back from their fund-raising efforts. But they, too, lacked viable alternatives and could not distance themselves too far from the LDP without running serious risks. Therefore, despite the well-intentioned efforts of reformers to curtail vote buying by well-organized groups in business and agriculture, those groups continued to support the only party capable of leading the government.

All these problems have seriously hampered smooth and effective policymaking. Personal and factional struggles for power within the LDP have made it difficult for the party to achieve consensus on controversial issues. Coalition governments that held office between mid-1993 and early 1996 were rent with internal conflicts. And the LDP that returned to power in 1996 was so chastened, weakened, and divided that it could take only slow, modest action.

Nevertheless, governments did pass laws that addressed critical issues in domestic affairs. Welfare concerns, especially for the elderly, attracted constant attention, which resulted in a new health law in 1982 and a revised pension law in 1985. Government debt financing in an era of slower growth led to the introduction of a 3 percent consumption tax in 1989, which was boosted to 5 percent in 1997. To deal with broader economic problems, the Diet passed laws in 1978 and 1983 to facilitate industrial readjustment, and it constantly debated and sometimes passed packages to stimulate the economy with tax cuts, public spending, and other measures. During the 1980s' administrative reform, or policies favoring small government, topped the political agenda, resulting in the privatization of the national railway in 1987 and the partial privatization of the telecommunications monopoly as well. Even though making policy became increasingly slow, difficult, and painful, the government eventually managed to deal in some measure with the most critical domestic issues.

International issues were equally vexing and even more difficult to resolve. Japan's large trade surpluses were a constant concern, especially to the United States and the European nations, which pressed Japan to control exports, stimulate imports, and remove trade barriers. Japan usually responded in a begrudging, piecemeal manner that sufficed to defuse crises but failed to resolve underlying problems. Security issues between Japan and the United States further complicated external relations. The Gulf War put Japan in an embarrassing position. Japan acted as a finance mercenary, obliged to put up large sums to support the anti-Hussein forces because it could not, according to its constitution, send troops to the Middle East. This incident brought the issue of constitutional revision (to abolish article 9) to center stage briefly, but political chaos after 1993 pushed it into the background again. Under ever more taxing circumstances, Japan has retained its military and economic dependence on the United States while trying at the same time to act more independently on the broader world stage.

ECONOMIC CONVULSIONS

Japan's political instability after 1974 was frequently related to economic conditions. A series of convulsions struck the economy, gradually pushing it into recession. The first convulsion was an oil crisis that began in late 1973 and caused deep distress for the next two years. When another oil crisis struck in the late 1970s, Japan was better prepared to deal with it. Nonetheless, several years of readjustment followed before the boom of the 1980s. Based on excessive speculation, that boom ended around 1990, when Japan descended into a recessionary condition from which it could not escape.

After sailing along at real rates of growth of 10 percent per year for nearly two decades, Japan's gross national product actually declined by about 1 percent in 1974. During the following decade and a half, positive growth returned at rates averaging about 4 percent per year. Although this was significantly lower than before, it was still high enough to sustain a sense of domestic economic well-being. This growth rate was also more than enough to provoke envy and resentment in North American and European countries, where real growth rates were still lower. Such envy and resentment stirred the trade disputes of the 1970s and 1980s. When the speculative bubble of the 1980s burst, however, real growth rates fell to barely 1 percent a year in the early 1990s. Many people in Japan began to feel the pinch of recession in the form of lower real wages, downsizing, and unemployment.

The convulsive economic instability after 1973 had many causes. Some were associated with the constant change in the international economy and Japan's extensive participation in it. Politically inspired actions taken by OPEC (Organization of Petroleum Exporting Countries) in 1973 drove up the price of raw materials. This was especially costly for Japan, because it has to import so many raw materials to make the finished goods it sells at home and abroad. Currency practices also fell victim to political aims. Exchange rate stability, based on currencies tied to gold, had been a major support for the expanding commerce of the early postwar era. In the 1970s, however, the United States forced nations to abandon the gold standard and to adopt a system of floating exchange rates tied to the dollar. This made exchange rates more volatile, gradually driving up the value of the yen, and making Japanese exports more expensive.

International trade competition also challenged Japan after 1974. At the same time the value of the yen was rising, many countries in East Asia, Southeast Asia, Latin America, and Eastern Europe began competing with Japan by exporting goods of comparable quality produced and sold at lower prices. Those nations also began developing their own industries to substitute for imports—such as steel, ships, and home appliances—that Japan had once sold to them. Japan thus encountered a new set of external economic challenges, and it confronted them with mixed success.

There also were domestic reasons for Japan's economic decline. One was saturated markets. Some of the products for which Japan had become well known—such as calculators, television sets, video cassette recorders, and cameras—were now available in every home, sometimes in multiple numbers. People simply did not need more of them. Innovation was constant, and although firms tried to come up with new and improved devices to tempt consumer desires, they were not always successful.

These outcomes were an indication of another problem in the economy after the 1970s. Having tapped most of the new technology available by then, Japan, like other nations, was forced to rely more on new research and development. This slowed the rate of innovation, especially in comparison with the period before 1974. Related to this technological dilemma was Japan's surprisingly slow entry into the world of computers and business software. Countries such as the United States depended heavily on rapid growth in these sectors to propel frenzied development in the 1990s, but Japan failed to capture these opportunities on a comparable scale.

One visible consequence of these economic dilemmas was the decline of older, major industries. Steel and shipbuilding were especially hard hit. In steel communities across Japan, fires were banked, mills were closed, and factories were dismantled. Some steel firms developed new enterprises, such as amusement parks and computer services, but they could not create enough new positions for all their employees. Unemployment thus rose sharply in many old steel cities. In addition, thousands of small affiliates, subcontractors, and retail shops were put out of business entirely, and their workers had great difficulty finding new jobs. The same story was repeated time and again in shipbuilding communities. Workers lost jobs and income, younger families fled, and once-vibrant communities became ghost towns. National and prefectural governments did institute a wide range of readjustment programs aimed at ameliorating distress and retraining workers but had only partial success.

While these proud old industries declined, others thrived. Automakers, consumer electronics firms, and machine makers expanded rapidly in the 1980s. Although they hit some bumps in the late 1980s and early 1990s, such firms as **Toyota** and Honda, **Sony** and **Matsushita**, **Hitachi** and **Mitsubishi** generally flourished both domestically and internationally. Their increased sales, employment, and profits compensated to some degree for the decline of steel and shipbuilding.

Even greater compensation for those losses came from the small- and medium-size enterprises. These firms still make up 98 percent of all establishments in Japan, employ about 60 percent of the labor force in manufacturing, and add about 50 percent of the value to manufacturing output. Many smaller firms retain their close relationships as subcontractors to final assemblers, especially in automaking and electrical manufacturing. And some once-small subcontractors, such as Nippon densō, have become major firms in their own right. In addition, many newer small enterprises possessing flexibility and organizational skills are well suited to exploit opportunities in such fields as biotechnology and consumer product development. Firms in this sector have always had a high failure rate. But those that have survived have created many of the new jobs in Japan since 1974, especially in manufacturing, and they are responsible for much of the energy driving the economy forward.

During the boom of the 1980s, banks were also among the most profitable concerns in Japan. Indeed, lists of the largest banks in the world were constantly dominated by such giants as Fuji, **Sumitomo**, Sanwa, and Daiichi-Kangyō. But they began to fall on hard times in the late 1980s, as they had made too many bad loans to finance real estate development and stock speculation. When the stock market plummeted, land prices fell, and commercial occupancy rates dropped, the borrowers could not pay interest or principal. By the mid-1990s, Japanese banks were holding uncollectable loans in such huge amounts that neither banks nor the Ministry of Finance would disclose the full sum.

Banks thus grew understandably hesitant to extend new loans, and their restraint became a critical cause of the downturn of the 1990s. Entrepreneurs, especially in manufacturing, also were reluctant to invest in the face of widespread economic uncertainties. This combination of bank distress and investor reluctance prolonged the economic sluggishness.

Another sector that declined considerably during this period was agriculture. In the two decades after 1975, the number of farm families fell from about 5 million to about 2.6 million, and the number of agricultural laborers fell from more than 23 million to about 12 million. The amount of land under cultivation also fell slightly, as suburban and exurban growth intruded on agriculture. The amount of rice produced dropped under pressure from domestic policies and foreign governments, not to mention a decline in demand as food preferences shifted. Japanese farmers are simply less able to produce what domestic consumers prefer to eat. They still supply nearly all the nation's rice and edible cereal grains and most of its fresh vegetables and eggs. But increasing shares of wheat, soybeans, pork, beef, fish, fruits, sugar, and oils are coming from abroad.

Although farming itself continued to decline, farm families (according to official designations) managed to do quite well for themselves. In some years, the total income of an average farm household exceeded that of a typical urban family. This was so, however, only because most income in most "farm" families actually came from employment outside agriculture. Many farmers were municipal officials, schoolteachers, railway employees, or businessmen, and many of their wives had full- or part-time jobs in nearby towns. In many ways, therefore, such families were farmers in name only, and they bore many of the attributes of the broad middle class. In particular, they enjoyed the same purchasing power as their city cousins, bought the same consumer products, and thereby sustained the widespread affluence that characterized the years after 1974.

International trade was putting Japan's true farmers out of business at a rapid rate, but it also had more beneficial effects. Many of the prosperous, large-scale industries—especially automaking, consumer electronics, and electrical manufacturing—relied heavily on exports for markets and profits. In most years after 1974, the value of Japanese exports rose, as did the value of imports into Japan, but never at the same rates. Therefore, Japan often incurred trade surpluses with the United States and Europe which caused the trade disputes noted earlier. In part, this happened because Japan imported large quantities of petroleum from areas of the world to which it could not sell enough exports to balance its trade. To some extent, trade surpluses with other areas were thus inevitable, perhaps even defensible. Japan either could not or did not defend such surpluses, however, for which it received a great deal of criticism.

The geographic distribution of Japan's trade shifted only slightly during this period. The United States remained its principal trading partner and Europe, a minor one. Indonesia and the Middle East provided Japan with most of its petroleum, and they also bought some imports from Japan. Southeast Asia attracted the largest increases in trade, by providing Japan with low-cost consumer items and raw materials while buying a wide range of manufactured goods. Given this increasing export dependence on the region, the drastic decline in the economic standing of many Southeast Asian nations that began in 1997 implied persistent difficulties in Japan's trade relations.

CULTURAL DISTRACTIONS

Many Japanese tried to forget their worries about economic convulsions, political instability, and social malaise by turning enthusiastically to cultural distractions. A new dynamism brought new departures in literature, popular culture, and religion.

In the 1960s, new ideas rekindled values inherent in the prewar cultural orthodoxy. One purpose of the exponents of these ideas was to explain, to both Japanese at home and foreigners abroad, why Japan was so successful economically. Japan's even greater economic successes in the 1970s and 1980s only confirmed such thinking. In the 1980s, a group of academic intellectuals closely associated with leaders of the LDP wrote a book entitled *The Ie Society as Civilization*. The *ie* in the title refers to the Japanese household as a distinctive phenomenon, a socioeconomic unit managed effectively in trust by the current son out of obligation to a long line of ancestors and also out of duty to his successors. This unit is an embodiment of the hierarchy associated with parents guiding children, the sense of unity inherent to the family as a social entity, and the impulses toward cooperation that have sustained the household through time.The authors applied these core observations to an understanding of Japan's high-performance economy in the 1980s, arguing that Japan succeeded where others nations did not because it possessed a unique set of values conducive to economic growth. These included an acceptance of hierarchy, a respect for elders, a commitment to diligence, and a natural inclination to cooperate for the sake of the common good. In contrast with the competitive self-interest driving capitalist societies in the West, Japan, they claimed, harmonized social interests behind a collective endeavor that produced not only material gains but social cohesion as well.

Such ideas articulated a form of Japanese triumphalism. The country had enjoyed remarkable economic success in the 1950s and 1960s and continued to do so in the 1970s and 1980s, when its counterparts in North America and Western Europe were struggling with nagging problems. It is not surprising that assertions of national pride arose under those circumstances, but it is surprising that they sometimes took a very shrill tone, as they did in an inflammatory book entitled *The Japan That Can Say No*. Coauthored by Sony's **Morita Akio** and a conservative LDP politician and former novelist named Ishiwara Shintarō, this book marked the crescendo of triumphalist ideas. When the economic dilemmas of the 1990s struck, a mad scramble for new ideas began.

The most strident voices in the world of ideas, and the ones that commanded the media, advanced views that were neither very inspired nor inspiring. This lack of inspiration also influenced the fate of Japan's established religions. There were no major doctrinal innovations or controversies. Shinto priests concentrated on ritual duties, and Buddhist priests conducted funerals and memorialized the dead. With increasing affluence, more people were able to attend shrine festivals, visit temples, and make religious pilgrimages, so activities at religious sites thrived. Whether the visitors did these things for religious reasons or for entertainment value was, however, difficult to discern.

Neither Shinto nor Buddhist priests had the time or inclination, it seems, to provide extensive pastoral care. Most of them were too absorbed by their ritual obligations and other duties to counsel parishioners on personal and practical matters. In a society still undergoing pervasive social changes and in a population with enough leisure time to reflect on deeper questions, the established religions thereby created a religious vacuum.

New religions, and what came to be dubbed new-new religions, moved to fill this vacuum. In the 1970s and after, religious organizations continued to form and to attract many new adherents. The older "new" religions, those established between the mid-1800s and 1970 thrived, too. Many people in Japanese society continued to seek out the kind of social community and psychological balm that the newer religions had always provided.

The newest religions brought sometimes curious innovations to religious life. A sect called Agonshū emerged in the late 1970s under the leadership of a man who called himself Kiriyama. A repeated business failure in his late fifties, he had spent time in prison before undergoing a religious conversion just as he was about to commit suicide. Seeing the light, he transformed himself. The secret to his success was the recognition that unappeased ancestral spirits were obstructing his ability to approach life with a confident, positive attitude. This became the doctrinal core of Agonshū. Using glossy publications, television programs, and shrewdly crafted videos, Kiriyama attracted a body of followers that grew from 30,000 to nearly 300,000 in the course of one decade. He built a huge temple complex near Kyōto, staged annual festivals, and nurtured a flock of volunteers devoted to helping themselves by helping others. Through collective efforts carried out under Kiriyama's tutelage, Agonshū adherents won individual release from troubling personal constraints to make new lives for themselves.

Another of Japan's newest religions brought horrifying twists to the scene. Aum Shinrikyō was founded by yet another troubled individual, a partially blind man called Asahara. Developing a body of doctrine that included snippets of Shinto, Buddhism, Christianity, and even Marxism, he used his charismatic powers to attract many bright, college-educated, middle-class adherents to his sect. Providing a network of social relations for people adrift in the world, Asahara persuaded the scientists and physicians under his control to produce nerve gas and to distribute it at subway stations in downtown Tōkyō. The deaths and injuries from this incident in 1995 prompted a quick response from the authorities. Eventually, Asahara was tracked down, arrested, and tried for his crimes, and his sect was disbanded.

Another religious development, or intriguing return, took place beginning in the 1970s. It displayed a Buddhist influence but also had its own unique features. This was the spreading practice of *mizuko kuyō*, or the commemoration of dead children, often children who had been aborted. The foundation of this practice rests on the Buddhist belief that if the spirits of the dead are not properly appeased, they will create problems for those who remain behind in the realm of the living.

These practices began when priests learned from older women that they felt uneasy about abortions and the spirits of their dead/unborn children. Because women in postwar Japan have frequently relied on abortion as a form of birth control, many have such feelings. Recognizing a need, priests began to set out small statues that symbolized the dead child, and they offered to commemorate the dead and to accept small donations for their services. Other, more entrepreneurial, figures recognized a gold mine. Some of them established temples that specialized in memorials for dead children, sold statues placed on temple grounds in the thousands, solicited contributions for regular ritual offerings and observances, and sold smaller statues that could be used in the home. These men advertised their services in the way that commercial firms did, and they attracted thousands of takers. Public criticism mounted against quacks preying on vulnerable women, and there certainly was some exploitation. But the practice itself did resolve a source of emotional, psychological, and religious distress, and it may have brought a sense of peace and repose to some women.

Repose was among the last feelings generated by the writers of this period. Male authors were insistent on taking off in new directions. Perhaps the most famous of Japan's novelists was **Ōe Kenzaburō**, who won the Nobel Prize for literature in 1994. Although Ōe had been a major figure in Japan for some time, his work was controversial, as it dwelt on his personal and highly subjective reactions to his son who was born with birth defects. Younger writers, such as Murakami Haruki (b. 1949), gradually surpassed Ōe and his predecessors in popularity. Their surreal fantasies written in a hip, cosmopolitan style appealed more to young, affluent readers.

Women writers also introduced new approaches. A group of Japanese women born around 1930 produced some of the most varied and imaginative prose ever written by Japanese authors. **Mukoda Kuniko** wrote about the sleazy conduct of urban, middle-class men and women, as these ruminations by one of her male characters attest:

"More often than he cared to remember, he had indulged in safe little love affairs on business trips. Shiozawa disliked knowing that this other, shady side lived behind the facade of the reputable, respectable businessman, but he comforted himself: That's how we men are. Everyone does it some time or other."[2]

Ōba Minako relied on her residence abroad to inject a note of anguished liberation into stories about women trapped in awkward marriages. **Ariyoshi Sawako**, who suffered health problems throughout her life, drew a vivid portrait of a dying parent and his caregiver. Her novel generated popular support for improving welfare for the elderly. And **Tomioka Taeko** published surreal but penetrating tales about the plight of the urban poor.

A younger cohort of female writers born after the war carried these new departures even further. **Tsushima Yūko**, herself a mother rearing children on her own, wrote moving but cloying stories about divorced women, their travails, and the ineffectual men in their lives. **Yamada Eimi** (or Amy Yamada) exploited her bawdy life to write thinly veiled autobiographies about lust and love at sex clubs and with American soldiers. And **Banana Yoshimoto** wrote a famous novella depicting personal loss and the tremulous nature of social relationships among the young in a rich, urban society. Women's writing thus engaged in frank explorations of female, and male, concerns, not the least of which was sex.

So much candid commentary in literature written by women for women shaped social conduct in disconcerting ways. The first section of this chapter discussed a new form of prostitution among teenage girls that mimicked in some ways the tales of Yamada Eimi. A rather different form of conduct began in the 1980s among girls known as "cuties." Cuties were between about twelve and fifteen at the outset, but as the cutie phenomenon persisted, it extended to females in their late teens and early twenties. Cuties wrote in a distinctive, childish script on paper festooned with friendly little cartoon animals. They ate cream-filled eclairs while dressed in childlike, unisex clothing, and they intentionally acted immature. We can discern in their behavior a resistance, especially as they got older, to the demanding social norms imposed on them, marriage in particular. The cutie phenomenon thus exemplified the pervasive tendency toward self-regard and self-indulgence that affluence brought to Japan, and it may have accounted in part for the increasing refusal of young women to marry "on time." If they could postpone the responsibilities of marriage by immersing themselves in an adolescent subculture, many young women seemed to be saying, why not?

Another youth subculture also emerged in this period to endorse self-indulgence and to refute the demands for diligence and conformity. Known as the "new species," the participants were males and females in their late teens who avoided regular jobs. Instead, they took well-paying, part-time jobs, accumulated some money, quit work, bought trendy clothing, partied till they were broke, recovered, and got another part-time job. They thought they were rejecting the kind of commitments their fathers had to their firms and their mothers had to their families. Few seemed to appreciate, however, that members of the new species displayed a similarly obsessive devotion to their ultimately feeble rebellion. Like the youth of the Meiji era and the modern boys and modern girls of the 1920s, the cuties and the new species kept alive the cultural generativity of the young.

Older Japanese distract themselves in different ways. They participate in sports, especially bowling, golf, swimming, baseball, skiing, and tennis. They are voracious readers. Every household takes an average of two daily newspapers and spends large sums on books and magazines. Families also spend heavily on sports equipment, audio and visual equipment, musical instruments, and cameras. Domestic tourism extends to nearly every family in the country, and international tourism is rising rapidly, too. In the late 1990s, more than 15 million Japanese are going abroad each year, most to the United States and other parts of Asia. Women often use their spare cash and extra leisure to take lessons in foreign languages, flower arranging, and tennis. Men with spare time do what they have been doing since the Tokugawa era: they go off with their male friends to eat, drink, and be merry.

JAPAN IN 2000

Nakagane Hitoshi groans and holds his head, his hungover mind grappling with the demands of a new day. Last night's drinking bout with some prospective business partners has left him feeling lower than usual. At forty-five, maybe he is getting too old for this kind of thing, even though it is good for business. If his firm can just close the deal he is negotiating, better times will follow.

Struggling to get up, he nearly falls off the Western-style bed his wife bought for their new home. She saw it in a glossy women's magazine and just had to have it, even though he would have been perfectly happy to sleep on Japanese-style bedding on the floor. At 7:15, it is too late for him to soak in the tub, so he takes a quick shower in their private bathroom. This is an innovation that he does like, because it frees him from waiting for Ken'ichi's interminable visits to the facilities.

At fifteen, Ken-chan, as his parents affectionately call him, is entering a difficult period. At five feet nine inches, he is gawky, already three inches taller than his father. His parents have smothered him with television sets, audio equipment, and video games for years, but he is still doing poorly in school. Hitoshi's wife, Yoshiko, wants to send Ken-chan to a good cram school. In fact, that is the first topic of conversation over breakfast. She has found one with an excellent reputation that charges a reasonable fee. Wouldn't it be a good idea to go ahead with the application? Too preoccupied with his own concerns, Hitoshi puts her off.

While Ken and Yoshiko eat cereal, toast, orange juice, and milk, Hitoshi gulps down a bowl of rice, some seaweed, and a cup of tea. He has never abandoned the breakfast diet on which he was reared in a small village west of Tōkyō. Noting the time, he says quick good-byes and rushes out to catch the express. This means a fast, fifteen-minute walk to the station, but he gets there just in time to grab a seat before the train pulls out. For the next fifty minutes, he is able to skim the newspaper he has brought along and to think about the day ahead.

Hitoshi feels pressured in a lot of ways. The new house carries a whopping mortgage that eats up 40 percent of his monthly salary. With lower annual raises and smaller bonuses, he is barely keeping up. Yoshiko has taken a job grading exams at home for a cram school, but the work is sporadic and pays poorly. Several new expenditures are on the horizon. Hitoshi's aging Subaru needs an expensive tune-up. Ken'ichi does have to enter a cram school. And the family has to go on a vacation to Los Angeles; they have been planning it for three years.

Hitoshi's job is a problem, too. He is a middle manager in a small firm that makes electronic products. The company was doing well until competitors from Korea and Taiwan began horning in on their markets. His firm has been trying to negotiate a deal with the men he was with last night to produce a new medical instrument. Success in this venture would put the firm on steady footing, win Hitoshi a promotion, and give him a much-needed raise.

Before Hitoshi realizes it, the train arrives at his destination and he is nearly lifted off by the tide of humanity. His company offices are located in a small building near Shinjuku, one of downtown Tōkyō's most important transport hubs, commercial districts, and entertainment quarters. By the time he staggers into the lobby, most of his coworkers have already arrived. For the next two hours, Hitoshi busies himself with paperwork in preparation for a meeting with the company leaders.

He slips out just before noon for lunch at a nearby Indian restaurant. The food is tasty, not too spicy, filling, and cheap. Gulping it down in seven minutes, he dashes along the crowded main street to a sports shop nearby. His major task for the day is to buy a pair of alligator golf shoes that he has been eyeing for weeks. He has squirreled away some of the allowance that Yoshiko gives him each month and managed to save enough to cover the $300 selling price. The shoes are just what he needs to impress the company president during their golf outing at a prestigious suburban course this Sunday. Just then, his cell phone rings.

Yoshiko is calling him. Fortunately, she has no way of knowing where he is. She is in Akihabara, where she has gone to see if she can get the video camera they want for the Los Angeles trip. In a discount shop, she has found one that will save them $50, so she is calling to tell him. And by the way, the PTA chair called to ask Yoshiko to help with the upcoming sports day at school, but she begged off again. With her job, Ken-chan's needs, and the forthcoming trip to Los Angeles, she is just too pressed for time.

On his return to the office, Hitoshi passes the shuttered doors of a Hokkaidō bank that recently declared bankruptcy. His own firm has had difficulty acquiring the financing it needs to carry out the prospective deal, and Hitoshi himself has had to visit five commercial banks as well as three lesser banks catering to the small-enterprise sector. But he has obtained verbal assurances of financing from four different institutions, so the deal should be secure, even in this shaky financial environment. He would be delighted if the nation's politicians showed more resolve in addressing Japan's economic problems. They all are a bunch of crooks, and if given the chance, he would throw them out in a moment. Unfortunately, that will have to wait. He is going to be on the golf course when the next lower house election is held, on Sunday. It is just as well. Hitoshi does not know the candidates running in his district anyway, and he no longer feels an allegiance to any political party.

Getting back to work again, Hitoshi chats with colleagues about the deal he is spearheading. The meeting with company officers goes well, and they designate him the point man for the final negotiations next week. To celebrate this progress and to lay the groundwork for next week's meeting, Hitoshi accompanies four coworkers to a nearby beer hall around 6:30. He orders a steak and fries. Just as he is about to tear into his meal, his cell phone rings.

Yoshiko again. Will he be home for dinner? She and Ken-chan have just eaten some fried chicken she brought home from KFC. Ken-chan is finishing his homework before turning on the television. She is about to leave for the cram school, where she will discuss application procedures and financing with the director. There is no time to start Hitoshi's bath, but he will probably be home too late to take one anyway. She will see him in the morning.

Thus informed, Hitoshi is able to spend a relaxing two hours with his friends. He rides home on the train with an associate who gets off at his station. They stop at a small bar where Hitoshi keeps a bottle of whiskey for just such occasions. After a glass or two, they part ways, and Hitoshi trudges home. It is

11:30. He notices on the kitchen table a thick envelope and a note from Yoshiko. She has booked a package tour for Los Angeles on a special deal, and she will show him the new camera in the morning. Heading upstairs, he finds that Ken-chan appears to be playing a video game. Taking note of the late hour, Hitoshi kindly says hello and urges Ken-chan to go to bed. Silence greets him. On this note, Hitoshi calls it a day. It will be a real pleasure to spend a leisurely week in Los Angeles. If only the business deal goes through.

NOTES TO CHAPTER 4

1. Gary D. Allinson and Yasunori Sone, eds., *Political Dynamics in Contemporary Japan* (Ithaca, N.Y.: Cornell University Press, 1993), p. 49.
2. Mukoda Kuniko, *The Name of the Flower: Stories by Mukoda Kuniko*, trans. Tomone Matsumoto (Berkeley, Calif.: Stone Bridge Press, 1994), p. 35.

PART II

Topical Compendium

This part of the guide is a kind of miniencyclopedia whose thirteen topical categories contain 150 individual entries. One purpose of the compendium is to provide more detail about the items treated briefly in the Historical Narrative and highlighted in boldface. Each item can be found in the index, where the page on which it appears in the Topical Compendium is noted in boldface. The compendium also can be used as a reference and learning source in its own right. The entries in each category are arranged (in nearly all cases) in chronological order. This enables readers to identify a topic—such as Political Leaders; Business Associations, Enterprises, and Firms; or State-Guided Organizations—in which they are interested and to follow its evolution from 1850 to the present. The third purpose of this compendium is to complement the Historical Narrative. For example, the entries under Male Writers and Female Writers contain biographies relating the lives of those authors to their works. Reading through these two topical categories in sequence reveals both the diversity of human experiences in Japan since 1850 and many aspects of its cultural, intellectual, social, and gender history. The same entries also list works of fiction—valuable sources for understanding Japan's modern history—and note their availability in English translation.

JAPAN

Japan's **geography** consists of four principal islands, one important island chain, and some seven thousand smaller islands. Moving from north to south, the principal islands are Hokkaidō, Honshū, Shikoku, and Kyūshū, stretching about twelve hundred miles from the northeast to the southwest. The important island chain lies southwest of Kyūshū and forms the prefecture of Okinawa.

In addition to the islands, Japan contains eight different regions. The regions have little administrative standing; rather, they are geographic areas displaying some differences in customs. The three most important are the Tohoku region, or northeastern Honshū; the Kantō region, where the Tōkyō-Yokohama-Chiba metropolitan area is situated; and the Kansai region, sometimes also called the Kinki region, where Kyōto and Ōsaka are located.

Japan covers about 146,000 square miles, most of which are hilly or mountainous. On the main island of Honshū, tall mountains form a spine running the entire length of the island. Shikoku and Kyūshū also have mountains, some of them active volcanoes. Only 14 percent of Japan's land is used for agriculture, and nearly all the nation's people are concentrated on less than 5 percent of the islands' surface.

Japan's **climate** varies greatly from north to south. Northern Hokkaidō lies at 45 degrees latitude and has cold winters and cool summers like those of North Dakota. As one moves southward, the winters become milder and the summers become hotter. The climate of the Tōkyō metropolitan area is similar to that of Washington, D.C. The winters are usually mild with little snow, and the summers are hot and humid. In southernmost Japan, on the islands of Okinawa, the climate is almost tropical.

Climate has had a major influence on the evolution of Japan. Those regions with short, cool growing seasons have been inhospitable to rice cultivation, and so the Tohoku region has suffered economically from its location in the colder north. Those regions with long growing seasons and warmer weather, however, have always been able to grow two crops per season. Thus, Kyūshū, Shikoku, and southern Honshū have historically been the country's most populous and economically productive areas. Never a major rice producer, Hokkaidō has nonetheless exploited its cooler climate and more open lands to become the center of the Japanese dairy industry.

In regard to Japan's **demography**, in the late 1990s, the nation's population was approaching 130 million. Given a landmass slightly smaller than the state of California, the population densities in Japan are very high. Indeed, in habitable areas, the population density is thirty times greater than in the United States. Many cities, and even affluent suburbs, have population densities that exceed 35,000 persons per square mile, a figure four times higher than the densities of such cities as Cleveland and Pittsburgh.

More than 80 percent of the Japanese population live in urban areas. More than one-fourth are in the large metropolitan region centered on Tōkyō, and another one-eighth live in the Kyōto-Ōsaka conurbation. In the late 1990s,

Japan had eleven cities with populations of more than 1 million. The six largest were Tōkyō, Yokohama, Ōsaka, Nagoya, Sapporo, and Kyōto.

Both birthrates and mortality rates are low in Japan. By the 1990s, birthrates had fallen from an early postwar high of about thirty-five per thousand to fewer than ten per thousand. Death rates also fell, from fifteen per thousand to about seven per thousand. Consequently, Japan has not been able to reproduce its own population naturally, so the population has been growing very slowly.

Japanese is the only official **language** in Japan and the language used by virtually all permanent residents. Despite some local dialectical differences, most people speak and understand the standard Japanese that is taught in the schools and spoken on television. Many Japanese know at least a little English, but to read newspapers and books, to watch television, and to conduct business effectively, a knowledge of Japanese is necessary.

Japanese seems to have derived from the Turco-Altaic languages of Central Asia, probably having been brought to the islands by continental emigrants thousands of years ago. The basic elements of the language consist of five vowels (*a, i, u, e, o*) and a number of vowel-consonant combinations (such as *ka, ki, ku, ke, ko*), for a total of forty-six units. Japanese uses three different written systems. It is possible to reproduce the forty-six units using either of two *kana* syllabaries. One is called *hiragana*, which has a cursive form, and the other is called *katakana*, which has a more angular form. The third element of the written language is *kanji*, or Chinese characters. These are the ideographs introduced into Japan from China sometime during the sixth century. *Kanji* are used for nouns, verbs, and word roots, and *hiragana* and *katakana* are used to indicate verb tense, to decline nouns, and to form connecting syllables. In order to read newspapers and popular books and magazines, a person must know about three thousand *kanji* and both the *kana* syllabaries.

Ethnicity is a controversial issue in Japan. Although many Japanese regard themselves as members of a pure race whose blood has not been mixed with that of other races, most scholars believe that contemporary Japanese are descendants of peoples from the Asian continent who entered Japan through the Korean peninsula some two thousand years ago. Since then, however, there has been little migration into Japan, and so the Japanese are quite homogeneous with respect to physical attributes, language, and customs.

Three groups in contemporary Japan differ from mainstream Japanese. One is the *burakumin* or *dowa minzoku*, people who, though physiologically the same as the Japanese, have been forced to reside in separate districts because they have followed occupations proscribed under religious custom, such as tanning hides and caring for the dead. Their segregation has fostered some-what different language usages and customs. A second group is the Ainu, de-scendants of the original settlers of Hokkaidō. They do differ physiologically from the Japanese, as they have Caucasian features, and they have historical-ly spoken a different language and lived according to different customs. The third non-Japanese group consists of the foreign nationals residing in Japan, the largest groups being Koreans and Chinese. Together, these three non-mainstream groups constitute less than 5 percent of the total population.

EMPERORS

In the modern era, Japan's emperors have been selected according to the prin-ciple of primogeniture, in which the oldest son succeeds his father. Four men have occupied the throne since the Restoration of 1868. The first was the Meiji emperor, followed in succession by his son, his grandson, and his great-grand-son. Japan's imperial family does not have a surname; instead, emperors are known by either their posthumous reign names—Meiji, Taishō, Shōwa, and Heisei, or their given names.

The **Meiji emperor** occupied the throne between 1867 and 1912, a period marked by momentous changes in Japan's history. Born in the imperial capi-tal of Kyōto, Mutsuhito (his personal name) (1852–1912) was the son of the 121st emperor and his consort, the daughter of a high-ranking official at court. Court tutors taught Mutsuhito a knowledge of Chinese and Japanese texts dur-ing the years that preceded the Restoration, and he developed a love for writ-ing poetry. He was only fifteen when he ascended the throne.

Mutsuhito's reign is noted for the sweeping changes that brought Japan into the modern era, such as the centralization of the nation-state, the promulga-tion of a constitution, the advent of industrialization, and Japan's expansion abroad following its victories in the Sino-Japanese War of 1894–1895 and the Russo-Japanese War of 1904–1905. In contrast with his successors, the Meiji emperor did make a number of significant public pronouncements and may have played a personal role in the affairs of state. However, the real leaders of the Meiji government, former samurai who held the post of prime minister and those of other cabinet ministers, gradually used him more as a figurehead imparting a religious aura. Pomp and pageantry surrounded the emperor's public appearances, and his real powers seem to have waned after the 1880s, when he began to style himself a constitutional monarch and to suffer the ef-fects of diabetes. The Meiji emperor was a heavy drinker with a large sexual appetite (he sired at least fourteen offspring by imperial concubines), but he always behaved decorously at public events.

The **Taishō emperor** governed in his own right for only nine of the fourteen years he was on the throne between 1912 and 1926. Yoshihito (1879–1926) was the son of the Meiji emperor and an imperial consort, a woman from an aristocratic family in Kyōto. When he was an infant, Yoshihito contracted meningitis, which left him physically frail, hyperactive, and perhaps mentally impaired. Like his father, he enjoyed poetry, horses, and women, but he never had his father's powers of concentration or personal presence. A series of strokes forced the Taishō emperor in 1921 to cede his powers to his son as regent, and he died five years later. Owing to his debilities and his short time on the throne, the Taishō emperor had little influence on affairs of state.

The **Shōwa emperor** is well known to the world as Hirohito (1901–1989). He occupied the throne for sixty-three years between 1926 and 1989, during a period of change comparable in significance to that of his grandfather's reign. Hirohito was the eldest son of the Taishō emperor and his wife, the daughter of an aristocratic court family. Between 1908 and 1916, he attended the Peers' School, then under the headship of General Nogi Maresuke. Hirohito followed a spartan military regimen and developed a propensity to play by the rules. In 1916 he entered a special school at court directed by a navy admiral. Perhaps as a result, at an early age, Hirohito cultivated an interest in marine sciences that he maintained throughout his life.

When he ascended the throne in 1926, Hirohito had already had five years of experience serving as regent to his father, which may have been fortunate because during the next decade, he faced constant political problems caused by aggressive military groups at home and in Manchuria. Hirohito's desire to function as a constitutional monarch and his own diffident personality, however, limited his ability to take action publicly to keep the military in check. Twice, however, he risked the prestige of the throne to rein in the military. The first occasion was in 1936 when he ordered that the leaders of a military coup be arrested and tried. The second occasion took place in 1945 when he interceded to force reluctant army leaders to accept the country's surrender.

After Japan's defeat in 1945, Hirohito remained on the throne but, under the terms of the 1947 constitution, gave up all but his "symbolic" powers. Besides consciously working to erase the aura of religious invincibility that had surrounded the throne in the prewar era, he also tried to conduct himself in a more democratic fashion, by touring the country, staying at ordinary inns, and attending sports events. He thus served as a symbol of unity for the Japanese people during the period of rapid growth after 1955. In 1989 hundreds of thousands of mourners on the streets of Tōkyō and millions at their televisions watched his funeral procession.

Upon his father's death, the **Heisei emperor** ascended the throne. Akihito was born in 1933 to Hirohito and his wife, Nagako, the descendant of a major daimyō house. Akihito was educated in properly imperial fashion during his youth in the wartime and early postwar eras. After 1945 he also received instruction in American studies and the English language from an American tutor, Elizabeth Vining. Akihito was praised for his democratic inclinations when he chose to marry a "commoner," Shoda Michiko. Even though she was not the daughter of a court official or former daimyō, she was hardly common, as her father owned one of the largest milling firms in Japan. The Heisei emperor traveled abroad on several occasions when still a prince, and since ascending the throne, he has continued to travel overseas. Although his formal political powers are limited, he is able to speak for and represent Japan in subtle ways, as he did during a visit to China when he almost apologized for Japan's conduct in the Pacific War.

POLITICAL LEADERS

During the Tokugawa period (1600–1868), members of a hereditary military class ruled Japan, the dominant figure being the shōgun, the head of the Tokugawa house, who controlled the largest allotment of land and the largest single army in the country. Another 260 lords, or *daimyō*, shared control over the rest of the country and its soldiers, in domains of various sizes. Finally, the shōgun and the daimyō relied on their loyal vassals, or *samurai*, to support them in war and to serve as their subordinates in peace. Under the Tokugawa regime, the court nobility in Kyōto held no real power.

The coup d'état that brought down the Tokugawa house was a political pincer movement joining lower-ranking samurai from domains in western Japan with some court nobles from Kyōto, all rallying around the emperor as the rightful ruler of Japan. For the next decade, as victors sharing the spoils, the men who led the Restoration were the central figures in the new national government.

Iwakura Tomomi (1825–1883) was a court noble who allied with samurai from Satsuma and Chōshū to overthrow the Tokugawa house and establish the Meiji government. Born to a high-ranking official at court, he was adopted by another noble family and reared in the protected environment of the imperial capital. His opposition to the Tokugawa house began in 1858, when it signed the Treaty of Amity and Commerce with the United States. Subsequently Iwakura joined with other nobles in opposition to the shōgun. In time, he began to plot with representatives from Chōshū and Satsuma to overthrow the Tokugawa house entirely. When their efforts succeeded in 1868, Iwakura assumed a leading position in the new government. He is best known for leading the Iwakura mission on a tour of the United States and Europe between 1871 and 1873. The mission failed in its task to renegotiate the unequal treaties and became instead a grand tour and fact-gathering effort for its members. In his later years, Iwakura used his position to bolster the status of the throne and to lay the groundwork for a constitutional monarchy.

Saigō Takamori (1828–1877) was one of the three samurai leaders of the Meiji Restoration and a tragic figure in the new government. He was the son of a low-ranking samurai in the domain of Satsuma, located in southern Kyūshū. With his large stature and garrulous ways, Saigō was a popular figure among his peers. When he was in his twenties, Saigō's domain lord noticed his abilities and appointed him to responsible positions in the domain bureaucracy. But during the early 1860s, Saigō often offended domain authorities with his opposition to the unequal treaties and the Tokugawa house. He nonetheless managed to preserve his influence and by 1866 was leading his associates in Satsuma into an alliance with like-minded samurai from Chōshū. Saigō led the Restoration armies in their takeover of the shōgun's capital, but he returned to Satsuma for two years before entering the government in 1870. After only three years, he left Tōkyō in a dispute over policy toward Korea. Helplessly entangled with samurai who gathered on Kyūshū to oppose the Meiji government in 1877, Saigō died while fighting the government he had helped create.

Ōkubo Toshimichi (1830–1878) was the second Satsuma samurai among the three leaders of the Restoration. A boyhood friend of Saigō Takamori, Ōkubo was also the son of a lower-ranking samurai. Like Saigō, he, too, demonstrated his leadership abilities at an early age, caught the eye of the domain lord, and found himself in unusually high-ranking official positions for a person of his background. Serving as a mediator between conservative higher officials and more radical lower samurai, Ōkubo worked with Saigō to create the Satsuma-Chōshū alliance in the late 1860s. Unlike Saigō, Ōkubo relished the political infighting of the new government and the power and responsibility that went with high office. In short order, he became the equivalent of minister of finance and then minister of home affairs. He worked to revise the tax system, to promote industrialization, and to ease the plight of the peasantry. Ōkubo also took the lead in reducing the status and privileges of the former samurai and ruthlessly suppressed the rebellion that some of them started in 1877. This cost him his life in the following year, when an outraged former samurai assassinated him.

Kido Kōin (Takayoshi) (1833–1877), a samurai from the Chōshū domain in western Honshū, was the third member of the samurai triumvirate that led the Meiji Restoration. As a teenager Kido studied at a private academy established by Yoshida Shōin, a Chōshū samurai who developed a love-hate relationship with the foreign powers. Yoshida was intensely curious about, even approving of, their technical accomplishments, but he was distressed by the threat they posed to the Japanese way of life. Kido embraced more of the open, inquisitive aspects of Yoshida's personality and consistently took advanced positions on government issues. He played a major role on the Chōshū side in cementing the alliance with Satsuma and later assumed influential positions in the Meiji government. Kido drafted the Five Article Oath (see Appendix), opposed a military expedition to Korea in 1873, and devoted his attention to domestic reform. Always frail in constitution and fond of women and drink, Kido died at age forty-four during the 1877 conflict.

Within two years, the key leaders of the Restoration had passed from the scene and been succeeded by the influential **genrō**, or Meiji oligarchs. Between 1889 and 1912 the Meiji emperor bestowed the status of *genrō* on twelve men, all second-generation revolutionary elites about ten years younger than Saigō, Ōkubo, and Kido. Most of them were former samurai from either Satsuma or Chōshū; one was a court noble. During and immediately after the Restoration, the *genrō* were top-ranking subordinates to the triumvirate. Then, between the late 1870s and the late 1910s, they dominated the Japanese government through their formal positions and informal influence. By recognizing them as *genrō*, the emperor authorized them to select and approve candidates for prime minister and cabinet posts, and he formally acknowledged the need for their advice during times of crisis. Biographies of six of the twelve *genrō* follow.

Inoue Kaoru (1835–1915), a low-ranking samurai from the Chōshū domain, was an influential leader in government and business circles from the 1870s to the 1910s. In his late twenties, he traveled illegally to England to see at first hand the accomplishments of the foreign powers. When he returned to Japan, he joined with the forces in Chōshū that eventually overthrew the Tokugawa house. After 1870 Inoue held a number of increasingly more important positions in the Meiji government, eventually serving as minister of both finance and foreign affairs. Unlike many of his contemporaries, he moved in and out of government service in order to assume private-sector positions as well.

Closely tied to the Mitsui *zaibatsu,* he played a leading role in developing both the Japanese economy and a corps of professional businessmen.

Matsukata Masayoshi (1835–1924) presided over the creation of Japan's system of public finance during the 1880s and 1890s. He was a low-ranking samurai from the Satsuma domain who had acquired economic expertise even before the Restoration, by serving in his domain's shipping bureau. He joined the Meiji government in 1871, taking a position in what became the Ministry of Finance. Between 1881 and 1898, Matsukata served as minister of finance, during which time he led a program of deflationary adjustment, introduced a new paper currency, developed the government's budgeting and financial systems, and laid the groundwork for a modern banking system. He also served twice as prime minister, between 1891 and 1892 and again between 1896 and 1898.

Yamagata Aritomo (1838–1922) was one of Japan's most powerful army and government leaders between the 1880s and the 1910s. A former samurai from the Chōshū domain, Yamagata began his career as a military leader by joining a special force in Chōshū in 1863. After the Restoration, he played a key role in developing the modern conscript army, by serving as an official in the Ministry of the Army and as an officer in the army itself. During the Sino-Japanese and Russo-Japanese Wars, Yamagata held some of the highest-ranking posts in the army, including that of chief of general staff. In the 1880s he began to take an interest in domestic politics by working through the Ministry of Home Affairs to create a system of local government patterned after that of Prussia. Between 1889 and 1900 he served on two occasions for nearly four years as prime minister. The contacts he made through the army and domestic ministries provided him with sources of influence that he continued to exercise for two decades after his retirement from office.

Itō Hirobumi (1841–1909) was, along with Yamagata, the most powerful figure in the Meiji government between the 1880s and his death in 1909. Itō also was a low-ranking samurai from Chōshū. He had accompanied Inoue Kaoru on his trip to England in 1863 and early on joined the anti-*bakufu* (shōgunate) forces. After the Restoration, Itō—still only in his twenties—ingratiated himself with Iwakura Tomomi and Ōkubo Toshimichi and became an expert in domestic political affairs. When Ōkubo was assassinated, Itō moved into his positions. In 1885 he became the first prime minister under the new cabinet system, holding the post on four different occasions for a total of nearly eight years. In 1888 Itō became the first president of the Privy Council. During the 1880s he took the lead in preparing the new constitution that was introduced in 1889. Unlike Yamagata, who was adamantly opposed to political parties, Itō recognized their necessity under a constitutional monarchy, establishing the

Seiyūkai (political party) at the turn of the century and serving as an elected representative in the national Diet (parliament) for many years. In 1909 Itō was assassinated in Manchuria while on duty as governor-general of Korea.

Itō was a vain and arrogant man who liked women and drink. His attitudes were summed up nicely in the following ditty, a favorite among his chauvinistic samurai buddies: "Drunk, my head pillowed on a beauty's lap; awake and sober, grasping power to govern the nation."

Katsura Tarō (1848–1913) was an army general and prime minister who had a major influence on Japanese foreign policy between 1895 and 1913. Katsura, a samurai from Chōshū, entered the domain's special military forces and played a role in overthrowing the Tokugawa house. From then on, he helped create and administer Japan's modern army. In this role, he was a protégé of Yamagata Aritomo, who groomed Katsura as his successor. During the Sino-Japanese War, Katsura served briefly as governor-general of Taiwan. In 1898 he began a long tenure as minister of the army, and in 1901 he formed the first of his three cabinets serving as prime minister for eight of the next twelve years. He governed Japan during the Russo-Japanese War and during the annexation of Korea. Katsura used his influence to bolster Japan's military strength and to expand its presence in Asia. By 1912, however, the public had grown weary of his bellicose ways, and controversies surrounding his last cabinet brought to an end both his political career and his life.

Saionji Kinmochi (1849–1940), the youngest of the *genrō*, exercised his greatest influence over Japanese politics between the 1900s and the 1930s. Saionji was the only *genrō* to come from the aristocratic court in Kyōto. After his tenure as an officer in the Restoration armies, he spent nine years in France during the 1870s as a student and observer. On his return to Japan, Saionji became a protégé of Itō Hirobumi, accompanying him on his European study tours while Itō drew up the Meiji constitution. Saionji served in the late 1880s as Japan's ambassador to Germany, Austria, and Belgium. He was appointed to his first cabinet post in 1894, as minister of education under Itō. He succeeded Itō as head of the Seiyūkai between 1903 and 1914 and served twice as prime minister between 1906 and 1912, for a total of four years. Following the end of World War I, Saionji headed the Japanese delegation to the Versailles Peace Conference. As the last living *genrō*, he continued into the 1930s to approve the selection of prime ministers and cabinet ministers.

One contemporary of these men was also a major political figure during the Meiji era, although he never won recognition as a *genrō*. **Ōkuma Shigenobu** (1838–1922), born into a high-ranking samurai family in the domain of Hizen in northwestern Kyūshū, was both an educational and a political leader dur-

ing the late nineteenth and early twentieth centuries. Although Hizen supported the Restoration, Ōkuma was always an outsider among the samurai
from Satsuma and Chōshū who dominated the Meiji government. But he did
hold a variety of positions in the government during the 1870s and 1880s, often
dealing with sensitive foreign policy issues. Ōkuma also served briefly as prime
minister in 1898. But because he opposed men like Itō and Yamagata during
much of the 1880s and 1890s, he was forced to concentrate on building a political party and promoting a private school he had established (later Waseda
University). He then used his party leadership as a vehicle to return to the
prime ministership in 1914 for two years.

By the 1910s, most of the men who had participated in the Meiji Restoration had disappeared, and Japanese society was becoming far more diversified.
In addition, a still small but crucial electorate was exercising more influence
on the choice of political leaders. Until 1945, therefore, the men who formed
Japan's governments came from a variety of backgrounds and represented
many different interests and constituencies.

Takahashi Korekiyo (1854–1936) was a bureaucrat, financier, and politician
who helped shape Japanese economic policy for nearly four decades. He was
born to a vassal of the Tokugawa house but was adopted into a samurai family
as its heir. At the age of only thirteen Takahashi left Japan to spend two difficult years as a student-apprentice in the United States. On his return, he
served for the next twenty-two years as a government official, leaving in 1892 to
enter the Bank of Japan. In 1905 he was selected as a member of the House of
Peers, where he got his first taste of politics. In the 1910s, after heading two
major banks, he entered the Seiyūkai and also took his first cabinet post as minister of finance, a position he held intermittently until his death. Takahashi
also was prime minister briefly in 1921–1922. He was best known for crafting the
reflationary policies that brought Japan's economy out of recession in the early
1930s. Unfortunately, however, those policies played into the hands of the military, and when he tried to alter them in the mid-1930s, a young officer assassinated him.

Inukai Tsuyoshi (1855–1932) was a career politician who worked throughout his long life to create a system of competitive party politics. Born in a village in western Honshū, Inukai studied at Keiō University and began a career
as a journalist. When the Diet first convened in 1890, he won a seat in the first
election and retained it through the next eighteen contests. During his early
Diet career, he was associated with Ōkuma Shigenobu and parties opposing
the Satsuma-Chōshū clique that controlled the government. Inukai was appointed to his first ministerial post in 1898 under Ōkuma but spent many of the

following years in the political wilderness. By the 1920s, Inukai had reached an accommodation with his former opponents in the Seiyūkai, who called on him to form a cabinet in 1931. He governed for barely half a year before being assassinated by a right-wing terrorist, an event that brought down his civilian-dominated cabinet and paved the way for a series of governments led by army generals and navy admirals.

A bureaucrat, businessman, and politician famous for establishing Japan's first party government, **Hara Kei** (1856–1921) was born into a samurai family from a domain in northern Japan. He had only a modest formal education and spent three years as a journalist before entering the Foreign Ministry. During the next fifteen years, Hara held a variety of bureaucratic appointments, finally rising to the top position in the Foreign Ministry. He retired in 1897 to assume the presidency of a major newspaper, but in 1900 he took another position with an important private firm and also joined the Seiyūkai. From then on, his political career flourished. Hara was a skillful tactician who built a broad base of electoral support through pork-barrel politics. He accepted his first ministerial post in 1901, won election to the Diet's lower house in 1902, became president of the Seiyūkai in 1914, and governed as prime minister between 1918 and 1921. In 1921 a young man, troubled by the widespread corruption under Hara's cabinet, assassinated him.

Katō Takaaki (1860–1926) was a prominent diplomat and political leader during the first quarter of the twentieth century. Born in central Japan, he graduated from Tōkyō Imperial University in 1881 and immediately entered the Mitsubishi *zaibatsu*. For the next seven years, he had a meteoric career as a manager in the enterprise, impressing the founder, Iwasaki Yatarō, so much that he allowed his oldest daughter to marry him. Katō left Mitsubishi in 1888 to enter the Ministry of Foreign Affairs, where he had an equally notable career as official and ambassador. In 1902, Katō won a seat in the lower house from a district in Shikoku and began his career as an elected politician. Exploiting his contacts with Mitsubishi, he gradually assumed leadership of the Kenseikai (political party), served frequently as the minister of foreign affairs, and formed two short-lived governments in the mid-1920s. Katō sought conciliatory ties with England but advocated aggressive policies toward China while maneuvering opportunistically on domestic policy issues.

Konoe Fumimaro (1891–1945), the scion of one of the five most prestigious families in the old Kyōto aristocracy, was the most enigmatic political leader in prewar Japan. As a student at Kyōto Imperial University, he studied with a philosopher noted for his pro-Marxist views. While attending the Versailles Peace Conference, he developed antagonistic attitudes toward the victors for what he construed as their racist policies toward Asians. Then, while serving as a member of the conservative House of Peers during the 1920s, Konoe established ties with politically radical officers in the military. In the 1930s, Germany's Nazi policies won his favor to such an extent that he appeared in Nazi garb at his daughter's wedding rehearsal. Between 1937 and 1941, Konoe presided over two cabinets. During the first, one of his public pronouncements ensured a long-term war with China. During the second, he put the government on a wartime footing. Four months after the Allies entered Japan, he committed suicide.

At the end of the war, Japan faced a leadership crisis. The Allies carried out a political purge that removed from office almost all wartime politicians, many wartime business leaders, and a number of important bureaucrats. Although the country then could have turned to a younger set of leaders, men in their thirties or forties, instead, it opted for older men in their sixties who had been out of political favor during the war.

In keeping with his nickname "One-man Yoshida," **Yoshida Shigeru** (1878–1967) nearly monopolized the prime ministership between 1946 and 1954. Born to a family from Shikoku, he was adopted by the Yoshida house of Yokohama and educated at Tōkyō Imperial University. Upon his graduation in 1906, he entered the Ministry of Foreign Affairs. He completed his bureaucratic career before the war by winning the highest post in the ministry and serving as Japan's ambassador to Great Britain. During the war, he maintained a pro-Anglo-American stance that prompted investigations by the thought police. These incidents, along with some disputes with the military while on duty in China during the 1930s, conferred on him a political correctness that made him acceptable to the Allied occupiers. He served as Minister of Foreign Affairs in the first two postwar cabinets before forming, as prime minister, the first of his five cabinets in mid-1946. Following an eight-month hiatus in 1947–1948, he governed continuously until late 1954, usually heading the Foreign Ministry concurrently. He thus led the governments that negotiated reforms with the Allies and implemented the Occupation policies. Conciliatory toward the foreign occupiers, he took a hard stance against domestic opponents, especially labor unions, and smoothed the return to power of some wartime leaders.

Ishibashi Tanzan (1884–1973) was an influential prewar journalist and important postwar political figure. Born in Tōkyō, he graduated from Waseda University in 1907 and began his career as a journalist, editing between 1925 and 1946 a major economic publication known in English as the *Oriental Economist*. After the war, Ishibashi served briefly as minister of finance, left office owing to the purge, and returned in 1952 when he won a seat in the lower house. He joined Yoshida Shigeru's opponents to form the Liberal Democratic Party (LDP) in 1955 and served briefly as prime minister in 1956–1957. Ishibashi was an outspoken proponent of free trade and Keynesian policies, ideas that aided Japan in its economic recovery following the war.

To compensate for the absence of qualified legislators caused by the purge, Yoshida Shigeru recruited many former bureaucrats into his Liberal Party. These men, most in their forties and fifties, had already had distinguished careers, and Yoshida often assigned them major cabinet portfolios shortly after they began their political careers. As a consequence, these former bureaucrats dominated the leadership positions in the LDP and the government into the early 1970s.

Kishi Nobusuke (1896–1986) was a prominent bureaucrat and politician whose career spanned both the prewar and postwar eras. He was born into a family descended from samurai in the Chōshū domain and was educated at Tōkyō Imperial University. After graduating in 1920, he entered the bureaucracy and spent his career climbing to the top of the Ministry of Commerce and Industry. In the 1930s he was posted to Manchuria, where he developed ties with a rising army officer, Tōjō Hideki. When Tōjō formed his first cabinet in 1941, he assigned Kishi to head his old ministry. Kishi then won a lower house seat in the 1942 election but left the cabinet in 1944. Incarcerated as a Class A war criminal after the war, Kishi was released without being convicted. In 1953 he regained his old seat in the lower house and began organizing the LDP. In 1957 he became prime minister, but his cabinet fell amid the controversies caused by renewal of the U.S.-Japan Security Treaty in 1960. Kishi was a fervent anti-Communist, taking a hard line against internal dissent and seeking amicable relations with the United States.

Ikeda Hayato (1899–1965) was another prominent bureaucrat and politician during the early postwar era. The son of a landlord from Hiroshima and a graduate of Kyōto Imperial University, he was a bureaucrat in the Ministry of Finance between 1925 and 1948. Resigning after reaching the highest post in the ministry, Ikeda won a Diet seat in 1949 and was immediately tapped to head his old ministry. For the next eleven years, he frequently served as minister of finance and also as minister of international trade and industry. Ikeda formed his own cabinet when Kishi's fell in 1960 and served for the next four years as prime minister. Ikeda advanced his career by promoting the Income-Doubling Plan around 1960, and he was a central figure in laying the political groundwork for the high-speed growth of the 1960s and early 1970s.

Another influential postwar bureaucrat and politician, **Satō Eisaku** (1901–1975) set a record for tenure in office and also won a Nobel Prize. A brother of

Kishi Nobusuke, Satō graduated from Tōkyō Imperial University and entered the prewar Ministry of Transportation, rising in 1948 to its highest post. In 1949 he was elected to the lower house and won a seat that he retained for the duration of his career. Like Ikeda, Satō was quickly tapped for ministerial posts and key party posts as well. When Ikeda had to step down owing to cancer in 1964, Satō became prime minister for the next nearly eight years. Although he presided during an eventful period in Japan's domestic history, his major accomplishment was to secure the reversion of Okinawa to Japan in 1972, for which he won the Nobel Peace Prize in 1974.

The bureaucrats who dominated the LDP after the war established bureaucratic procedures in the party that eventually favored politicians, rather than recently retired bureaucrats, for the party's top posts. After the 1950s, the party required legislators to acquire experience in low-level positions and cabinet posts before they would be considered for the party presidency and the position of prime minister. Because such experience usually required nearly a quarter-century to obtain, by the early 1970s, the leaders of the LDP, and thus of the government that it monopolized, were chosen from the ranks of elected, professional politicians.

Tanaka Kakuei (1918–1993) was the first pure politician to win the prime ministership after the war. Born into a farm family in the mountainous prefecture of Niigata, Tanaka obtained a degree in engineering from a modest institution in 1936 and established a small construction firm. Taking advantage of the disorder prevailing at the end of the war, he made a lot of money on the black market while buying up vacant land in the Tōkyō area. This he used to build the financial base for one of the LDP's largest and most powerful factions. Entering the lower house in 1947, Tanaka soon caught the eye of Satō Eisaku and, beginning in 1957, won major ministerial portfolios for finance, international trade and industry, and transportation. Tanaka deftly turned those posts to his advantage in expanding his political base and handily succeeded Satō when he retired in 1972. But only two years later, the Lockheed scandal exposed some of Tanaka's shady dealings, and he had to resign in disgrace, though he remained in the Diet from then until his death, continuing to wield power until 1989. Although Tanaka's principal aim was to rebuild the Japanese archipelago by developing rural Japan, his indictment shattered that dream.

Nakasone Yasuhiro (1919–), a career politician, governed Japan during the conservative mid-1980s. Born into a wealthy family in Gumma, northwest of Tōkyō, Nakasone graduated from Tōkyō Imperial University and served briefly in the navy before entering elective politics in 1947. He rose gradually in the party ranks, being appointed to his first ministerial post in 1959. Subsequently he held several important party posts as well as four significant ministerial positions. Known as a hawk on defense matters and a nationalistic conservative, Nakasone finally became prime ministers as a compromise candidate in 1982. He governed for an unusually long five years, during which he oversaw the privatization of government monopolies, tried in vain to restore the political influence of the Shinto religion, and strove to enhance Japan's international status—while shamelessly courting favor with Ronald Reagan and Margaret Thatcher.

Miyazawa Kiichi (1920–), a leading figure in the LDP from the 1960s into the 1990s, was the son of a distinguished family from Hiroshima Prefecture. After graduating from Tōkyō Imperial University, he entered the Ministry of Finance, becoming private secretary to Ikeda Hayato while Ikeda was minister. Leaving the ministry in his thirties, Miyazawa twice was elected to the upper house before taking a lower house seat traditionally held by members of his family. A very intelligent man who speaks excellent English, Miyazawa was given major ministerial posts early on, in finance, economic planning, international trade and industry, and foreign affairs, as well as key party and government posts. After more than thirty years as an elected politician, he finally won the prime ministership in 1991, only to lose it when the party split and the LDP was defeated in 1993. In 1998, Prime Minister Obuchi Keizō appointed Miyazawa finance minister in the hope that he could lead Japan out of its financial turmoil.

Women are conspicuous by their absence from this list. Before the war, women could not vote or hold elective office. After the war, they could do both. Nonetheless, since 1945, female Diet members have always been a small minority; few women have ever held cabinet posts; and no woman has ever been prime minister.

Doi Takako (1928–) is one of the few women to have served in the postwar Diet and the only one ever to head a political party. Doi graduated from the law division of Dōshisha, a private university in Kyōto, and stayed on to conduct research and lecture. As a legal scholar, she has a long-standing interest in freedom of expression and the emperor's war guilt. An activist in local politics until winning a seat for the Japan Socialist Party in the lower house election of 1968 and climbing gradually through the party's ranks, Doi was designated head of the party in 1986. By taking advantage of the widespread discontent with a new consumption tax during the 1989 lower house election, she led her party to an unprecedented victory. In the following year, however, a stunning defeat in an upper house election forced her resignation. In 1993 she became the first woman ever to serve as speaker of the House of Representatives. (See the related entries in Political Parties.)

MILITARY LEADERS

The tradition of military rule personified by the samurai persisted after the Meiji Restoration, as many of the new government's leaders were former samurai who infused martial values into their roles as both civilian officials and military leaders. In addition, both the army and the navy relied heavily on former samurai and sons of samurai to staff their officer corps after the 1870s. The army played a more intrusive role in national politics. Moreover, during the 1930s the army took the lead in driving Japan toward war. The following entries give the life histories and military accomplishments of four prominent army officers who shaped Japan's history in significant ways before 1945.

Nogi Maresuke (1849–1912) was the descendant of a samurai family from the domain of Chōshū. He served as an officer in the Seinan War of 1877, when the new army defeated samurai dissidents trying to overthrow the Meiji government. Nogi was also a field officer during the Sino-Japanese War of 1894–1895 and during the Russo-Japanese War a decade later. In 1907 he was appointed head of the Peers' School, a private institution where the children of the nobility were educated, and his spartan regimen influenced the early life of the Shōwa emperor. General Nogi is perhaps best known for committing *junshi* (suicide out of duty to one's lord) following the death of the Meiji emperor in 1912. Nogi's suicide may have inspired Natsume Sōseki to write *Kokoro* when and as he did (see Male Writers) and thus to immortalize Nogi's death.

Araki Sadao (1877–1966) was a prominent leader of the Imperial Way faction that promoted militant nationalism during the 1930s. He was born in Tōkyō and educated at the Army Academy. After fighting in the Russo-Japanese War, he graduated from the Army War College as the top student in his class. During the 1910s Araki visited Russia as a member of the Army General Staff and may have developed then his strongly anti-Russian, anti-Communist attitudes. During the 1920s he held many, increasingly more powerful, positions in the army hierarchy. Araki was appointed in 1931 as minister of the army in the Inukai cabinet and used this position to advance his ideas about Japan's racial uniqueness, its military destiny, and its role in Asia. Between 1937 and 1939 he was the minister of education and likewise used that position to spread his views officially through the public schools. General Araki thus exerted his influence primarily as an ideologue and propagandist and not as an officer in the field. He was sentenced to life in prison as a Class A war criminal after the war but was released in 1954 owing to poor health.

Nagata Tetsuzan (1884–1935) was a key figure in the Control faction, a group in the army that opposed the views of General Araki. Nagata was unusual among army officers because he was the third son of a physician from Nagano, a region known for its political dissidence. He graduated in 1904 from the Army Academy and in 1911 from the Army War College. Between 1915 and 1917 he served as an army researcher in Denmark and Sweden. This experience in Europe, during World War I, must have driven him toward the issues that preoccupied him thereafter: strategic planning and total war. After returning to Japan, Nagata was assigned to a series of policymaking and strategic-planning positions, which he used to develop his own understanding of the relationships between a nation's economic strength and its military preparedness. He also began openly to oppose the more emotional and aggressive officers associated with the Imperial Way faction, one of whom assassinated him in August 1935, a critical time when Nagata's views might have brought about greater moderation in the army.

Tōjō Hideki (1884–1948) was prime minister and general of the army when Japan attacked Pearl Harbor in late 1941, thereby bringing the United States into the war. Tōjō had pursued an undistinguished career for almost thirty years. Although he had graduated from the Army Academy and the Army War College, he did not make his mark until 1932, when he became head of the military police forces in Manchuria. By 1937 he had ingratiated himself with the powerful bureaucrats and businessmen associated with Manchurian development and won appointment as head of the general staff for the Japanese army in Manchuria. He presented himself as an advocate of planning and a member of the Control faction. In 1940 Tōjō was appointed minister of the army, at which time he advocated military expansion and helped bring down the government. After being appointed prime minister in 1941, he immediately began planning the attack on Pearl Harbor. During the war, Tōjō served not only as prime minister but also as minister of the army, minister of home affairs, and chief of general staff before reversals in the Pacific forced his resignation in 1944. He was designated a Class A war criminal after the war, tried—but failed—to kill himself, and was hanged in 1948.

BUSINESS LEADERS

When it began to industrialize in the late nineteenth century, Japan was an agrarian society with a small merchant class. It thus had no body of natural leaders on whom to rely as it strove to raise capital, build factories, and manage industrial enterprises. Accordingly, Japan's future leaders came from merchant, samurai, landlord, and poor farm households. Few of them had a good education or prior experience in their calling, and they were only in their twenties or thirties at the time of the Restoration. They were very efficient, however, at exploiting the opportunities offered by the chaotic world of the early Meiji era. Many of these early leaders are referred to as *seishō*, or political merchants, because they relied on government contacts, orders, and support to develop their firms.

Iwasaki Yatarō (1835–1885) was the founder of the Mitsubishi enterprise. The son of a rural samurai from the Tosa domain in Shikoku, he had worked in the domain's business facilities in Nagasaki and Ōsaka as a youth. After the Restoration, Iwasaki established a small shipping company with several boats on loan from the domain. He profited by serving the government and quickly enlarged his company, in time to reap even greater profits from serving the military during the domestic war of 1877. Iwasaki used his capital to enter the money exchange and marine insurance businesses, to expand his shipping firm into an oceanic enterprise, and to develop extensive coal mining operations. He died before his successors—his brother and his own son—were able to develop Mitsubishi into a comprehensive *zaibatsu*.

Ōkura Kihachirō (1837–1928) was the founder of a family enterprise based on a profitable trading company. The son of a wealthy merchant from western Japan, he left home in the mid-1850s to seek his fortune in Edo and found his calling in a job selling rifles. Ōkura first made money at the time of the Restoration, and the contacts that he developed then served him well during later conflicts fought by the new government in 1877, 1894–1895, and 1904–1905. His trading company used its profits to create a construction firm, to invest in major hotels (including the Imperial Hotel) and entertainment facilities, and to buy an interest in a large coal and steel facility in Manchuria. The Ōkura Hotel, well known to Tōkyō's foreign visitors, sits on the site of the Ōkura family's prewar mansion.

Yasuda Zenjirō (1838–1921) laid the foundation for the prewar Yasuda *zaibatsu* and the postwar Fuji Bank, moving to Edo from his home in western Japan at about the same time as Ōkura did. Yasuda found work as an apprentice in a money-changing firm, and in less than a decade, he had saved enough money to establish his own business. Serving after 1868 as a financial agent for the new government, he profited immensely from currency manipulation in the chaotic early years of the Meiji era. By 1880 he had established the Yasuda Bank and purchased an insurance company. These two entities thereafter became, along with a family holding company, the nerve center of the Yasuda *za-*

ibatsu. In contrast with many Japanese entrepreneurs, Yasuda was a philanthropist who endowed a famous building in Hibiya Park and a tower on the campus of Tōkyō University.

Shibusawa Eiichi (1840–1931), an entrepreneur who played a major role in creating a self-conscious Japanese business community, was the son of a wealthy landlord. He left for Edo in the last years of the Tokugawa era and worked briefly in the *bakufu* (Japan's central administration under the shōgun) before it fell. He then joined the financial section of the Meiji government, leaving in 1873 to enter the private sector permanently. The locus of Shibusawa's efforts was the Tōkyō-based Daiichi Bank, which he headed between 1875 and 1916 and which functioned as a kind of venture capital firm. Through the bank, Shibusawa assisted the development of more than five hundred businesses during his career, including textile, brewing, transport, and utilities firms. He also worked to enhance the status of businessmen, by creating business associations and speaking and writing about the need for talented people to enter the business world.

Masuda Takashi (1848–1938) created Mitsui bussan in 1876 and presided over its fortunes until 1913. He was also known as a collector of pottery and utensils used in the Japanese tea ceremony. The son of a low-ranking samurai in the Tokugawa house, Masuda began learning English at age ten in a school his father ran in Hokkaidō. Later he studied in Edo and worked as a translator at the American embassy and in an American business firm. Between 1872 and 1873, Masuda held a post at the Ministry of Finance, where he met Inoue Kaoru and Shibusawa Eiichi. He obtained a position with one of Shibusawa's firms until he joined Mitsui in 1876 to establish its international trading firm. Masuda presided over the firm for several years, taking on increasingly wider responsibilities in the Mitsui enterprise and helping make it the preeminent *zaibatsu* before 1945.

The preceding five figures laid the foundations for major firms and enterprises during the early years of the Meiji era. The men who succeeded them and were active between the 1890s and 1945 differed in some important ways. Many of them had had a formal, university-level education and had often been managers of expanding enterprises, rather than founders of new ones. They worked to win more political autonomy for the business community by reducing close ties to the government, and several of them promoted the development in Japan of technological and production capabilities that would render the nation less reliant on foreign imports.

Nakamigawa Hikojirō (1854–1911) was a leading figure in the Mitsui enterprise between the 1880s and 1910s. He was related through his mother to

Fukuzawa Yukichi, the founder of Keiō University. Nakamigawa studied at Fukuzawa's academy between 1869 and 1874 and then spent seven years studying in England. After being introduced to Inoue Kaoru, Nakamigawa worked in two government ministries before taking positions as head of a newspaper and a railroad. When he began working at Mitsui in 1888, he tried to sever its close ties with the government, to deal with a bad loan crisis, to expand into manufacturing, and to recruit well-educated young managers. Although he succeeded at many of these tasks, he also made powerful enemies in the process and died at fifty-seven.

A leading figure at the Mitsui enterprise between 1888 and 1932, **Dan Takuma** (1858–1932) was the adopted son of a high-ranking samurai family from Fukuoka. He was unusual among his contemporaries because he had obtained a degree in metallurgy from the Massachusetts Institute of Technology. Returning to Japan in the late 1870s, Dan worked for a decade as a bureaucrat supervising government-owned mines. When one of those mines was sold to Mitsui in 1888, he joined Mitsui to become the on-site superintendent of the Miike Mines. In 1909 he was appointed a director of the Mitsui holding company, and five years later he succeeded Masuda Takashi as chairman of the board. Dan was a leading spokesman for the business community and a key figure in the creation of the Japan Industrial Club and its subsidiary organizations. His public standing cost him his life, however, in 1932, when he was assassinated by right-wing opponents of the *zaibatsu*.

Toyoda Sakichi (1867–1930) was an inventive genius whose work led to the establishment of the Toyota enterprise. Born into a farm household in Shizuoka, Toyoda began his career as an apprentice in a weaving factory in Nagoya. Throughout his life he worked to perfect weaving equipment, starting with wooden implements and progressing to electrically driven metal machinery. In 1926 he invented a machine that won international acclaim. In addition, during his life he earned more than one hundred domestic and more than fifty international patents. Toyoda relied on his brothers and wife to manage the early spinning and weaving establishments that underwrote his work. Later the family created the Toyoda Automatic Loom Company to produce his advanced weaving equipment, and out of that firm grew the auto company. Toyoda Sakichi's son, Toyoda Kiichirō, an engineer, founded Toyota Motors seven years after his father's death.

Mutō Sanji (1867–1934) was the leader of the Kanegafuchi Spinning Company at its peak and an important spokesman for the business community. Born in central Japan, Mutō's father was a wealthy landlord and, later, a Diet member. After graduating from Keiō University in 1884, Mutō spent the next three years studying abroad. His first job on his return to Japan was with a small trade firm. He also worked for one year in the Mitsui Bank before joining Kanegafuchi in 1894, where he remained until 1930, rising through the presidency to the chairmanship. Mutō held a seat in the House of Representatives between 1923 and 1932, edited a major newspaper, and worked actively on behalf of various business associations to advance his progressive views on labor relations.

Kobayashi Ichizō (1873–1957) was a corporate leader with a novel strategic vision that has left a deep imprint on urban Japan. Kobayashi hailed from Yamanashi, where his wealthy family was active in sake brewing and commerce. After graduating from Keiō University in 1892, he took a job with the Mitsui Bank, leaving the bank in 1907 to become a director of a private railway in the Ōsaka area that later became Hankyū. Kobayashi's business genius rested on a vision that linked the railway with a large body of captive consumers. He began by creating subdivisions along the rail route where the expanding urban middle class could build single-family homes. He next purchased a resort and established a troupe of female performers who attracted customers of the rail line to the area northwest of Ōsaka where they were located. Later he developed the first department store located at a railway terminal site, where riders could have a meal, visit a gallery, and go shopping. Even later in life he helped set up one of Japan's major movie studios. In the 1940s Kobayashi twice held ministerial posts in national cabinets and served in the House of Peers.

Odaira Namihei (1874–1951) fostered the evolution of Hitachi while serving as a strong proponent of Japanese technological development. He was born in a small community north of Tōkyō and graduated from Tōkyō Imperial University in 1900 with a degree in electrical engineering. For the next six years he worked for several firms in the Tōkyō area before taking a position in a division at Hitachi responsible for repairing electrical machinery. In 1910 that division began to build electrical equipment as well as to repair it. Because Odaira was driven by the desire to rely less on imports and to replace them with equipment designed and manufactured in Japan by Japanese engineers, this has been ever since Hitachi's mission. Odaira's division was incorporated as a separate firm in 1920. Besides being the moving force at Hitachi from the outset, Odaira was its president from 1929 to 1946.

Ōkōchi Masatoshi (1878–1952) was an engineer who promoted the need for Japanese-style technological development. Far more privileged than many of his business cohorts, Ōkōchi was the heir to a baronetcy and a member of the House of Peers from 1915 to 1946. He graduated from the engineering division of Tōkyō Imperial University in 1903 and studied in Germany and Austria before returning to his alma mater as a professor. In 1921 he became head of the university's Institute of Physical and Chemical Research, holding that position until 1946. Ōkōchi wanted Japan to develop more rationalized manufacturing processes, combine high wages with low-cost production, and turn out inexpensive, high-quality goods. By patenting discoveries made in the institute and establishing private firms to exploit them, he gradually built a large conglomerate that by the end of the war numbered more than forty firms. Although the conglomerate was broken up after the war, one element has survived as Ricoh, the copy machine maker.

Aikawa Yoshisuke (Gisuke) (1880–1967) was an innovative entrepreneur who created and developed the Nissan *zaibatsu*. Aikawa was born into a family that had numerous ties by birth and marriage to the elite of the business and political world. After graduating from Tōkyō Imperial University with an engineering degree in 1903, he took a job with an electrical manufacturer, resigned to study abroad, and returned to enter a metals firm. In 1928 he assumed the presidency of a mining firm that became the base of the Nissan enterprise. Aikawa raised enormous sums of money, often relying on his family contacts, and invested heavily in new industries (shipbuilding, autos, and chemicals) that expanded with Japan's militarization in the 1930s. In 1937 he used similar funding schemes to establish the Manchurian Development Corporation, which he headed until 1942. He was declared a Class A war criminal after the war but returned to public life as a member of the House of Councillors for six years and as a leader promoting the organization of small- and medium-size enterprises.

The final seven business leaders are men active after the 1920s, a highly varied group, in large part owing to a purge of more than three thousand businessmen after the war. When a firm lost its top executives, it could either promote younger men or recruit older ones. Although many in this group had been professional managers in private firms, others were self-made entrepreneurs, such as Honda Sōichirō and Matsushita Kōnosuke, along with political facilitators, such as Uemura Kōgorō. The diversity of this group bespeaks Japan's difficult passage during this period from war and occupation, through recovery, to growth and affluence.

Ishizaka Taizō (1886–1975) was the wartime head of an insurance company who escaped the purge and returned after the war to assume major leadership roles at Toshiba and Keidanren. Born in Tōkyō, he followed the elite educational course through Tōkyō Imperial University. After graduating in 1911, he spent four years as a bureaucrat before taking a position at the Daiichi Insurance Company. Rising steadily through the ranks, he became president in 1938 and retired at sixty in 1946. Drawn out of retirement in 1948, he served as president of Toshiba between 1949 and 1957, when he directed a turnaround effort that was especially ruthless in its treatment of workers. In 1956 he became president of Keidanren, serving for twelve years before stepping down in 1968. Ishizaka personified a kind of hard-nosed postwar executive whose outspoken support of big business contributed significantly to Japan's postwar economic ascent.

Tsutsumi Yasujirō (1889–1964) was an unscrupulous entrepreneur and politician who laid the foundation for the Seibu enterprise. He was the son of a wealthy landlord and, following his graduation from Waseda University, used his family's inheritance to begin accumulating land in the western suburbs of Tōkyō in the 1910s. Because his attempts to develop that land into suburban subdivisions were ahead of the times, he turned his attention to vacation sites in the prestigious highlands of Karuizawa. In 1924 he was elected to the House of Representatives and served for thirty-three years. Later he bought a sagging private railway serving a rural area northwest of Tōkyō. Profiting handsomely during the war, he used his capital to upgrade the railway, to buy land and build the Prince hotel chain, and to purchase a dowdy department store in Ikebukuro. Thus was laid the foundation for the Seibu enterprises, which two of his sons and a body of loyal company executives later developed into a massive commercial, transportation, entertainment, and real estate empire.

Matsushita Kōnosuke (1894–1989) created and oversaw the development of the consumer electronics giant that makes Panasonic and National brandname products. Born in a community south of Ōsaka, Matsushita's first job was as an apprentice at the docks in Ōsaka when he was thirteen. Four years later, he took another position at the local power company, and in 1918 he established his own small firm to make electrical adapters and bicycle lamps. As sales grew, he expanded his product line, in 1935 incorporating Matsushita Electrical Industries to consolidate control over nine smaller firms. Matsushita presided as president of the firm until 1961 and as chairman until 1973 while it grew into a major producer of electrical goods and household appliances. He was also a generous philanthropist who established a small foundation in 1946 to promote peace, happiness, and prosperity, as well as an advanced institute for the study of political economy in 1975 and other foundations.

Uemura Kōgorō (1894–1978) was a bureaucrat and business association leader, whose father, a prominent, well-connected businessman, introduced him at an early age to many business figures. After graduating from Tōkyō Imperial University in 1918, Uemura entered the Ministry of Agriculture and

Commerce and then moved to the new Ministry of Commerce and Industry when it was formed in 1925. Between 1927 and 1940 he held high-level positions in central government planning agencies at which he came into contact with a wide range of business leaders. During the war Uemura was the executive director of the quasi-governmental body controlling the coal industry. Purged after the war, he frequented the Japan Industrial Club and carried on informal conversations with many business leaders about how to revive the economy. When the purge was lifted in 1952, he became the executive director and vice president of Keidanren, and in 1968 he became president for six years. Uemura's broad contacts in the bureaucratic, business, and political worlds enabled him to serve as a facilitator who nurtured the cooperative economic environment of Japan's high-growth period.

Nagano Shigeo (1900–1984) was a prominent executive in the steel industry and a leading political spokesman for the business community. His father was a well-placed judge, and his four brothers all became leading figures in the political and business communities. Graduating from Tōkyō Imperial University with a law degree in 1924, Nagano spent a year with a trading firm before entering Fuji Steel. For almost half a century, he was an executive in the steel industry. When Fuji Steel was reestablished as a separate firm in 1950, he served as its chairman until 1970, when he became the chairman of New Japan Steel. He was also a high-ranking officer of Nikkeiren between 1948 and 1970, as well as president of the Japan Chamber of Commerce between 1969 and 1984. Using his formal roles, political contacts, and personal charisma, Nagano was a powerful advocate of government support of the steel industry.

Honda Sōichirō (1906–1991) was a self-taught technician who created the Honda auto firm. He was born in a village in Shizuoka and was educated only through the eighth grade, at sixteen taking a job as an apprentice in an auto repair shop in Tōkyō. Five years later, the firm assigned him to open a branch in Hamamatsu. After twelve years, Honda left to establish his own small firm to make piston rings, and in 1946 he established the Honda Technology Research Institute to manufacture motor bikes. Two years later he created Honda Technical Industries, the foundation for his auto enterprise. For the next quarter century, he led the firm through an astonishing expansion that sometimes was opposed by the government, which earned him an international reputation as a spunky, technical genius leading an innovative, independent company.

Morita Akio (1920–) was a leader of the Sony Corporation and a flamboyant spokesman for the Japanese business community. Morita was born in central Japan into a family that operated a sake brewery. After receiving a science degree at Ōsaka University in 1944, he immediately entered the navy. An officer during the war, he was assigned to a special technical facility where he met the owner of a small firm making radar for the military. After the war, that man, Ibuka Masaru, established a small firm in Tōkyō to make communications equipment and persuaded Morita to join him as a director. While Ibuka concentrated on technical matters, Morita specialized in marketing. The firm's first big seller was the transistor radio, developed in the mid-1950s, which Morita marketed in the United States under the brand name Sony. Strong sales persuaded Ibuka and Morita to rename the firm itself Sony in 1958. A year later, Morita became vice president, rising to the presidency in 1971 when Ibuka retired. A dapper, energetic man who speaks good English, Morita was the quintessential confident, successful, aggressive Japanese businessman of the 1970s and 1980s. (See the many related entries in the following section, Business Associations, Enterprises, and Firms. For the historical context, see the sections on economics in Historical Narrative.)

BUSINESS ASSOCIATIONS, ENTERPRISES, AND FIRMS

Modern Japanese businesses have organized themselves in various ways to pursue both economic and political objectives. This section sketches the evolution in the modern world of three types of organizational venues: business associations, enterprise groups, and individual firms.

Business Associations

Individual firms in the same industry sometimes form trade or industry associations in order to promote their members' economic and political interests. When most firms in most industries organize to promote their interests through one body, it is referred to as a *peak association*. Japan has had two major peak business associations in the modern era, one operating before the war and the other, after.

The **Japan Industrial Club** was formed in 1917 for the purpose of providing a collective forum through which the leaders of Japan's largest commercial, financial, and industrial firms could reconcile their interests and articulate their political demands. The club built a grand, European-style building on a site near Tōkyō Station in downtown Tōkyō and soon began to lobby on behalf of big business. In the early 1920s it established a separate organization charged with the task of political lobbying, and in the early 1930s it established a second organization to specialize in labor and labor-management relations.

Before the war, these two bodies took center stage in expressing the political views of the business community, and the club itself retreated from the front lines to become mainly a social organization.

Keidanren is the abbreviated Japanese term for the Federation of Economic Organizations. Since its formation in 1946, it has been the most important of Japan's four major postwar business associations. Keidanren is the direct descendant of the organization established by the Japan Industrial Club in the 1920s, which was reestablished after the war under terms that satisfied the occupying powers. Since 1952 the members of Keidanren have consisted of Japan's largest firms, most of its major trade associations, and some individuals noted for their economic achievements. Its leaders—who include the president, vice presidents, and committee chairs—are senior business figures who represent the most prestigious firms and trade associations. Keidanren contributes to political parties (especially the ruling party); it lobbies government leaders to adopt probusiness legislation; and it exploits the media to win its way on both domestic and international issues.

Nikkeiren is a more specialized peak association, a federation of employers' organizations responsible for dealing with labor matters on behalf of the big-business community. Like Keidanren, Nikkeiren is a postwar descendant of the prewar organization established in the 1930s to deal with labor affairs. Nikkeiren's members are big businesses that join the federation through trade associations or regional bodies. Its leaders are usually current or former presidents of major firms who are noted for their expertise in labor affairs, often as hard-nosed bargainers. This organization has played a major role in regulating wage increases in the economy, especially since the early 1970s.

Enterprises

The term *enterprises* is used here to refer to groups of individual firms. In the Japanese context, only a relatively few enterprises have played a major role both before and after the war in shaping economic developments. Before the war, such enterprises were known as *zaibatsu*. Resembling giant German concerns in some ways, they also had distinctively Japanese features. Although the Allied authorities tried to eliminate the *zaibatsu* after the war, they have persisted, albeit in an altered form.

Zaibatsu is a term that first was used during the 1910s to refer to large-scale, family-controlled enterprises that spanned many fields of financial, commercial, and industrial endeavor. Some of the *zaibatsu* originated in the 1600s as retail or industrial firms and, by the end of the Tokugawa era, had expanded into additional activities, especially moneylending and domestic trade. After 1868, these family businesses began to expand even more rapidly, into such fields as banking, shipping, coal mining, international trade, and manufacturing.

When Japan introduced new types of corporate law after the late nineteenth century, these firms began to consolidate under the control of family-owned holding companies which functioned like privately held merchant investment banks. They financed new ventures and provided the centralized leadership under which firms in the *zaibatsu* were coordinated. The four major *zaibatsu* were Mitsui, Sumitomo, Mitsubishi, and Yasuda.

During their period of maturity between the 1910s and 1945, *zaibatsu* usually consisted of three layers of firms operating with the financial assistance, and under the leadership, of the holding company. The top layer of firms bore the name of the family (or the family's trade name, in the case of Mitsubishi) and usually numbered around ten. This stratum of named firms usually included a commercial bank, a trust bank, a real estate entity, an international trading firm, an insurance company, and a number of manufacturing firms in a variety of industries, especially shipbuilding and metals manufacture. Most shares in such firms were owned by the family through the holding company or sometimes by other firms in this stratum and by their leading managers. Below this top stratum, most *zaibatsu* also had a second layer of firms. Some bore the *zaibatsu* name, though others did not. These firms, too, were heavily owned by the holding company, by other firms in the first stratrum, and by enterprise managers. Finally, some *zaibatsu* included a third layer of much smaller firms, usually subcontracting firms attached to the larger firms in the two top strata.

A *zaibatsu* was thus a large, well-financed combination of firms operating under the control of a single family or family group that exercised its influence through a holding company. The *zaibatsu* played a central role in promoting Japan's industrialization and economic development both before and during the war. Although they were similar in many ways, each *zaibatsu* evolved in a somewhat different fashion.

Authorities of the Allied Occupation tried to dissolve the *zaibatsu* after the war, but their reform efforts were only partly successful. Consequently, many former *zaibatsu* firms still operate today, under a different organizational form known as the *keiretsu*.

Keiretsu refers to a "set" of firms or a group of affiliated firms. When organized around a financial institution, they are called *bank-centered keiretsu*, and when they are focused on a final manufacturer, they are called *industrial keiretsu*.

Bank-centered *keiretsu* are, in most cases, the postwar descendants of the prewar *zaibatsu*. When the reformers tried to dissolve the old *zaibatsu*, they confiscated the stock of the family owners, eliminated the former holding companies, and subdivided individual firms in the top layer of the former *zaibatsu*. They also forced the passage of laws that impeded the *zaibatsu's* reconsolidation. But the reformers stopped before they had broken up the old *zaibatsu* banks. Therefore, during the 1950s and 1960s, as Japan's economic recovery accelerated, the old *zaibatsu* banks served as both the financial and the advisory centers for the former firms in their *zaibatsu* group. A new pattern of alliance and affiliation grew around these banks, thereby creating the *keiretsu*.

The banks provided the bulk of the affiliated firms' financial needs in the form of loans, through which they gathered around them what the Japanese call *wan-setto*, or one set, of firms. A set nearly always includes a trust bank, an insurance company, an international trade firm, a real estate entity, and manufacturing firms, especially steelmaking, shipbuilding, electrical manufacturing, coal mining, automaking, beer brewing, and precision equipment making. Four of the bank-centered *keiretsu* are descendants of the major *zaibatsu*: Mitsui, Sumitomo, Mitsubishi, and Yasuda. Two other bank-centered *keiretsu* emerged: the Sanwa group, in the Ōsaka area, and the Daiichi-Kangyō group, in the Tōkyō-Yokohama region. Through the 1970s, these bank-centered *keiretsu* included many of the largest, most successful firms in Japan, and they counted for a large share of paid-up capital, value added in the production process, exports, and profits in the Japanese economy.

Industrial *keiretsu* are somewhat different, consisting of a giant firm functioning as a final assembler resting on top of a hierarchy of progressively smaller firms supplying it with parts and components. Industrial *keiretsu* are common in the automobile industry and in the electrical and electronics industry, in which firms such as Toyota and Nissan, or Toshiba and Matsushita, developed complicated hierarchies of subcontractors and suppliers to meet their needs as final assemblers of cars or electrical appliances.

The **Mitsui enterprise** originated in the early 1600s as a dry goods firm operating out of the Matsuzaka area of central Honshū. The Mitsui house gradually established shops in Kyōto, Ōsaka, and Edo, steadily building a sound business foundation. In the latter part of the Tokugawa period, the Mitsui group expanded into finance by becoming money exchange specialists and loan agents. After the Meiji Restoration, the enterprise moved quickly to establish beneficial political ties with some of the government's key leaders.

Relying on its capital and financial expertise, the Mitsui group expanded into even more activities. Its *sōgō shōsha*, or general trading company (known in Japanese as Mitsui bussan), was consistently the largest in Japan before the war. The group also entered a range of industrial activities, including coal mining, metals manufacture, and shipbuilding, and expanded into trust banking and insurance as well. Throughout the prewar era, Mitsui was always the largest *zaibatsu* in the country, relying on its financial might and its trading prowess to build a comprehensive enterprise.

After the war, the Mitsui group was gradually eclipsed. It had never been deeply involved in the heavy industries that dominated the early postwar economy, such as steelmaking and chemicals. Nor did Mitsui firms develop a presence in the newer industries that prospered after the 1960s, such as automaking and consumer electronics. In addition, the Mitsui Bank fell on hard times and merged with another company to form the Sakura Bank, which still ranks well behind its former *zaibatsu* cohorts. Although the Mitsui *keiretsu* did play a significant commercial and financial role in the early postwar decades, its influence paled in comparison with that of the prewar Mitsui *zaibatsu*.

The **Sumitomo enterprise**, like the Mitsui group, originated in the Tokugawa era when the Sumitomo family purchased a copper mine in Shikoku in the 1690s. Throughout the Tokugawa period, the Sumitomo house concentrated on metal mining, smelting, and manufacture, continuing after the Restoration and into the early twentieth century. Although it did enter the banking, insurance, and warehousing businesses and establish its own trade firm, they never equaled those of Mitsui or Mitsubishi before the war. Instead, Sumitomo relied on its metals-making expertise and developed close ties first with the navy and then with the army. During the war, it was a major supplier of metals products to the military.

After recovering from the initial shock of the *zaibatsu* dissolution, Sumitomo returned to its concentration on metals and mining and also expanded its banking and trade firms, developed a major chemical firm, and used its expertise in metal making to create new firms in electrical manufacturing. Sumitomo was thus more successful than Mitsui in making the postwar transition into a comprehensive enterprise group based on finance, commerce, and heavy industry.

The **Mitsubishi enterprise** was started after the Meiji Restoration when a former samurai from the Tosa domain, Iwasaki Yatarō, created, with the use of a few borrowed boats, a small shipping company. In 1873 he established a commercial firm with the trade name Mitsubishi shōji, which has survived to the present as one of the top two *sōgō shōsha* in Japan. In the late nineteenth century, the Mitsubishi enterprise moved quickly and deftly to establish its presence in many, often very lucrative, endeavors. It dominated commercial ocean shipping; it owned and operated some highly profitable coal mines; it purchased at fire-sale prices in 1887 a shipyard in Nagasaki that became the core of its heavy industry division; it entered commercial banking in the 1890s; and it established a real estate division that still controls a valuable parcel of land in downtown Tōkyō. In the early twentieth century, Mitsubishi also ventured into electrical manufacturing, aircraft assembly, and insurance. Nevertheless, despite its dramatic successes in a wide range of activities, Mitsubishi was always the second largest *zaibatsu* before the war.

The story of Mitsubishi's postwar endeavors is different. Although it suffered as much as from the Allies' dissolution as did the other *zaibatsu*, it gradually began to reconsolidate during the 1950s. Since then, Mitsubishi firms have played a major role in the chemical and petroleum industries, and with a heavy industry component manufacturing automobiles and ships, Mitsubishi flourished in the 1960s and early 1970s. Its financial institutions have outstripped those of Mitsui, and its firms in electrical manufacturing have grown apace with the boom in consumer electronics and business machines. As a consequence, more Mitsubishi firms have ranked high on the lists of Japan's postwar enterprises than have those of its former *zaibatsu* competitors.

The **Yasuda enterprise** dates formally from the 1880s, when the Yasuda Bank was incorporated. Its founder, Yasuda Zenjirō, accumulated a small fortune between the 1850s and the 1880s by serving as a moneylender and currency specialist. Yasuda always differed from the other *zaibatsu* because it was primarily a financial entity; it did not develop a comprehensive set of firms in commerce and industry under its direct control. Rather, the bank made loans or direct investments and, through those mechanisms, exercised supervisory control over firms that seldom bore its name. Although Yasuda exercised a great deal of control over financial, commercial, industrial, and real estate development in the Tōkyō-Yokohama area before 1945, it always ranked a distant fourth to Mitsui, Sumitomo, and Mitsubishi.

After the war the Yasuda Bank changed its name to Fuji Bank, and in due course Fuji became one of the largest banks in the country, thanks to its strategic location in the Tōkyō area. Gradually it gathered around itself a *keiretsu*, sometimes referred to as the Fuyō Group. Including major industrial firms in eastern Japan, such as Hitachi, Nissan, and Japan Steel Tube, the postwar Fuji Bank alliance has enjoyed even greater stature than the Yasuda group possessed before the war.

Firms

The following nine major firms in six industries trace the evolution of the modern Japanese industrial economy from its origins in the textile trades, through large-scale manufacturing, to the current emphasis on computers and consumer electronics.

Kanegafuchi Spinning was typical of the large, comprehensive textile firms that dominated the Japanese economy between the 1880s and the early 1930s. The firm was started in 1889 by a group of cotton dealers in the Tōkyō area who pooled their assets. Although spinning cotton thread was the firm's principal undertaking at the outset, Kanegafuchi soon expanded into other materials, such as wool and silk, and other processes, such as dyeing and weaving. Through links with Mitsui bussan, the firm carved out a profitable market for its products in China and Korea and eventually built factories in both countries. During the 1930s, Kanegafuchi began to experiment with synthetic fibers, and although the war years were difficult for all textile makers, they staged a brief comeback in the 1940s and 1950s. By the 1960s, however, lower-cost competitors forced natural fiber makers to adopt new business strategies. Kanegafuchi responded by expanding its output of synthetic fibers. Taking advantage of its expertise in chemical manufacturing, it also developed new lines of business in food products, cosmetics, and medicines. Then, to reflect the firm's changing character, it took the name Kanebo in 1971. Once known for its huge, dirty mills, Kanebo is better known today for its up-scale shops selling women's cosmetics and accessories.

New Japan Steel is the current name of one of Japan's oldest, largest, and most important industrial firms. The firm originated as a government-owned and -operated enterprise in the late 1890s, beginning operations in 1901 as the Yahata Steel Works at a site on the northeast coast of Kyūshū. For the next thirty-three years, Yahata was the country's largest producer of raw steel. When war seemed imminent, this government-owned firm merged with several, smaller private firms to form Japan Steel. The new semiprivate entity played a major role in meeting the nation's steel needs during the war. In 1950 the Allied authorities forced its breakup, and Japan Steel functioned as a smaller entity until 1970, when it merged again with another company to form New Japan Steel. Since then, global competition has created severe difficulties for the firm, and it has been forced to close mills and lay off workers. For some time, New Japan Steel has been trying to develop new endeavors, such as the management of a leisure world on the site of its original mill. Nonetheless, even with the shrinkage of its steel business, it remains one of the largest firms in Japan.

Kawasaki Heavy Industries traces its formal origins to 1896, when a ship-building company with docks in Tōkyō and Ōsaka was incorporated. The firm flourished during periods of war and expanding trade, but it often faltered in times of peace and recession. During the 1920s, Kawasaki entered new lines of production, establishing plants to build electrical products, rolling stock for railroads, and aircraft. Given its product line, it was well situated to profit from the war. Because it was a target of Allied reforms, the firm fell on hard times immediately after the war but revived with the expansion of Japan's heavy industry beginning in the 1950s. With respect to its assets, Kawasaki was often the largest firm in Japan between the 1910s and the 1930s, and it was still among the top thirty firms as late as 1987.

Hitachi is one of the two major electrical manufacturers in Japan. Originally formed in 1910 as a division of a mining firm to produce its electrical equipment, Hitachi was incorporated in 1920 as a separate firm. It expanded quickly to manufacture a broad line of products, including generators, ships, and locomotives. During the war, it played a critical role in producing equipment needed by the military. But because Hitachi was concentrated in a small community northeast of Tōkyō, it suffered considerable damage from Allied bombing and recovered slowly after the war. Then Japan's economic revival in the 1950s renewed the demand for household appliances and for large-scale electrical equipment. In the 1960s, the firm entered the computer and business machine market, at the same time as its exports rose steadily. By the 1980s, it was building new factories in countries around the world to meet the global demands for its wide range of products. Hitachi consistently ranks among the top ten firms in Japan with respect to assets and employees.

Toshiba, the second of Japan's giant electrical manufacturers, was formed in 1939 with the merger of two older electrical firms in the Tōkyō area—the Shibaura Works (founded in 1875), which specialized in generators and small fans, and Tōkyō Electric (founded in 1890), which dominated the market for lightbulbs. The new firm thus competed with Hitachi for a similarly broad range of electrical products. Likewise, Toshiba's factories also were bombed during the war and had severe labor problems after the war. Its recovery also duplicated Hitachi's in nearly every respect, and it, too, consistently ranks among Japan's top ten firms in terms of assets and employees.

Nissan Auto emerged in 1934 under the pressures of war. Automobiles had been manufactured in Japan since the 1910s, but by American firms such as Ford and General Motors. In the 1930s, as relations between the two countries worsened, Japan sought to create a domestic auto industry and force out the foreign firms. Nissan thus arose to satisfy this need. With its factories lo-

cated mainly in the Tōkyō area, Nissan began producing small autos targeted to wealthy urban consumers. But before it could develop such a market,
the war intervened, and Nissan was obliged to fulfill the military's demand for
trucks—the Japanese military during the war and the American military during the Occupation. After it finally resolved some nagging labor problems in
the early 1950s, Nissan returned to producing small autos (the Datsun Blue-
bird) and began exporting them as early as 1958. For the next several decades,
it fought an intense, but usually unsuccessful, battle to win first place among
Japanese automakers.

Toyota Motors has always been Nissan's main competitor in Japan. It was
started when the Toyota Automatic Loom Company established a department
to explore auto production. Four years later, in 1937, Toyota Motors was incorporated, with headquarters in a small former castle town near Nagoya. Like
Nissan, Toyota manufactured vehicles for the Japanese army in its first decade
and trucks for the American army in the early postwar years. Taking advantage
of quick profits during the Korean War, the firm bought new equipment, developed innovative production processes, and laid the foundation for one of
the world's most efficient auto enterprises. Toyota began exporting its cars in
the 1960s and had dramatic success in the American market in the 1970s and
1980s. In the 1980s it also began building production facilities abroad. Today it
is not only one of Japan's most important firms but is also one of the world's
most profitable auto manufacturers.

Matsushita Electrical Industries is the maker of Panasonic and National
brand-name consumer products. It is renowned for its innovative research, efficient production, and reasonable prices. This firm originated in 1918 when
Matsushita Kōnosuke began making bicycle lamps and electrical sockets and
selling them out of his home in the Ōsaka area. In the next two decades, he
enjoyed considerable success and established a number of other companies to
make additional products. The present firm dates formally from 1935 when it
was incorporated to oversee the production of nine smaller companies. During the war years, Matsushita made electrical equipment and wooden pro-
pellers and also developed markets for small electrical appliances in East and
Southeast Asia. Targeted for breakup after the war, Matsushita began to revive
in the early 1950s through an alliance with a giant Dutch firm. Matsushita thus
was able to enter electronics production to ride the consumer boom of the
1950s, 1960s and 1970s by supplying batteries, radios, television sets, and small
electrical appliances to the domestic market. At the same time, it returned to
its prewar Asian markets and boosted its exports. In the 1980s, Matsushita also
invested heavily in overseas production facilities and has become a major glob-

al enterprise. It is consistently one of the three or four largest firms in Japan with respect to assets and sales.

Sony is the highly recognizable name of a firm that began after the war as Tōkyō tsūshin kabushiki kaisha (TTKK), making communication equipment out of a small factory in downtown Tōkyō. The head of the postwar firm, Ibuka Masaru, had operated an enterprise that made radar for the Japanese navy during the 1930s and 1940s. In the early 1950s, TTKK adapted transistors for use in small radios. They were an instant success. Changing its name in 1958 to Sony, the firm made its reputation by developing ever more consumer products known for their small size, low price, and convenient use, such as portable television sets and the Walkman. Sony's high visibility abroad belies the fact that it is not one of Japan's largest firms; Matsushita, Hitachi, and Toshiba all are about three times bigger than Sony. Nonetheless, Sony still is one of the top thirty firms in Japan and among the most profitable and innovative in the world. (See also the many related entries in the section on Business Leaders. For the historical context, see the sections on economics in the Historical Narrative.)

BUREAUCRACY

The term *bureaucracy* refers to the ministries of the national government. More specifically, it refers to the highest, policymaking positions in the national ministries, those at the level of section chief (*kachō*) and above. In this sense, the bureaucracy dates from the 1880s, when the leaders of the Meiji government established the administrative organs through which they ruled. A significant step in the evolution of the bureaucracy occurred in the 1890s when a system of competitive civil service examinations was put into place to test applicants.

The bureaucracy has always played an influential role in the affairs of state, its influence deriving from two general sources. One is the high quality of bureaucratic personnel. Ever since the introduction of the rigorous written and oral entrance exams, most bureaucrats have been selected from among the best students at Japan's most prestigious universities, Tōkyō and Kyōto. The second source of influence derives from the authority, both formal and informal, of the bureaucracy itself. Formal authority is a product of law, and the bureaucracy has both the legal authority to implement laws and the ordinance authority tantamount to lawmaking. Informal authority derives from the status and perceived influence of the bureaucracy, often in the form of guidance and counsel. Informal bureaucratic authority is also enhanced by the bureaucracy's critical role in shaping the political agenda, drafting legislation, and assisting with its passage.

Bureaucrats, especially those who attain the highest positions in a ministry, have long been prestigious, powerful people in Japanese society. While they are in office, they exercise the incumbent powers associated with the authority of the bureaucracy and their position in it. Even after they leave office, former bureaucrats enjoy continuing influence, and they are frequently offered prestigious positions in public organizations and private businesses.

Amakudari, meaning literally "descent from heaven," is the term used to describe a former bureaucrat's appointment to a postbureaucratic job. Through the practice of *amakudari*, many former bureaucrats continue to influence political and economic affairs from positions outside the ministries. Some of them have become officers of major corporations and banks; others have entered business associations or quasi-governmental organizations; and still others have run for elective office. In their new positions, the former bureaucrats use their knowledge of public administration and the contacts made during their bureaucratic careers, thereby exercising "ramifying powers" in Japan's political economy.

The number of ministries in the national government has varied over time. In recent decades there have usually been about twenty. The following describes three of the oldest and most powerful ministries, along with two significant postwar agencies. The ministries and their staffs often compete with one another for jurisdiction and authority over government affairs, thus belying the widespread claim that Japan's bureaucracy is a monolithic structure.

The **Ministry of Foreign Affairs** (MFA) was one of the first government organizations established (in 1869) after the Meiji Restoration, to manage Japan's relations with foreign powers. In 1885 the MFA received full status as a ministry in the newly formed cabinet system of government, and its head became a cabinet minister with portfolio. Since that time (with the exception of a seven-year period between 1945 and 1952), the MFA has conducted Japan's formal diplomatic relations with other countries, through both the foreign ministries and legations located on Japanese soil and the Japanese embassies and legations located abroad. Since the war, the ministry has been divided into nine bureaus, four regional and five functional. Because two of the functional bureaus deal with economic affairs and economic cooperation, the MFA often finds itself in conflict with other ministries that also have some jurisdiction over Japan's foreign economic relations.

The **Ministry of Finance** (MOF) also was instituted in 1869 and became a ministry under the new cabinet system in 1885. Since then, it has gradually accumulated more authority over a wide range of financial activities. The MOF collects government revenues, oversees government expenditures, draws up the national budget, serves as the government's official printer, plays some role in setting interest rates and controlling foreign exchange, issues government bonds, and supervises both the banking industry and the securities industry. In other words, this one ministry in Japan combines functions that in the United States are divided among the Treasury Department, the Internal Revenue Service, and a number of other federal agencies and regulatory bodies. For this reason, the MOF has been one of the most powerful ministries in the postwar era. It played a major role in promoting Japan's rapid growth in the 1950s and 1960s; it helped ease Japan into broader international participation in the 1970s and after; and it monitored the growth of some of the world's largest financial institutions. Unfortunately, in the 1980s, its supervision of those institutions may have been too lax. As a consequence, the MOF has come under ferocious political attack in the 1990s, aimed at reducing its powers.

The **Ministry of International Trade and Industry** (MITI) was organized in 1925 when a portion of the older Ministry of Agriculture and Commerce was broken off to form the Ministry of Commerce and Industry (MCI). This reorganization acknowledged Japan's growing importance as a commercial and industrial power. In 1949 the ministry was given the name under which it has become famous, along with the added responsibility of promoting Japan's role as an international industrial power. The tasks of MITI are to help develop large-scale domestic industry, to supervise small- and medium-size enterprises, to promote Japan's international trade and exports, and to manage the patent office and an energy agency. In these tasks, the MITI often finds itself in conflict with both the MFA and the MOF, because Japan's excessive exports have often caused diplomatic problems and financial stress.

The **Economic Planning Agency** (EPA) was established in 1955 as an agency (not a ministry) attached to the prime minister's office. Its head does hold a cabinet portfolio, and many former heads of the EPA have gone on to occupy very high positions in the government. The agency is charged with collecting data on the economy and devising long-term projections concerning economic development and people's livelihoods. Because the EPA is relatively new and has a small number of officials, a limited budget, and advisory authority, it is not regarded as a "powerful" entity. Nonetheless, its forecasts and economic plans, especially the Income-Doubling Plan, helped elevate Japan into the front rank of economic powers in the 1960s.

The **Self-Defense Agency** (SDA), like the EPA, functions under the prime minister's office. It is analogous to the U.S. Department of Defense in its supervision of Japan's military forces and the preparation of the nation's defense budget. Established in 1954, the SDA is headed by a civilian with a cabinet portfolio who is responsible to the prime minister and cabinet. The land, sea, and air forces that operate under the jurisdiction of the SDA number about 250,000.

STATE-GUIDED ORGANIZATIONS

During the Tokugawa period, Japan did not have a well-educated citizenry possessing legal rights, a desire to assemble voluntarily, and the motivation to promote its interests in a sustained, organized manner. Rather, popular political participation was often sporadic, isolated, and short lived. With the Meiji Restoration, the weak, fragmented system of government gave way to a centralized nation-state that exercised a monopoly over law and coercive force. The state did not hesitate to act authoritatively; in fact, Meiji leaders actually went so far as to establish mass organizations that operated under government control and direction. In this way the government was often able to co-opt popular political movements before they began, and it made organized interests dependent on the government for funds, leadership, and legitimacy. As Japan went on a wartime footing during the 1930s, even more state-controlled organizations were formed, for the express purpose of aiding the war effort.

These state-guided organizations are significantly different from the more voluntary interest groups characteristic of American or British politics. For example, Japan's state-guided organizations often incorporated their members involuntarily, required highly conformist behavior, and promulgated state goals that have not always served the best interests of the people. Consequently, such organizations have left an ambiguous legacy regarding the substance, quality, and consequences of political participation.

The **Patriotic Women's League** was formed in 1901 and dissolved in 1942. Its purpose was to mobilize women to assist the government during war and military emergencies. At the outset, the wives of nobles and men in the imperial family dominated the leadership positions. Although the membership gradually expanded to include the wives of high-ranking bureaucrats, the league was always an upper-class entity that operated in tandem with the government to support the military. In the wake of the Manchurian takeover in 1932, a new organization known as the **Greater Japan Women's Defense League** was legally incorporated and brought under the direction of the military. Drawing its membership from the middle and lower ranks of Japanese society, this new organization grew rapidly and began to compete for contributions and membership with the Patriotic Women's League. To resolve the conflict, government authorities in 1942 merged these two organizations with a third to create the **Greater Japan Women's Association**. Regardless of their name or membership, these organizations were patriotic undertakings that infused society with martial values, encouraged material sacrifices, and aided the war effort. Although they did try to ease the emotional costs of war, they did so in a martial atmosphere that supported war. The association disbanded in June 1945.

The **Imperial Agricultural Society** was a state-administered organization that dealt with economic problems in rural Japan. Based on prior organizations dating back to the 1880s, the society was established in 1910 and continued to function until 1943. Landlords dominated its leadership, even though its purpose was to improve agricultural practices, stabilize agricultural prices, and conduct agricultural research. In step with its leaders' sentiments, the organization usually sided with landlords in tenancy disputes. The society thus functioned to promote the government's agricultural policies while shoring up the political and economic position of the strongest, most progovernment groups in the countryside.

The **Imperial Reservists' Association** (IRA) was established in 1910 by leaders in the Japanese army to clarify military issues and to sustain military preparedness among former army recruits. Its membership expanded quickly to include former navy recruits, with branches in nearly every community in the country and in some factories by the 1930s. In 1936 a national law made the organization an official external entity of the Ministries of the Army and Navy. Both before and during the war, the IRA fostered popular acceptance of the military's policies and contributed to the gradual acquiescence of the Japanese people to the military's war aims. The IRA was abolished in 1945.

The **Greater Japan Alliance of Youth Organizations** was formally established by the Ministries of Home Affairs and Education in 1925. Before then, youth organizations had been informal associations of young men between the ages of twelve and twenty-five who joined together to participate in leisure activities or to assist with local festivals. During the twentieth century, however, the government began to penetrate these informal entities in order to contain juvenile delinquency, cultivate patriotic sentiments, and build support for the military. Mayors and school principals often played the leading role in achieving these aims at the local level. The national unification of these groups in 1925 marked the maturation of such efforts and also provided the organizational vehicle with which the government controlled young men on the home front until it disbanded in 1945.

Neighborhood associations (*chōnaikai*) were initially formed in Tōkyō in 1927. Usually overseen by elderly, long-standing residents of a specific neighborhood, these associations operated with the expectation that everyone eligible to join would, using the household as the membership unit. In a city that was growing rapidly, government agencies had great difficulty in keeping pace with the demands for social services, and the neighborhood associations offered them an essentially tax-free way of mobilizing the citizenry to communicate government decrees and to clean streets and gather garbage. By the late 1930s, the national government was relying on these associations for other purposes, too. They served as the distribution channels for rationed goods and as a surveillance mechanism to ensure popular compliance with the war effort. In 1945, the Allied authorities abolished the prewar-style neighborhood associations.

The **Greater Japan Patriotic Industrial League** was formally established in 1940, patterned on the local organizations that had first emerged in 1938, and officially disbanded in 1945. Relying on bureaucrats and corporate managers, rather than union leaders or workers, for its leadership, this was nonetheless Japan's patriotic labor front during the war. Although it had great difficulties achieving its primary goals of sustaining morale and boosting production, owing to the chaos in the domestic economy, the league did show workers how to organize and articulate their grievances at the factory level. After the war, workers used this experience to launch a brief but vigorous union movement that challenged managerial control of the workplace.

The **Imperial Reserve Assistance Association** was the final, culminating effort at organizing state control during the prewar era. In the eyes of its proponents, it was modeled after Germany's Nazi Party. Established in 1940, this association was the most encompassing of all wartime bodies, created as a symbol of national unity. Theoretically it embraced the functions of the political parties and labor unions—as well as business, agricultural, and other associations—that had dissolved to join the IRAA and to cooperate in the war effort. In fact, however, in 1940 Japan was already wracked with divisions that the war only deepened, so the association was never able to carry out effectively the high aspirations it held for itself. It disbanded in June 1945.

By the late 1930s, these many state-guided organizations had gathered nearly all of Japanese society under their embrace. Women, farmers, former soldiers, young men, urban residents, and factory workers all were mobilized under the state's tutelage in these organizations. Although each had originated under somewhat different circumstances, during the war they combined to unite—and keep in check—the Japanese populace, as the nation's leaders sought to prevail in an unwinnable war. Even before Japan's defeat, some of these organizations were disbanded; the remainder were eliminated by the Allied occupiers in 1945.

We might assume, therefore, that this episode of organizational history was closed. But after the war, Japan's central government continued to use its laws, influence, resources, and moral suasion to cajole, guide, counsel, and administer various groups and movements. These efforts were never so widespread as before and during the war, and they were not oriented to the military purposes that prewar organizations had served. Instead, the state-guided organizations and movements had more innocuous objectives in postwar Japan, promoting hard work, clean living, family planning, careful budgeting, steady savings, and caring for the elderly. But the persistence of this type of state-fostered activity attests to the continuity of the organizational, psychological, and political patterns that distinguish Japan from many other democracies. (For comparisons, see Political Parties and Opposition Movements.)

POLITICAL PARTIES

Political parties are social organizations of like-minded people whose primary purpose is to elect their representatives to legislative assemblies. According to this definition, political parties exist only in nations with elected legislatures. Japan's first genuine political parties originated with the opening of the national legislature (Diet) in 1890 and have gradually grown stronger over time. Large parties of a conservative bent have nearly always dominated Japan's party-led governments, both before and after the war, competing for power against a wide variety of opposition parties that have always been hampered by their small size, fragmentation, and political infighting.

The **Seiyūkai** was the first major political party in Japan. Formed in 1900, it survived until 1940, when it dissolved under the pressures of war. Itō Hirobumi, a leading member of the Meiji oligarchs, formed the party and set its tone thereafter. The Seiyūkai always drew its leadership from the ranks of progovernment elites: generals, admirals, and former bureaucrats. Only on rare occasions did elected politicians lead the party. Its policies reflected the nature of the party's leadership: hawkish on military matters and conservative on domestic issues. These positions suited well its electoral constituency, which consisted mainly of landlords in rural areas and the upper classes in the cities. The Seiyūkai was the dominant party in prewar Japan, consistently holding majorities in the Diet between the turn of the century and the mid-1920s and then sharing power with its conservative opponents until party governments disappeared in the 1930s.

The **Kenseikai** was the principal opponent of the Seiyūkai from its founding in 1916 until its reorganization in 1927. At that time it joined with another party to create the new **Minseitō**, which is thus a direct successor. The Kenseikai-Minseitō party lineage differed from the Seiyūkai in several ways, however. The leaders of the Kenseikai and Minseitō were opponents of the former samurai from the Satsuma and Chōshū domains who dominated both the government and the Seiyūkai. Outsiders, such as Ōkuma Shigenobu, and elected politicians, such as Hamaguchi Osachi, presided over the party. They tried, especially after the 1920s, to carve out a constituency in the cities of Japan, where the electorate expanded greatly after the vote was extended in 1925 to all males over twenty-five. The Kenseikai had in fact pushed this development, one illustration of its slightly more progressive policies. These parties were less hawkish than the Seiyūkai and sometimes supported defense cutbacks. In fact, it was a Minseitō government that negotiated the limits on naval expansion in 1930. These parties were also more generous in their social policies and more likely to favor progressive treatment of workers and unions. Although the Minseitō presided over some governments in the 1920s and 1930s, after the Manchurian incident in 1932, its powers and unity declined, and in 1940, it, too, disbanded.

Socialist parties in prewar Japan were numerous but also small, fragmented, and volatile. They were initially formed in the early 1900s, and the expansion of the electorate in 1925 offered them a boost, because they appealed primarily to the lower socioeconomic orders: tenants and poor farmers in the countryside and workers and lower-level white-collar workers in the cities. In fact, the socialist parties often worked in tandem with the tenant and labor movements (see Opposition Movements) to create a legal environment that improved the conditions and rights of tenants and workers. In this effort, they were hampered by many obstacles: a general aversion throughout Japanese society to left-wing politics; constant surveillance and repression by the government; laws restricting freedom of assembly, speech, and organization; modestly educated leaders drawn from the lower ranks of Japanese society; and, not least, by their own internal bickering, often over fine points of political theory. Consequently, the socialist parties in prewar Japan never won even a tenth of the popular vote and never formed a government. Like the larger, more conservative parties, they, too, dissolved in the late 1930s under the pressures of war.

After the war, the Allied Occupation authorities created a more tolerant legal environment that increased the freedoms of opposition parties. More, and more effective, opponents thus emerged. Nonetheless, a single, dominant, conservative party and its predecessors have exercised a near monopoly over Japan's postwar governments.

The **Liberal Democratic Party** (LDP) is a distant descendant of the Seiyūkai and Minseitō and a direct descendant of the Liberal Party and the Democratic Party, two parties that governed for all but eight months between 1946 and 1955. In that year, they joined to create the LDP, in large part to forestall the steady growth of the progressive parties. From 1955 until 1993, the Liberal Democrats formed every government in Japan. In 1993 a dramatic setback drove the LDP briefly from office, but it returned in a coalition government in 1994 and has governed ever since.

The LDP initially relied heavily on former bureaucrats to provide its leadership, but since the 1970s, elected career politicians have dominated the top ranks of the party. This reflects the party's steadily growing task of meeting the political needs of a highly diverse constituency, including farmers in rural areas, workers in urban areas, some members of a broad middle class, and key segments of the postwar elite (bureaucrats, businessmen, and professionals). Promoting economic growth has been the LDP's major policy and achievement. The party has long worked to help farmers, big business, shopkeepers, and small enterprises, often at the expense of a middle-class, urban electorate. The party also has sometimes taken surprisingly progressive positions on health and welfare issues.

When it tries to attract younger constituents, the LDP has always faced opposition, especially from its older members. In the early decades of the postwar era, the "progressive parties" were the LDP's major opponents. The progressive parties were those on the left pushing communist or socialist programs. In the 1960s, a second stream of opposition arose from "centrist" parties advocating moderate policies. Finally, in the 1990s the LDP's opposition came from the ranks of its own former members who had created new "reform" parties. They have tried, though with little success, to dislodge the LDP from its political predominance.

The **Japan Communist Party** has been the LDP's most radical and durable opponent since 1955. This party began in 1921, suffered constant repression before the war, and was virtually eliminated with the incarceration of its leaders in the 1930s. After the war, its leaders were released, and its legal status was assured. Since 1945 the Japan Communist Party has espoused a Marxian program aimed at an urban constituency made up of both disadvantaged workers and elite intellectuals. The party has maintained its independence and rarely allies with other progressive or centrist parties. It has never won more than about 10 percent of the popular vote, which translates into an even smaller percentage of seats in the Diet.

The **Japan Socialist Party** (JSP) reappeared in 1945 and was the largest single opponent of the LDP until the JSP's virtual demise in the mid-1990s. The JSP tried to gather under its umbrella the groups, parties, and movements that had supported the prewar socialist parties, mainly rural tenants and urban workers.

By taking advantage of growth in the industrial economy during the 1950s, the party grew to embrace almost a third of the voters, but thereafter, it confronted a string of obstacles that it was never able to overcome. In 1960, the party split. During the 1970s, Japan's industrial expansion slowed and, with it, growth of the unions. Meanwhile, the JSP's union allies in the private sector were becoming politically more moderate while its allies in the public sector were becoming highly adversarial. These internal splits and a preoccupation with the union movement complicated the JSP's ability to expand its base among the fastest-growing segment of the electorate, the urban white-collar voters. The JSP persisted as the main opponent of the LDP into the 1980s and won occasional victories as a protest alternative. But when it joined a coalition with its long-time opponent in 1994 and essentially abandoned its core principles in the process, the party destroyed whatever appeal it still retained. Then in 1996 it fragmented completely and all but disappeared.

The **Democratic Socialist Party** (DSP) was created in 1959 when a group of moderate socialists split off from the JSP. Many of them were former workers and union leaders who opposed confrontation. They disliked the shrill, Marxist programs of the left-wing factions in the JSP and preferred a more amicable approach to both political policymaking and union negotiation. Aligning with workers organized in private corporations under the Dōmei labor federation, the DSP still emphasized domestic welfare issues and opposed rearmament. But in time, the party drifted away from its progressive allies and carved out a centrist position, sometimes even supporting the LDP. It was never able to expand its base, however, and always had a small constituency and an equally small number of Diet seats. In 1994, it dissolved to enter a new "reform" party.

The **Clean Government Party** (CGP) is one of the most unusual political parties in modern Japan. Its political base rests almost exclusively on the membership of an evangelical Buddhist sect called the Value-Creating Society (Sōka gakkai). Formed in the early 1960s, the CGP first elected members to the national Diet in 1967. Its leaders and constituents are mainly urban residents from the lower and middle ranks of society, many of them people adversely affected by the events of the Pacific War. Owing to the strong ties between the party and the society, it has been almost impossible for the CGP to expand its constituency to other segments of society. The CGP always had an interest in social welfare policies, but it followed a rather hawkish line on military matters. This made it possible for the party to cooperate with both the DSP and the LDP during the 1970s and 1980s. In 1994, the national party dissolved to form a new "reform" party, although the provincial parties retained their identity. Given the fate of the "reform" parties, the CGP could stage a comeback by rebuilding on the base of these local branches.

The first **1990s' "reform" parties** appeared in 1992 and blossomed after 1993. Because these parties are so new and volatile and have formed, functioned, and dissolved with such frequency and in such number, it is most useful to discuss them as a group. All of them have in common one desire: to break the LDP's monopoly on national governance. These reform parties also have often shared a second, more surprising, feature: many of their leaders and members have been former LDP politicians who left the party to win power, to restart their political careers, to seek revenge, or to pursue new policies. Most of the reform parties have tried to distinguish themselves from the LDP by advocating deregulation and administrative change, but when forced to describe their programs, they have differed from the LDP's only in detail. Some of these parties have taken a stronger stance on the issue of constitutional revision, which in their eyes would clear the way for Japan to play a larger military role in the world. The reform parties have tried hard to attract younger, urban, middle-class voters disaffected with the LDP, but with only partial success. (See also Political Leaders and Opposition Movements.)

OPPOSITION MOVEMENTS

Since the late Tokugawa period, many popular movements in Japan have arisen to oppose groups in power. These opposition movements have always had three features in common. First, their members have been drawn from the ranks of the disadvantaged, people not part of the mainstream or establishment order. During the late Tokugawa era, such people often were landless farm workers, and in the late nineteenth and early twentieth centuries, they were poor tenant farmers and industrial laborers. Then and later, the disadvantaged also included women and university students. A second striking feature of the opposition movements has been their infrequent, sporadic nature. They have cropped up, often unexpectedly and spontaneously, in different places and at different times. Finally, the objectives of Japan's opposition movements have usually been limited. Many movements were provoked by economic crises, and once the demands were met and the crisis had passed, the movements usually withered or disappeared.

Over time, however, the opposition movements became larger in scale, developed more enduring organizations, and started using written documents and references to the law. As a consequence, some of these movements became institutionalized as organized, durable bodies regularly opposing the groups in power. On some occasions, the opposition groups even accepted the concessions that powerful groups offered them, which often led to their co-optation and their becoming part of the establishment, thereby losing their identity as opponents.

Uchikowashi, "trashings," were among the first credible incidents of rebellion that appeared in the years after 1850, and they always resulted in damage to property. Such incidents usually occurred when rice prices rose sharply or rice supplies were low. Poor farm workers, desperate for food, would gather in small groups, march to the homes of wealthy landlords or rice dealers, shout their frustrations, and tear down fences, gates, homes, and warehouses. These incidents were usually confined to a village or a few villages, involved only a score or more of protesters, and had limited objectives. The protesters and their targets were generally able to reach amicable settlements, and the participants were not severely punished for their actions, because both parties recognized that advantaged groups (landlords and rice dealers) had a moral obligation to help the disadvantaged (poor workers) during times of crisis.

Insurrections were another type of opposition movement that cropped up in Japan during the 1860s. They had more ominous implications than the *uchikowashi* did. Insurrections were usually larger in scale, sometimes involving thousands of participants on both sides. They often took place over larger areas, spanning not just a few villages but many domains. They also encompassed a wider swath of society, including not just poor farm laborers but also priests, townsmen, and samurai. Because insurrections drew their leaders from educated groups, the participants often stated their grievances in written form. For all these reasons, insurrections posed a greater threat to the political standing of the established authorities than did the more inchoate, smaller-scale trashings. One famous insurrection in 1864–1865, caused by the Tengu Party from the Mito domain northeast of Edo, lasted for nearly a year, involved several thousand participants on both sides, and threatened the very existence of the shōgun. It was violently suppressed, and nearly four hundred participants were punished for their actions. In the last years of the Tokugawa shōgunate, dozens of events like this took place at different times in scattered locales across the nation, indicating both outright opposition to established political powers and a pervasive loss of respect for authority.

The **ee ja nai ka incidents** were the third and final type of opposition movement. They appeared during the 1850s and 1860s as a somewhat humorous commentary on the declining respect for authority. Such movements, characterized by rowdy or disruptive crowd behavior, sometimes began among large, drunken groups on religious pilgrimages. At other times they started in crowded urban areas where thousands of people might be gathered for a fair or festival. Confronted by police and others representing the political powers, these groups would taunt them with the phrase *"ee ja nai ka,"* a challenge to authority backed up by the unpredictability of behavior by hundreds of drunk revelers. Even though these incidents did not lead to real revolution, they were one more sign that the political integrity of the ruling authorities had become an object of public ridicule.

The actions of the proimperial forces that carried out the Meiji Restoration of 1868 were, strictly speaking, an opposition movement. The revolutionaries established a new government, which almost overnight became the established authority, and its new army successfully suppressed the rebellion by disgruntled former samurai in 1877 during the Seinan war. Meanwhile, significant popular opposition had already begun to take shape.

The **Freedom and People's Rights Movement** is a perhaps overly general term that encompasses several different opposition movements against the Meiji government, beginning about 1874 and ending about 1889. The opposition during this period was united around four political objectives: the creation of an elected, national legislature; the reduction of taxes on agriculture; the revision of the unequal foreign treaties; and the achievement of freedom of expression and assembly. In social terms, the opposition encompassed a broad cross section of Japanese society. At different times and with different intensity, it attracted the participation of former samurai leaders of the central government, wealthy merchants and farmers, less prosperous farmers, and poor tenants.

Between 1874 and 1889, these groups were often driven apart by different concerns and aspirations. The former samurai were mainly concerned with regaining power in the national government. They consistently advocated the need for a legislature and treaty revision, and they also sought freedom of expression, especially in the face of the government's repression of their activities. The wealthy landlords wanted land taxes reduced in order to ease the financial pressures they faced during periods of deflation. And the poor tenants, staggering under heavy debt when prices fell, wanted both lower taxes and lower rents. Therefore, these groups eventually quarreled among themselves, and the unity of the movement, which seemed so promising in the 1870s, essentially disappeared by the late 1880s.

In part—and only in part—because of the public pressure imposed by this broad movement, the leaders of the Meiji government did produce a constitution, promulgated in 1889. The national legislature that took office one year later provided a forum for some of the government's former opponents, who later became part of a slightly larger political establishment.

The **Hibiya riots** lasted for nearly a week in late 1905 and were an almost unprecedented form of spontaneous urban opposition to government authority. The issue that set off the riots was the government's acceptance of a treaty ending the Russo-Japanese War. The riots began in the Hibiya section of downtown Tōkyō, where large crowds had gathered to hear speakers criticize the treaty as well as the evils of government by oligarchs and self-serving cliques. The speeches obviously tapped the public's distaste for the government's conduct, but the circumstances led to destructive mass action rather than reasoned opposition formally articulated. The crowds began to attack and burn trolleys and police boxes. The speeches, assemblies, and destruction quickly spread to other cities, and in the end, more than two thousand people were injured, seventeen killed, and more than two thousand arrested. The treaty was not changed, nor was the structure of government, but this incident may have signaled a growing desire by city dwellers, most of whom still were not eligible to vote, to play a greater role in national affairs.

Rice riots first broke out in a small fishing village on the coast of western Japan in the summer of 1918. From there they spread to such cities as Kyōto and Nagoya, to mining communities in Honshū and Kyūshū, and eventually to scores of other cities and towns. Ostensibly, the high price of rice caused the outbreaks. But in each area, distinctive local grievances fanned dissent into something more significant. In some areas, the protesters trashed the property of landlords or rice speculators; in mining communities, a wave of strikes broke out. What began as an isolated incident became a nationwide protest. Like many opposition movements in the late Tokugawa period, this one was provoked by a short-term economic crisis. But unlike those movements, this one employed faster means of communication and drew on a better-educated populace to exploit the crisis as a vehicle to express broader grievances. Again, many segments of Japanese society seemed to be indicating that the government had to be more responsive to popular needs and that the people themselves deserved to play a greater role in the affairs of state. Because the rice riots took place just as the labor movement, the tenant movement, and the *buraku* liberation movement were first organizing, it offered them all an unexpected opportunity to develop their political skills.

The **labor movement** has been a principal base for the opposition in twentieth-century Japan. As a serious national force, the labor movement began during the late 1910s. Both the ideas spread by the Russian Revolution and the economic conditions of World War I and its aftermath formed the movement. In the early years, despite serious obstacles, workers sought better employment conditions, higher wages, and greater status. The prevailing laws, however, made the organization of unions in most sectors illegal, and they prohibited collective bargaining and the right to strike. Moreover, both governments and employers worked strenuously to prevent union activities. Finally, the industrial sector was still small; most factories were scattered in isolated rural areas; and many industrial laborers were young women who usually worked for only four to six years before leaving the labor force to marry. Accordingly, before the war the labor unions never organized more than 8 percent of the eligible labor force, and they were unable either to achieve their own objectives or to oppose government policies that damaged their standing.

After the war, the Allied authorities legalized unions, collective bargaining, and the right to strike. Immediately, many workers joined unions, and for about six years after 1945 the union movement thrived. But then a counterattack by the government and managers with the approval of the occupying authorities began in 1949. Their actions removed many influential labor leaders, created an atmosphere of intimidation in labor ranks, and gradually weakened the movement. Nonetheless, from the early 1950s through the late 1980s, an organized union movement did provide the financial, administrative, and electoral foundation for an opposition in Japan. Two national labor federations, Sōhyō and Dōmei, spoke for about two-thirds of union workers, who themselves comprised about a fourth of the national labor force. By allying with the socialist parties, the unions gained a small but consequential voice for themselves in national, regional, and local politics.

As Japan became more affluent after the 1960s, labor unions in the private sector became more moderate, gradually devoting more attention to job stability than to wage increases or broad political change. By the 1980s, this moderation underlay a willingness to negotiate and compromise with the LDP and the bureaucracy. In 1987 a new labor federation called Rengō was created to give voice to this cooperative, moderate behavior. Shortly thereafter, the other national labor federations disbanded to join Rengō, which represents about two-thirds of organized workers in Japan and provides a unity for the union movement that it never had before. However, the number of union workers now totals less than 20 percent of the labor force, so this unified voice speaks for only a small portion of the Japanese population. Rengō thus does not carry great weight in a polity still dominated by big business, the bureaucracy, and politicians tied to the establishment.

During the prewar years, the **tenant movement** grew in tandem with the labor movement. That is, while the labor unions were organizing workers in rural and urban factories, the tenant movement was organizing farmers in the countryside who owned little or no land. They worked collectively to secure more explicit tenant contracts, to lower tax payments, and to reduce rents. Sometimes the tenant unions adopted extreme tactics reminiscent of the trashings of the Tokugawa period. More often, however, they issued petitions, sought to bargain collectively with landlords, and worked to change laws to their advantage. At the peak of their organizational strength in the mid-1930s, the tenant organizations still embraced only a minority of the families in rural Japan. They were not a large force. Nonetheless, their voice did win a hearing among bureaucrats who took some small steps to improve their conditions beginning in the late 1930s and continuing through the war. After the war, the Allied authorities conducted a land reform that virtually eliminated tenancy in the countryside and, with it, the tenant movement.

In some regions of the country, the tenant movement had allied before the war with the socialist parties to advance its aims. When strong personal and political networks had been established under those circumstances, the farmers in such regions continued to support socialist parties after the war, thereby preventing the LDP from completely monopolizing the farm vote after 1955.

The **women's movement** in modern Japan has been a fitful, fragmented undertaking involving only small numbers. Without a large, centralized organization to articulate their demands and promote a movement, women have continued to suffer inequalities that are startling to Americans and Europeans in the late twentieth century.

As in most societies, Japan's first women's groups were dominated by women from elite families. The first of these appeared in the late nineteenth century, when women had no right to vote and worked under severe legal disabilities in many other ways. The early organizations tried to improve educational opportunities for women and to expand their political freedoms and rights. Later, in the early twentieth century, women's organizations formed to win female suffrage. Throughout the prewar era, however, women's organizations had to walk a dangerous tightrope between contention and compliance. By wartime, they had opted for compliance and largely abandoned their opposition.

Following the war, Allied reforms granted many rights and freedoms that women had never been able to obtain before the war. Nonetheless, customary views of women and their roles in society persisted largely unchanged. Women thus found it difficult to attend prestigious universities, win secure jobs, and participate as equals in Japanese society. Many small, short-lived women's groups have arisen in the postwar era to address these inequalities, but they have seldom been taken seriously. Perhaps more than pressure from within, it is pressure from without that is gradually altering the roles of women in Japan, as they experience life abroad, read about foreign women in magazines, watch foreign practices on television, and hear pronouncements from international organizations.

The **buraku liberation movement** is a political undertaking conducted to improve the legal and material conditions of the *burakumin* ("designated hamlet people"), or *dōwa minzoku* ("discriminated-against" people), descendants of people who have historically pursued occupations, such as tanning and caring for the dead, that are proscribed under religious law. Such people have been forced to live in separate residential settlements, where they have adopted customs and language usages that can distinguish them from mainstream Japanese, even though they are physically the same.

The liberation movement began in the late 1910s and continues into the present. At the national level, the movement has striven to win legal victories that prevent or punish discrimination against *burakumin*. At the local level, the movement has often engaged in raw political bargaining aimed at winning policy concessions and material rewards for their members. The movement has always had a strong public relations orientation, designed to keep the problems of their members in the public eye. Unfortunately, in recent decades it has used the technique of denunciation — humiliating an opponent in public — to advance its cause, which has been counterproductive in many ways. Partly in consequence, the *burakumin* remain an isolated minority subject to many kinds of informal discrimination.

Japan's **student movement** has been much like the women's movement. It has suffered from elitism, its small scale, and a profound fragmentation based on ideological differences among groups on the political left. Historically, the student movement has drawn its leaders and followers from university students and, in that group, from students at the best universities, such as Tōkyō and Kyōto. The first student groups were formed at Tōkyō Imperial University in the 1910s and 1920s, some of them benevolent organizations combining survey research with assistance to the poor. Others were study groups devoted to Marxist texts and the finer points of political ideology. After 1945, when students organized into Marxist-dominated political societies on many campuses, they advocated the general causes then popular on the left, such as democracy, pacifism, and diplomatic neutrality. These issues came to the fore during the security treaty crisis in 1959 and 1960. Students joined with labor unions, socialist parties, and others to oppose the renewal of the treaty on American terms. Although they did help topple the Kishi government, the treaty was passed as negotiated. The students paid a price for their participation, however, because the once-unified student movement broke down during the 1960s into a variety of bickering factions. The students reappeared on the scene again briefly in the late 1960s, when on many campuses they organized efforts to revise curricula and to protest the Vietnam War. Nonetheless, the students' actions produced few of the changes they sought, and the movement continued to splinter. Some extreme factions left Japan and embarked on terrorist activities abroad. Other groups simply disappeared. No visible, large-scale student movement has existed since the early 1970s. (For comparisons, see State-Guided Organizations and Political Parties.)

EDUCATION

The Japanese people prize education, believing that learning is valuable in its own right. They also recognize that training and educational credentials are necessary for success in a complex, technically oriented society. Japanese governments have both promoted and shared these attitudes since the Meiji Restoration, and they have always provided educational opportunities to the Japanese people. Usually, however, these opportunities have been defined by bureaucrats operating a highly centralized system of education.

The **Ministry of Education** is the organ through which bureaucrats have controlled Japan's educational system. First established in 1871, it became a ministry under the new cabinet system in 1886. From that time onward, it has been primarily responsible for organizing and managing education from kindergarten through university and for supervising a number of scholarly academies and government research institutes.

The Ministry of Education has unusually broad powers. It establishes educational standards; it determines pedagogical requirements and procedures; it approves textbooks; and it sets the pace of classroom instruction. Consequently, there is great uniformity in Japanese education. On any given day, most students in most schools are doing the same lessons in the same textbooks in the same way.

The structure of Japan's **public education system** has changed frequently since the 1870s. Before 1945, Japan's educational institutions had evolved to serve the needs of an agricultural nation undergoing rapid industrialization. Six, and sometimes eight, years of elementary school formed the base of the system, in which students developed a basic competence in reading, writing, and arithmetic. Many children completed their education at that point and entered the labor force. Those who wished to continue their education, how- — ever, had several alternatives. Those on an elite educational track completed five years of middle school followed by three years of higher school before en- tering a three-year university curriculum at about age twenty. Before 1945, only a tiny portion, barely 1 percent, finished university. Many students, both male and female, pursued vocational studies in a wide range of institutions, includ- ing business colleges, women's finishing schools, and technical colleges. Some of these students entered teachers' colleges, where they were trained to be educators in the public schools.

Reforms during the Allied Occupation drastically altered the structure of Japan's educational system. A new 6–3–3–4 system was established under which everyone was required to complete six years of elementary and three years of middle school. Those who wanted to continue could attend another three years of high school, followed by four years of college or university. The proportion of students completing high school rose steadily after the 1950s. By the 1990s, almost every student completed high school, and about 40 percent went on to some form of postsecondary education.

Nearly all students attend public schools through the ninth grade. Those who want to enter an elite university often try to enter a private secondary school through a highly competitive examination system. In the last two decades, an unusually high percentage of students entering the most presti- gious universities have been educated at private secondary schools. This fact implies that a student's family's wealth, and not just the student's abilities, has become an important ingredient in winning entry to the universities that shape a person's life chances in Japan.

Tōkyō University has always been the most prestigious institution of high- er education in Japan. Its graduates have long dominated the upper ranks of the bureaucracy and the business community, and they have played a preem- inent role in education and the arts (as the biographies of male writers show).

Tōdai, as Tōkyō University is commonly known, traces its origins to 1855 and the creation of a shōgunal office for the translation of texts and the study of foreign languages. In 1877 the successor of that office joined with a medical school to form what was until 1945 Tōkyō Imperial University. The university originally consisted of four divisions: law, natural sciences, humanities, and medicine. In subsequent years, divisions for engineering, agriculture, economics, education, and pharmacy were added. The faculty at Tōdai has always included many of Japan's leading scholars, and they have always received the lion's share of the funds supporting public higher education.

Kyōto University, or Kyōdai, is another old, proud, and prestigious public university. Formed under pressure from political interests in the Kyōto and Ōsaka area in 1897, it began with divisions for engineering and natural sciences and over time added law, medicine, humanities, economics, agriculture, education, and pharmacy. In the 1990s a number of new, interdisciplinary centers were created. In contrast with Tōdai, Kyōdai has not always seen itself as an incubator for leaders of business and bureaucracy. Instead, it has prided itself on its search for the truth, its intellectual independence, and its strong institutions of self-governance. During the prewar era, its philosophy faculty was especially famous, and in recent years, its law professors have made their mark on international scholarship.

Waseda University is one of the two most prestigious private universities in Japan. The foundation for Waseda was laid in 1882 when Ōkuma Shigenobu (see Political Leaders) established Tōkyō semmon gakkō. Having just been forced out of government by the men from Satsuma and Chōshū who controlled it, Ōkuma wanted to establish a school at which political opposition could be freely discussed. The school's first divisions were created to study economics, politics, and law. Humanities and other divisions have been added over time. The original school became Waseda University in 1902, and it has been noted since the 1910s for its School of Political Economy and for the many elected politicians among its graduates.

Keiō Gijuku University is Japan's other most prestigious private university. As a university it dates from 1902, but its origins are much earlier. The founder of Keiō was a samurai from a small domain in Kyūshū named Fukuzawa Yukichi, a prominent intellectual who played a major role in the cultural debates of the 1860s and 1870s. He always, however, insisted on retaining his freedom by refusing to serve in the government. To disseminate his views and to train students who could serve in other careers and private organizations, he had operated a number of small academies from as early as 1858. In 1871 he moved his recently renamed Keiō Academy to a site in Mita (near downtown Tōkyō) where the central campus of Keiō University is still located. Possessing many of the same divisions as Tōdai, Kyōdai, and Waseda, Keiō has differed by emphasizing economics and business management, so as to preserve Fukuzawa's original desire to train students for jobs in the private sector and in the broader world of practical affairs.

Tsuda Women's College exemplifies the kind of institution that was responsible for training women at the university level before other universities began accepting them, in most cases after 1945. The founder of the college was an unusual figure named Tsuda Umeko (1865–1929). At the age of six, she accompanied a Japanese government delegation to the United States, where she stayed for the next eleven years. In 1885 she took a position at a school for children of the nobility and taught there for fifteen years, making another three-year trip to the United States between 1889 and 1892. In 1900 she resigned her position and established the Tsuda English Academy which originally emphasized instruction in the English language and the importance of the individual in education. Women from elite families who were likely to marry government officials or prominent businessmen dominated its classes before the war. Although it has evolved since the war into a comprehensive liberal arts college, it still concentrates on cultivating individualism among its female students. (See also Bureaucracy.)

MALE WRITERS

The history of prose literature in Japan dates from the Heian period (794–1185), when a court lady, Murasaki Shikibu, produced what many regard as the world's first novel. *The Tale of Genji* describes the cultural and romantic mores of the Kyōto aristocracy during the eleventh century. Such writing virtually disappeared, however, when the warlike medieval era began a century or two later, to be replaced by tales of martial valor. Socially realistic literature returned during the Tokugawa period (1600–1868) with the appearance of a new style of commoner writing. Inspired by the work of such men as Ihara Saikaku (1642–1693), this literature depicted the varied lives of urban merchants and the flamboyant customs of the entertainment districts. Saikaku and his successors had a significant influence on the men and women who at the end of the nineteenth century began to develop a form of prose writing modeled on the social and psychological realism of the nineteenth-century European novel.

Mori Ōgai (1862–1922), along with Natsume Sōseki, is regarded as one of the two literary giants of the Meiji period (1868–1912) and one of the first practitioners of modern prose literature. Ōgai was a medical officer in the Japanese army. His family had been physicians for generations, and his father and grandfather, both samurai, were trained in foreign languages as well as medicine. Ōgai was a precocious child who excelled in school and was able to enter the medical division of the new Tōkyō Imperial University in 1877, two years early at the age of fifteen. After graduating in 1881, he accepted a commission in the army and spent the next thirty-seven years as an officer, physician, and health administrator.

The pivotal event in Ōgai's life occurred in 1884 when the army sent him to Germany. Having already studied German for many years, he took advantage of this opportunity to immerse himself in European literature, philosophy, and psychology. After his return to Japan in 1888, Ōgai devoted himself to translating foreign works, engaging in critical commentary, and writing his own stories and novellas, all while pursuing his army career.

Ōgai's three major works that have been translated are *Vita Sexualis* (1909), *Youth* (1911), and *The Wild Geese* (1915). Each of these is important in its own right, but they do not compare in quality with the novels of Natsume Sōseki, for the simple reason that Ōgai was not a very deft storyteller. Rather, he was an intellectual, mainly interested in getting across a body of ideas that often meshed poorly with the imaginative literature he was struggling to write. His short stories were more successful, especially "The Courier" (1891), because it ignores his habit of expounding at length in the first person on some intellectual position, and it avoids the awkward, brooding, and pessimistic style of his more autobiographical prose. Ōgai's translations of European novels, plays, and poetry and his role as a critic in the debates about aesthetics were his greatest contributions to the cultural life of turn-of-the-century Japan.

Futabatei Shimei (1864–1909) was a contemporary of Mori Ōgai and Natsume Sōseki and is credited with writing Japan's first modern novel. Futabatei was the pen name of Hasegawa Tatsunosuke. He was born in Edo (later Tōkyō) to a well-placed samurai family and attended good schools in the capital. Between 1881 and 1886, Futabatei was a student at a government-operated foreign language institute where he specialized in the study of Russian language and literature. He was a talented linguist who, while still in his twenties, translated difficult works on literary theory, as well as the novels of Turgenev.

Futabatei was an idealistic person, and like many idealists, he was stubborn and inflexible. He refused to concede to authorities in 1886 and failed to graduate from the language school, which prevented him from entering the civil service. Instead, he turned to writing and spent the next several years producing Japan's first modern novel. *Floating Clouds* (1889) offers a realistic portrayal of early Meiji society while introducing Japanese readers to the psychological realism of the Western novel. It depicts the plight of a young civil servant who has just lost his job and cannot deal with the consequences. *Floating Clouds* perches uncomfortably on a bridge between Japanese commoner fiction of the Edo period, inspired by Saikaku, and Western literature of the nineteenth century, exemplified by Futabatei's favorite, Dostoyevsky. Futabatei artfully employs the vignettes, the quick and witty dialogue, and the scene setting of late Edo prose fiction to lend life and personality to his novel's characters. He also portrays the hapless hero as a characteristically Russian recluse, crippled by self-doubt and unable to take the actions that will win him a job or the hand of his loved one.

Disappointed by his work, even though it won critical acclaim, Futabatei spent the next seventeen years at a series of modest jobs and stopped writing novels entirely. Then, after taking a position with a newspaper, he wrote two novels in quick succession in 1906 and 1907, both still untranslated. A year later he contracted tuberculosis while traveling in Russia and died shortly thereafter at age forty-six.

Natsume Sōseki (1867–1916), usually referred to by his pen name Sōseki, was arguably the greatest novelist in Japan's modern history. Sōseki spent a lifetime struggling against mental and physical problems but left a diverse body of work capped by his masterpiece, *Kokoro*.

Sōseki was born Natsume Kinnosuke in Edo. His family had been locally influential for generations, but it fell on hard times with the coming of the Meiji era. For this reason, and also because Sōseki was the fifth of eight children born to a father in his fifties and a mother in her forties, the family immediately placed him with a foster family. Mistreated and ignored by them, he was soon returned to his family of birth. The father was determined to reject the child, however, and quickly placed him with a second foster family with whom he stayed between the ages of two and nine. Eventually he returned to his own family again, suffering the rejection of his father though winning the affection of his mother, who died when he was fourteen. These early childhood experiences certainly contributed to the low self-esteem that plagued Sōseki throughout his life, and they might well have disposed him to the mental problems that he suffered as an adult.

As a youth, Sōseki spent time at *kabuki* and *rakugo* performances, whose humorous, rapid-fire monologues left their mark on the style of some of his early novels. He also took the elite course of study at institutions affiliated with Tōkyō Imperial University, from which he graduated in 1893 with a degree in English literature. Sōseki spent the next seven years teaching at a variety of schools in the capital and in provincial cities, acquiring experiences that later appeared in some of his most popular novels.

During this period, he married and began rearing a family. His wife, like Sōseki, suffered mental health problems. Combined with Sōseki's own bouts of mental illness, their difficulties drove them apart throughout an unhappy marriage—similar to those in his novels.

In 1900 the Ministry of Education plucked Sōseki from obscurity and sent him to England for three years, a sojourn that gave him an opportunity to experience a "modern" Western society at first hand and to develop his already exceptional skills in English and English literature. The experience also produced mental depression and social isolation, fed by his lack of self-esteem, his inability to become a part of English society, and pervasive racial discrimination.

Upon his return to Japan, Sōseki won appointment to a position in English literature at Tōkyō Imperial University, replacing the famous American expert on things Japanese, Lafcadio Hearn. Sōseki did not like lecturing, however, and after four years he resigned to take a position with the Tōkyō *Asahi*, one of the country's major newspapers. His contract obliged him to devote almost all his attention to writing.

In the decade between 1906 and his death in 1916, Sōseki produced twelve novels that have been translated into English, as well as essays, poetry, and short stories. The novels are *I Am a Cat* (1906), *Botchan* (1906), *Three-Cornered World* (1906), *The Miner* (1908), *Sanshirō* (1908), *And Then* (1909), *Mon* (1910), *To the Spring Equinox and Beyond* (1912), *The Wayfarer* (1913), *Kokoro* (1914), *Grass on the Wayside* (1915), and *Light and Darkness* (1916).

Sōseki's masterpiece, and perhaps the greatest work of modern Japanese literature, is *Kokoro*. Divided into three parts, the first two introduce a young man who imposes himself on a reclusive figure called Sensei. Hints about Sensei's mysterious remoteness appear in the first two parts, but they are revealed fully only in the third, which is a lengthy personal confession written in the form of a suicide note by Sensei to the young acquaintance.

Kokoro is an exceptionally rich and multilayered text that invites a variety of readings. If it is not entirely autobiographical, the novel certainly uses Sensei as a proxy through whom Sōseki offers his commentary on his own personal, psychological, social, and cultural dilemmas. The relationships in the story also sustain a reading informed by Confucian values and norms. In this respect, the novel is a lament for the passing of an older era. Finally, the novel can be read as an anguished statement by a man who has failed to adapt to the challenges of modernity. *Kokoro* stands as a monument to Sōseki's literary genius.

As the careers of Ōgai and Sōseki were drawing to a close, a younger group of men were rising to prominence in the 1910s. Like their predecessors, these writers were experimenting with the language and form of modern writing. In their hands, however, prose writing took on a far more obsessive and self-indulgent quality, often turning its back on society at large and addressing the author's own idiosyncratic concerns.

Nagai Kafū (1879–1959) (the pen name of Nagai Sōkichi), the son of a government bureaucrat in Tōkyō, is best known for his short stories that depict the dying world of the old pleasure districts. Kafū became interested in the decadent world during his teens, when he read the popular literature of the Edo period and began to experience for himself the attractions of Tōkyō's bars, tea houses, and brothels. His father sent Kafū, after several years of idleness, on a tour of the United States and France. During his years abroad, he developed an interest in French literature, and the travel books he wrote about his journeys abroad established his reputation.

Kafū's fame won him a position at Keiō University, where he taught between 1909 and 1916. During this period, he also married, divorced, remarried, and was abandoned by his second wife. He was able to survive on his writings and an inheritance from his father, who died in 1912. For the rest of his life, Kafū wrote sporadically, grew increasingly more isolated, and devoted himself to the pleasures of the fading entertainment districts.

One of Kafū's novels, *Geisha in Rivalry* (1918), has been translated. Edward Seidensticker translated many of his best short stories in *Kafū the Scribbler*, and Lane Dunlop translated two of his finest novellas, *During the Rains* (1931) and *Flowers in the Shade* (1934). These works offer an evocative portrait of men and women flirting dangerously with life on the seamy margins of prewar Tōkyō. Kafū maintained a disapproving silence throughout the Pacific War, and he lived to see renewed interest in his works before he died in the late 1950s.

Shiga Naoya (1883–1971) is one of the most enigmatic authors in modern Japan. For years he was regarded as Japan's greatest writer, yet his reputation rested primarily on one novel that took him sixteen years to complete. Shiga's father was a wealthy businessman whose fortune assured his son a life of privilege and comfort. Shiga attended the Peers' School, a special institution for children of the nobility, where he came into contact with noble sons who were later collaborators in the Shirakaba-ha (White birch society), an important literary coterie in the early twentieth century. Shiga graduated from Tōkyō Imperial University with a degree in English and Japanese literature. Four years later he married the daughter of a noble family and lived an apparently simple and contented life thereafter.

Much of the impetus for Shiga's creative writing seems to have arisen from conflicts with his strong-willed father. When those struggles were at their height in the early 1910s, Shiga wrote some of his finest short stories. Seventeen of them have been collected and translated in *The Paper Door and Other Stories*. After he reconciled with his father in 1917, Shiga lost the conflictual stimulus and produced very little thereafter. His novel appeared in four parts between 1921 and 1937. *A Dark Night's Passing* is regarded by many as Japan's most exemplary I-novel (*watakushi shōsetsu* or *shishōsetsu*). It is noted for Shiga's exquisite use of language, the plausibility of its rhetorical displays, and the sincerity of its content. The novel seems to be based almost exclusively on Shiga's own life, thoughts, and aesthetic preoccupations, so many readers find its vision crabbed and its mere existence self-indulgent.

Tanizaki Jun'ichirō (1886–1965) never won the Nobel Prize for literature, but he can still be regarded as the preeminent man of letters in midcentury Japan. In quantity, quality, and diversity, his work far surpasses that of Kawabata Yasunari and Ōe Kenzaburō.

Tanizaki was born into a prosperous merchant family in the old commoner section of Tōkyō known as *shitamachi* (downtown), where he was exposed at an early age to the sensuous atmosphere of Tōkyō's entertainment districts. This exposure, along with Tanizaki's intimate ties to his mother and other women in his life, may have led to his obsessive interest in female erotica. As a youth, Tanizaki was an excellent student. He attended a succession of good schools in Tōkyō and completed the literature course at Tōkyō Imperial University, although he failed to obtain a degree because he did not pay his tuition. By then, however, he had already been recognized as a promising writer, having established his reputation and his ability to subsist on his writing while still in his twenties.

Tanizaki worked in many genres, including literary criticism and essays. One of his most insightful essays has been translated as "In Praise of Shadows," a nostalgic eulogy to the physical and aesthetic features of Japanese life before the 1920s. He was also a translator. During the 1930s he translated the classical masterpiece, *The Tale of Genji*, into modern Japanese. His major works, however, were novels, novellas, and short stories. A partial list includes *Naomi* (1924), *Some Prefer Nettles* (1929), *The Reed Cutter* (1932), *The Makioka Sisters* (1949), *Captain Shigemoto's Mother* (1949), *The Key* (1956), and *Diary of a Mad Old Man* (1961). At first glance, many of Tanizaki's novels and stories appear somewhat bizarre and pornographic. The central male figures seem obsessed with perverted sexual desire. In fact, however, Tanizaki's works are rich, playful, tantalizing, and deeply layered. They set out fantastical illusions inviting readers to explore not just male sexual conduct but also male-female relations, cultural aesthetics between Japan and the West, and the corrosive mores of a modernizing society.

Tanizaki's most important and accessible novel is *The Makioka Sisters*. Begun during the war and then stopped by censorship, this novel was not completed until the postwar Occupation period. Set in the late 1930s, it depicts the declining world of a once-distinguished Ōsaka merchant house contrasted with a flourishing household in the wealthy suburb of Ashiya. Tanizaki drew the inspiration for this story from both *The Tale of Genji* and his personal relationship with his wife's sisters. As a portrayal of strong-willed sisters, the dynamics of family life, shifting patterns of cultural behavior, and Japanese society on the brink of war, it has no equal in Japanese literature.

Tanizaki's collected works — the symbol of recognition as a major author — were published when he was in his forties. He won Japan's major literary prize in 1949, and he had apparently been under discussion as a Nobel recipient before his death in 1965.

Akutagawa Ryūnosuke (1892–1927) is an anomaly among Japan's modern authors. He is the only well-known author born between Tanizaki in 1886 and Ibuse in 1898. He wrote no novels and is acclaimed for only a small body of short stories. It is really the Akutagawa Prize for young writers, established by his classmate and friend Kikuchi Kan in 1935, that has immortalized his name in literary circles.

Akutagawa was born into the prosperous Niihara family of Tōkyō. His mother plunged into incurable schizophrenia just after his birth and lived for ten years as a housebound recluse. Akutagawa was raised in the home of her brother and was adopted by him in 1904. Fearful throughout his life about the hereditary consequences of his mother's illness, Akutagawa himself began to decline mentally following a trip to China in 1921. His health worsened; his mental problems deepened; and he began to take drugs. Finally, he committed suicide.

Akutagawa read voraciously as a youth, especially Japanese folktales, popular Chinese literature, and Japanese and European novels. He pursued his literary interests in college, graduating in 1916 from Tōkyō Imperial University with a degree in English literature. He had already published the story for which he is best known, "Rashōmon," a year before he graduated. In three years, he was able to support himself, his wife, and their growing family from his writing alone.

Akutagawa's early stories are often set in historical contexts. They are tightly written tales characterized by a lucid use of language and dwelling on the weaker, less appealing attributes of humankind: duplicity, hatred, immorality, self-deception, envy and murder. Akutagawa's later works, written after the onset of what may have been his own schizophrenia, are autobiographical. They are consistently morbid, bleak, and pessimistic, reflecting his declining mental state and the gradual dissolution of what may have been one of the keenest minds in modern Japanese literature.

Had Akutagawa lived longer, Japanese literature might have turned earlier from the self-centered themes that Kafū, Shiga, and Tanizaki often worked on. Consequently it fell to even younger writers to experiment with new themes, and one of them achieved international renown.

Ibuse Masuji (1898–1993) holds a special place in modern Japanese letters as the author of *Black Rain* (1966), a moving fictional statement about the long-term consequences of the atomic bombing of Hiroshima.

Ibuse was born in a village near Hiroshima where his family had been gentry for generations. His rural upbringing left a strong imprint on his stories, which are told in simple language with common sense and gentle humor. In his teens, he left home to enter Waseda University. There his literary interests blossomed and he began writing, publishing his first story in 1923. For the next two decades he cultivated helpful mentors in the literary world, helped organize new publications, and continued to write, trying to avoid close identification with any one school of fiction. Ibuse succeeded by developing his own distinctive style and by using unconventional subjects (such as animals) and themes (such as castaways during the Tokugawa period). During the war he had to spend a year as a "patriotic writer" under government sponsorship, but along with Tanizaki and Kafū, he maintained a disapproving silence after 1943.

Ibuse's greatest work appeared in serial form between 1965 and 1966. Using the simple, straightforward language for which he had become known, he told the story of a young girl whose possible affliction with radiation sickness darkened her family's life and her marriage prospects. The novel won numerous prizes for the author and the highest award from the Japanese government.

Ibuse's translated stories appear in the following collections: *Castaways, Lieutenant Lookeast and Other Stories, Salamander and Other Stories*, and *Waves*.

Kawabata Yasunari (1899–1972) was a writer, critic, and literary entrepreneur whose career began in the 1920s and flourished after the Pacific War. He is widely known as the first Japanese author to win the Nobel Prize for literature, in 1968.

Kawabata was born to a distinguished family in the Ōsaka area. His father was a physician who died when his son was only two. Kawabata's mother died in the following year, and the two grandparents who had been rearing him and a sister, died by the time Kawabata was fifteen. From then on, he always seemed to be preoccupied with loneliness, a recurring theme in his literature, in which he often referred to the "orphan's disposition" of the male figures in his stories.

Always a talented student, Kawabata attended Japan's best schools and graduated in 1925 with a degree in Japanese literature from Tōkyō Imperial University. Having been active during his college years in a wide range of literary activities, he stepped easily into the broader literary world. He had a powerful patron, Kikuchi Kan, a cultural leader who established the prestigious journal *Bungei shunjū* in 1923. For several years, Kawabata was on the journal's board and one of its noted contributors.

Over his lifetime, Kawabata exerted substantial influence as a literary entrepreneur. He worked on numerous journals, using his position to encourage young writers and to foster a tolerant environment for the publication of writing and criticism from all camps. In this way and others, he served as a valued mentor to younger writers, one of whom was Mishima Yukio. Between 1948 and 1965, Kawabata also presided over the Japan branch of PEN, an international writers' organization, and used that position to encourage a greater understanding of modern Japanese literature and to promote more translations of Japanese works.

The stories and novels for which Kawabata is best known often focus, as Tanizaki's do, on women and male-female relationships. In place of the passionate sensuality of Tanizaki's work, Kawabata uses a distancing sentiment that is chilling in its detachment. Some of his best-known works are "The Izu Dancer" (1926), *Snow Country* (1947), *A Thousand Cranes* (1952), *The Master of Go* (1954), *Sound of the Mountain* (1954), and *The House of the Sleeping Beauties* (1961).

Kawabata's collected works were published in 1947 when he was still in his forties. He won the highest literary award in Japan in 1961 and the Nobel Prize in 1968. Depressed by recurring health problems and overwhelmed by the fame his Nobel Prize brought, he died—probably by his own hand—in 1972.

The long period of war, which in some ways began in 1931, probably robbed Japan of many writers. Some men who might have become writers died in the war. Others were muzzled and gave up. And still others lost their lives under suspicious circumstances when governments crushed dissenters in the 1930s. One man, however, achieved lasting acclaim for his work in the 1940s and served as a transition figure between older writers such as Ibuse and Kawabata and the first generation of postwar writers.

Dazai Osamu (1909–1948) is best known for his novellas written shortly after the war ended. *Setting Sun* (1947) and *No Longer Human* (1948) present two despairing but vivid perspectives on postwar conditions in Japan.

Dazai was born Tsushima Shūji. His father was a wealthy landlord and politician in a village in northeastern Japan. Dazai always had a love-hate relationship with both the values of rural Japan and the high status of his family, a contradiction that shaped his life and gave form to his writing.

When his father died in 1923, Dazai began his journey through a succession of schools that finally brought him to Tōkyō Imperial University in 1930. He pursued a desultory course of study focused on literature, but already his real interest was in writing. He was able to publish some stories in the 1930s, and he had begun to win attention by 1940. Dazai was always a "difficult person," however, and he was not able to curry the favor with older writers that was necessary to win sponsorship and publication.

One major reason for Dazai's exclusion from the clubby world of male writers was his behavior. He either delighted in, or was drawn to, a wide range of nonconformist activities, including licentious relationships, heavy drinking, drug use, and suicide attempts. These activities often assumed center stage in the stories he wrote about his fictional counterpart, a figure he called Osamu. In her excellent critical biography of Dazai, Phyllis Lyons contends that Dazai's greatest "novel" actually consists of a large number of stories and one novella written between 1933 and 1948, all of which chronicle Osamu's life from birth to death.

When he completed *No Longer Human*, Dazai finally succeeded — on his fifth attempt — in committing suicide, in the company of a female companion. Dazai's daughter, Tsushima Yūko, born to another woman in 1947, later became a major author herself (see Female Writers).

Dazai Osamu set the stage for a new breed of postwar authors by undermining confidence in the established I-novel form. Shiga Naoya had become "the god of Japanese literature" in the 1920s by writing works celebrated for the sincerity and self-confidence of the first-person narrator. Dazai also followed the conventions of the I-novel by using his personal experiences and the first-person narration typical of the style. But by casting constant doubt on the integrity of the narrator and eroding the reader's respect for the narrator's often outrageous behavior, Dazai attacked the authority of the I-novel. It was this loss of authority that encouraged the younger writers to articulate the dilemmas Japan faced during the first postwar decade.

Yasuoka Shōtarō (1920–) in some ways took up where Dazai left off, by creating real antiheroes crippled by indecision and also by introducing more voices and perspectives into his writing. Yasuoka's early works thus convey a strong sense of the psychological devastation Japan faced in the late forties and early fifties.

Yasuoka was born in the old castle town of Kōchi. His father was a veterinarian in the Japanese army, and the family moved frequently while Yasuoka was a child. Attending so many different schools made him something of a truant who compiled a modest academic record. Nonetheless, he still managed to enter Keiō University and to graduate with a degree in literature. Just as the war ended, Yasuoka contracted a severe back disorder and had to spend nearly six years in bed. After he recovered, he married and began his career as a writer.

Yasuoka won early recognition for two stories, "Gloomy Pleasures" and "Bad Company," that won him the Akutagawa Prize in 1953. They are among the five short stories that appear in a volume with his greatest work, a novella entitled *A View by the Sea*. Published to major acclaim in 1958, it is one of the most significant and extraordinary works in postwar Japanese fiction, because it portrays so effectively the long-term costs of war to the Japanese people.

After these early successes, Yasuoka began writing essays and literary biographies and even translated Alex Haley's *Roots* into Japanese. Using it for inspiration, he wrote his own version of "roots" in a novel, *Ryuritan*, still untranslated. That book captured a major prize and secured Yasuoka's place in the top rank of Japan's literary establishment.

Endō Shūsaku (1923–1996), a contemporary and close friend of Yasuoka, was probably the most cosmopolitan writer among Japan's twentieth-century novelists. This cosmopolitanism plus his enduring interest in Christianity explain why Endō is especially well known to readers in the West. He was born in Tōkyō in 1923. Two events early in his life had a lasting impact on him and his writing: Endō's mother divorced when he was still a child. She then converted to Christianity and had him baptized a Catholic. As a consequence, his personal anguish as a Japanese Christian heavily influenced most of his writing. The second lasting influence was a series of health problems that began with pleurisy during his adolescence. This prevented Endō from entering the military, so he remained in Japan during the war, working as a student conscript in aircraft factories. Later in life he had more lung problems, forcing him to undergo near-fatal surgery and eventually causing him to lose a lung. These physical and wartime experiences appear frequently in his writing.

After the war Endō graduated from Keiō University with a degree in literature. In the early 1950s he lived for three years in France, where he pursued his interests in French literature and Christianity. Later, he traveled to the United

States, Southeast Asia, and India, experiences that gave his novels an international flavor rare among Japanese novelists.

Endō's fame as a writer began in 1955 when he won the Akutagawa Prize for a short novel entitled *Shiroi hito* (untranslated). He secured his reputation with *The Sea and Poison* in 1958, which won both a cultural award and a literary prize. Many of his subsequent novels have been translated, including *Wonderful Fool* (1959), *Volcano* (1959), *Foreign Studies* (1965), *Silence* (1966), *When I Whistle* (1974), *Samurai* (1980), *Scandal* (1986), and *Deep River* (1994), his last novel. Some of his best short stories appear in a volume entitled *Stained Glass Elegies*.

Controversy surrounds Endō's writing. Some of his work has been criticized for being a bit pedestrian. But even his serious work has been faulted for its forms, themes, characters, and message. Indeed, his work is repetitive in its preoccupation with Christian dilemmas and moral issues, and his novels overflow with self-sacrificing martyrs whose humility Endō deems the proper behavior in a humane society. Despite his detractors, however, Endō held a respected position in Japanese and international letters at the time of his death in 1996.

Abe Kōbō (1924–1993) was a contemporary of Yasuoka and Endō and is best known for his novel *The Woman in the Dunes* (1962), which won lasting fame through the movie version produced by Teshigahara Hiroshi in 1963. Abe was born in Tōkyō to a family from Hokkaidō, but he was reared in Manchuria. He often spoke of his rootlessness and his lack of a sense of place, from which emerged the Kafkaesque, surreal landscape of his fiction.

Although he graduated from the University of Tōkyō in 1948 with a degree in medicine, Abe never practiced. He turned instead to a writing career, initially joining a Marxist group that published an important literary magazine. Abe proved to be too independent to remain a member for long, however. He won his first prize in 1951 for some of his early short stories, collected in *Beyond the Curve*. In the early 1960s, *The Woman in the Dunes* secured his reputation. The novel offers a brilliant but terrifying commentary on the claustrophobic quality of human existence and is a devastating critique of the narrow-minded obsessiveness of some Japanese social behavior.

Abe continued to produce novels, stories, and plays for the next three decades, but his subsequent work never reached the same level of achievement as his early writing. Other novels are *Inter Ice Age 4* (1959), *The Face of Another* (1964), *The Ruined Map* (1967), *The Box Man* (1973), *Secret Rendezvous* (1977), and *The Ark Sakura* (1984).

Mishima Yukio (1925–1970) was a prolific author who is remembered as much for his notorious death by suicide as for his writing. Born in 1925 as Hiraoka Kimitake, Mishima was reared mainly by an elderly grandmother suffering from nervous disorders. He was treated as a girl and prevented from playing with other children. His grandmother, however, did tell him stories about traditional Japan and also took him to *kabuki* performances. Mishima's obsession with literature began during these years.

Mishima was weak and often sickly as a youth. His physical problems prevented him from being drafted during the war and enabled him to complete his degree from Tōkyō University. Under heavy pressure from his family, he accepted a bureaucratic post upon graduation. His real interest lay in writing, though, so he asked Kawabata Yasunari to serve as his patron. With Kawabata's encouragement and his own discipline and dedication, Mishima quickly won recognition as a writer and left his bureaucratic position.

Mishima wrote short stories, novellas, novels, and plays, ranging from sugary romances aimed at adolescents to erudite philosophical and religious novels. His writings fall into no ready categories; indeed, he often sought to destroy old paradigms and create dramatic new ones. A selected list of his translated novels includes *Confessions of a Mask* (1949), *The Sound of Waves* (1954), *Temple of the Golden Pavilion* (1956), *After the Banquet* (1960), and the four novels in the tetralogy called *Sea of Fertility* that he completed just before his death: *Spring Snow* (1967), *Runaway Horses* (1968), *Temple of Dawn* (1969), and *Decay of the Angel* (1970). Two collections of fine short stories are *Acts of Worship* and *Death in Midsummer*.

Beginning in his thirties, Mishima's personal life took some odd turns. Although he was married and had two children, he seems to have pursued homosexual relationships as well, some of them involving young men who belonged to a quasi-military sect that he organized called the Shield Society. Mishima also developed a fanatical interest in bodybuilding. Both the military sect and the bodybuilding were associated with his growing chauvinism. All these tendencies culminated in late 1970 when he, assisted by several members of his society, entered a military headquarters in downtown Tōkyō, tied up the commander, harangued the troops, elicited jeers of rejection, and committed suicide by disembowelment.

Ōe Kenzaburō (1935–) was the second Japanese writer to win the Nobel Prize for literature, in 1994. Ōe grew up in a small village in Shikoku, and as a child during the war, he witnessed some sadistic behavior by American airmen that left him with a strong opposition to war and an attraction to left-wing politics. Like so many of his predecessors, he graduated from Tōkyō University with a degree in French literature in 1957. In the following year he won the Akutagawa Prize for his short story "The Catch," and his writing career was launched.

Ōe married in 1960, and three years later his wife gave birth to a son with severe brain damage. From then on, Ōe's life and writings were profoundly influenced by his ambivalent reaction to having a handicapped child. In 1964 he wrote the novel for which he is best known, *A Personal Matter*. Several others followed: *The Silent Cry* (1967), *Teach Us to Outgrow Our Madness* (1972), and *The Pinch Runner Memorandum* (1976). A collection of essays dealing with the atomic bomb is available as *Hiroshima Notes* (1964). Ōe's writings are vague, elusive, caustic, fantastical, and often contradictory. When he accepted the Nobel Prize, he announced that he would no longer write novels, but in two years he had broken that pledge. (Also see the sections on culture in the Historical Narrative, and for comparisons, see Female Writers.)

FEMALE WRITERS

Male writers dominated the coteries that produced literary journals, and they nearly monopolized the writing establishment, known in Japanese as the *bundan*. Accordingly, women found it exceedingly difficult to win patronage, to get their works published, and to attract a readership. Few managed to overcome such barriers before the war ended in 1945, but those who did also established a forum for women's writing, returning to prose literature the woman's voice that had been almost silent since the Heian period (794–1185).

Higuchi Ichiyō (1872–1896) was the only noted woman writer during the Meiji period. Her work consists of premodern-style poems, personal diaries, and short stories and novellas. These works are infused with a sense of longing and despair that reflect the tragic circumstances of Higuchi's own short life.

Like the figures in her stories, Higuchi was caught between two worlds, the vibrant world of the Tokugawa era and the volatile world of Meiji. Her father and mother moved to the former capital of Edo just as the old regime was falling, and her father never found a secure position. When he died in 1889, he left the family in dire straits. Higuchi, her mother, and a younger sister were constantly forced to move, finally settling in a small shop on the edge of the old entertainment district. With no major breadwinner, the family was obliged to take in sewing and to sell sundries out of the house. Jilted by suitors and responsible for caring for her mother and sister, Ichiyō was crushed by the burdens and died from tuberculosis at age twenty-four.

Higuchi is best known for her short stories and novellas which are written in almost classical Japanese but whose subjects are often the humble people living around her. Thus, like Futabatei Shimei and others, Higuchi tried to reconcile language and form in a new type of prose medium.

Her stories illustrate how social conventions trap people in a world not of their own choosing and how they respond to such constraints. Higuchi's masterpiece is a story that Robert Danly translated as "Child's Play" (see his *In the Shade of Spring Leaves*). It depicts how the demands of a hereditary society steal the innocence of three young teenagers, raise barriers between them, and finally force them into unwanted vocations. This story vividly depicts the social tensions inherent in the lives of lower-class urban dwellers near the turn of the twentieth century. Several of Higuchi's other stories describe the struggles for place and status that such families faced, conveying a more perceptive and sensitive view of late Meiji society than many of her male contemporaries were able to do.

Yosano Akiko (1878–1942) was one of the few women born between 1872 and the turn of the century who made a mark on the world of letters. She was known not as a novelist but as a poet, essayist, editor, translator, and author of children's books, from the turn of the century until her death.

Yosano was born into a merchant house in a port city near Ōsaka. She was reared to be the wife of a merchant but as a child showed a strong interest in Japanese literature. Although she acquired much of her knowledge by reading the classics in her father's library, she also received a degree from a woman's school, finishing her formal education at fourteen. For the next decade she lived and worked at home while participating in a local poetry society. Around 1900 she established a relationship with Yosano Tekkan, a poet who also edited a new literary magazine. Tekkan published some of her poetry and in 1901 married her after divorcing his second wife. By the time he died in 1935, Akiko had given birth to twelve children, eleven of whom survived. Much of her life was devoted to caring for her large family.

Despite such domestic burdens, Yosano participated in a wide range of activities. She was a prolific composer of Japanese-style verse; in the 1920s she wrote constantly on women's issues for journals and newspapers; and she published children's stories. She also produced three editions of *The Tale of Genji* in modern Japanese. Her most famous collection of verse, *Tangled Hair* (1901), is available in English translation. The 1920s were years of openness and cultural experimentation in Japan, and Yosano both exploited that openness and advanced it.

Uno Chiyo (1897–1996) was one of the most talented and versatile women in twentieth-century Japan. Born in a small town in western Japan, Uno lost her mother when she was only two. Her father, who remarried shortly after, died when she was sixteen. From then on she lived a free and impulsive life, marrying or living with at least five men, divorcing three times, and having numerous affairs. Like the women who appear in her stories, she was a twenties-style "modern girl," or *moga* in Japanese. Nonetheless, she joined the women's chapter of the Japanese Literature Patriotic Association and assisted in the war effort during the 1940s. After the war, she started a new magazine, managed businesses, designed kimono, wrote essays and stories, and continued to marry and divorce. When she was in her early nineties, the Japanese government recognized her as a Person of Cultural Merit.

Uno wrote prolifically in several genres. Her best-known work is *Confessions of Love* (1935), about the amorous affairs of a young painter and three young women representative of the hedonistic, erotic, liberated world of urban, mostly upper-class, Tōkyō in the 1920s. *Ohan* (1957), available under that title in English translation, is another tale of love that involves a man and two women vying for his affections. Set in an earlier time and in the lower-class milieu of a rural town, it talks about the morality of love and is reminiscent of tales from the Tokugawa era. Uno's finest essay is "The Puppet Maker" (1942), a revised account, done in what she called *kikigaki* (hear-write) style, of a series of interviews with an elderly *bunraku* puppet maker from Tokushima. Rebecca Copeland's translation of this essay beautifully describes this vanishing segment of plebian society.

Hayashi Fumiko (1903–1951), like Higuchi Ichiyō, drew her literary material from surroundings where she was forced to eke out a living. Hayashi was born to the daughter of a small merchant and her fourth husband, a peddler. The marriage soon disintegrated and Hayashi had to accompany her mother and a new husband, another peddler, on their itinerant journeys. Between the ages of seven and thirteen, she lived in many different places, receiving only a haphazard education. In 1922, however, she managed to complete the curriculum of a higher girls' school while working at night in a factory. After graduating, she left for Tōkyō, where she was jilted by the young man she had intended to marry. This experience left her with a permanently negative view of men and forced her to support herself in any way she could. For the next several years, she survived by working as a waitress, cashier, office clerk, and barmaid.

Hayashi's career as a writer began in 1928 with the instant success of *Vagabond's Song*, published in book form in 1930. Based on a diary she had been keeping, with the addition of fictional elements, *Vagabond's Song* is a strongly autobiographical account of the travails of a wandering mother and her young child. It was one of the first works by a woman to reveal the plight of lower-class women striving to make a living outside the security of family, home, and respectability. In the open atmosphere of the 1920s, it attracted a large, appreciative audience.

Some of Hayashi's best writing appeared after the war, in the novel *Floating Clouds* (1951) and in such short stories as "Late Chrysanthemums," "Shitamachi" (Downtown), and "Narcissus" (all published in 1949). Many of her works reveal an acerbic attitude toward men and children, and they portray a dismal world in which women on the fringes of society are destined to die usually alone and in despair. Such images struck a responsive chord in a society devastated by years of war and by defeat.

Sata Ineko (1904–) is a representative figure from the proletarian literary movement that flourished during the 1920s and 1930s. She continued to write long after the war, so the eighteen volumes of her collected works span the half-century between the 1920s and 1970s.

In contrast with other proletarian writers, such as Miyamoto Yuriko, Sata was herself a product of Japan's lower classes. Born to unmarried parents in their teens, Sata lost her mother when she was only seven. Although her father later married, he was never able to provide her with a warm home or a stable family life. At an early age Sata was forced to work at a number of demanding, low-paying jobs, and from these experiences came the material for her early writing. Her first publication was a short story, "From the Caramel Factory" (1929), still untranslated. Depicting the poverty-stricken life of a thirteen-year-old girl, it established Sata's reputation as a commentator on the tensions between self and community, choice and resignation, and freedom and obligation.

Sata's adult years were marked by unstable marriages and a rocky association with left-wing movements, especially in the 1930s and 1940s. She used these experiences to inform her writing in the postwar era, when she often reflected on the heavy costs in human feeling that loyalty to a party exacted. The work of her late years shows her maturity, as revealed in the short story "The Inn of the Dancing Snow." In this story and others, she reflects on the way in which time and memory continually reshape one's place in the world.

Kōda Aya (1904–1990) had a famous father, the writer and scholar Kōda Rohan (1867–1947), who played a powerful role in shaping her life. The Kōda family was often an unhappy one. When still a young child, Aya lost her mother and had to spend years in the company of a cold, distant stepmother who was often sickly and at odds with Aya's father. Aya thus had to care for her father and do all the cooking and cleaning. This prevented her from obtaining a college education and even, it seems, from pursuing a program of reading on her own. Aya married in 1928 and gave birth to a daughter, but her husband failed at his business and the marriage ended in 1938. She then returned to her now ailing and still demanding father, caring for him until his death in 1947.

Only in that year did Kōda Aya's career as a writer begin. Her first published works were essays about her family's life, but gradually she began to produce novels and short stories, four of which are translated in Alan Tansman's *The Writings of Kōda Aya* (1993). Her work has provoked sharply differing reactions by critics, both Japanese and American and male and female. Her subjects are often downtrodden women who seem at first to be dutiful wives and daughters, serving the needs of either dependent or overbearing men. A closer reading reveals, however, strong, inventive women being crushed by social obligation. Whether one views Kōda's figures as exemplars of virtue or victims of oppression, they offer rich material for reflection.

Enchi Fumiko (1905–1986) was the daughter of Ueda Mannen (Kazutoshi), an authority on the Japanese language and a professor at Tōkyō Imperial University. Overflowing with books, Enchi's home was a private library where she read about Japanese literature, religion, and history and became a self-taught prodigy. Although she attended Japan Women's University for four years, she never obtained a degree. Enchi married at twenty-four and had a daughter two years later. She seems to have had a distant relationship with her husband, however, and for years carried on an affair with another man. Always plagued by a frail constitution, she twice suffered severe bouts with cancer, battled tuberculosis, and lost her eyesight in her final years. All these experiences found their way into her writing.

Enchi left a large body of works that filled nearly twenty volumes at her death. One of her major projects was a translation of *The Tale of Genji*. She also wrote many plays, numerous short stories, and a half-dozen major novels. Two of her novels have been translated, *The Waiting Years* (1957) and *Masks* (1958), as have some of her short stories. One of the most artful is "A Bond for Two Lifetimes— Gleanings." Enchi exploits her knowledge of classical Japanese literature, Japanese religious beliefs, and women's lives to explore sexual conceptions, identities, and relationships in the contemporary world. Conveying an often despairing view of women and their oppression, she nonetheless manages to bestow a perverse influence on her heroines, who often win their revenge in the end.

Nearly all the preceding five women, born at the turn of the century, were able to establish themselves as writers before Japan's long experience with war began and to build on their reputations after the war. But just as the war hampered the ability of male authors to establish their reputations in the 1930s and the early 1940s (see Male Writers), it also posed the same complications for female writers.

Setouchi Harumi (1922–) is one of the few women born in the 1910s and 1920s to have won acclaim as a writer mainly during the postwar era. The daughter of a wealthy merchant from Shikoku, Setouchi developed a deep interest during her childhood in Heian literature and in the commoner prose and puppet plays of the Tokugawa era. After receiving a degree in Japanese literature from Tōkyō Women's College in 1943, she married a professor and moved to China. She and her husband, along with a young daughter, returned to Japan in 1947. Shortly afterward, Setouchi divorced her husband, abandoned her daughter, and took up with a younger man.

Even amid the social chaos of the early postwar period, this kind of behavior by a wife and mother was scandalous. Ever since, Setouchi has exploited the sensational qualities of her life to produce a highly autobiographical prose describing adulterous men, their mistresses, independent women, and their search for love. Much to the surprise of her large audience, in 1973 Setouchi took religious orders at a Buddhist temple in Kyōto, where she has continued to write stories and novels. "The End of Summer," "Lingering Affection," and "Pheasant," all published in 1949, are among her works available in English.

One of the most diverse and talented groups of writers in twentieth-century Japan consists of women who were of school age during the war. Surprisingly, however, the war itself seldom appears as a subject in their writing. Rather, it may have exerted its influence by causing them to look at the world in new and unconventional ways. Indeed, the war does often seem to lurk in the background of their stories and may have stimulated these writers to explore such facets of the human condition as family life, medical problems, the plight of the elderly, and the role of witches.

Mukoda Kuniko (1929–1981) was a scriptwriter for radio and television, an essayist and critic, and a writer of short stories and novellas. Her father, of humble origins, was an executive in an insurance company. Because his job required frequent transfers, Mukoda attended schools in several parts of Japan before finally settling in Tōkyō. Upset by their unstable lives, she and her siblings purposely avoided attachments to the places where they lived. In fact, Mukoda herself never even married. Both the need to care for her father until 1964 and a bout with cancer ensured a life as a single woman.

After graduating from a Tōkyō women's college in 1950, Mukoda worked in radio and television and wrote essays for popular magazines. Her career as a novelist began in 1975, when she was in her forties. Her fictional treatment of her family's history attracted a large following, and her early short stories won a prize in 1981. She was just hitting her stride as a writer when she died in a plane crash.

Critics have denigrated Mukoda's work for being "popular," oriented toward a mass audience, and indeed it is. However, her short stories, such as those in *The Name of the Flower*, can be admired for their gritty, realistic images of Japanese society during the advent of affluence in the 1970s. Unlike many female writers, Mukoda devoted much attention to males, even going so far as to write from the masculine perspective and to discuss male psychology. She is especially skillful at depicting the cheerless destiny of salary men who live at or below the margins of success in Japan's competitive business world. Her women are often outspoken, assertive, and venturesome. They expect the worse and often experience it. But they seem more resilient and less self-destructive than the men and better able to adapt. In this respect, Mukoda's female characters represent the transition between those of her immediate predecessors and the liberated, manipulative women whom one encounters in the writing of the even younger female authors born after 1945.

Ōba Minako (1930–) is a novelist and short story writer whose work is noted for its use of international settings and its preoccupation with the fantastic. Ōba lived an unsettled life during the war, as her father was a physician in the Japanese navy and his job required frequent moves. A bright child and a voracious reader, Ōba was seldom challenged by her formal studies but graduated from Tsuda Women's College in Tōkyō. In 1955 she married a man she had met during her college years. Four years later they set out on the adventure that changed her life and stimulated her career.

Accompanying her husband to his new job in Alaska, Ōba spent the next eleven years living in the United States, studying at American universities, and traveling widely. Combined with her early exposure to myths and fairy tales, these opportunities nourished many of her best-known works: "The Three Crabs" (1967), "The Pale Fox" (1973), "The Smile of a Mountain Witch" (1976), and "Candlefish" (1986). Ōba employs myth and legend in a contemporary setting to create a netherworld in which she explores the texture and durability of male-female relationships. Her stories and novels have won numerous prestigious awards, and her collected works were published in 1991.

Ariyoshi Sawako (1931–1984) was a prominent author whose novels about health and social issues won her literary fame and even influenced national policy. Like Mukoda and Ōba, Ariyoshi found her life strongly influenced by the requirements for mobility during the war. Her father was a bank employee whose prominent family hailed from Wakayama, a city south of Ōsaka. When she was four, her father was transferred to Java, where the family lived between 1935 and 1940. Ariyoshi returned to Tōkyō in 1940 and completed a degree in English literature at Tōkyō Christian Women's University in 1952. In the immediate postwar period, she developed a deep interest in *kabuki* theater and took a position as a secretary to a *kabuki* dancer. She credits this interest with saving her from the despair of the early postwar years.

Ariyoshi suffered from malaria, chronic insomnia, and other health problems for nearly two decades before her death at fifty-three. Owing perhaps to these problems, much of her writing deals with the medical community and health issues. Her most famous novel, *The Twilight Years* (1972), is a moving depiction of a daughter-in-law forced to sacrifice herself to caring for a dying father-in-law. The book attracted a huge audience, brought political attention to problems of the elderly, and forced the government to take action. *The River Ki* (1959) and *The Doctor's Wife* (1966) have also been translated, along with a short story, "Tomoshibi" (1961). At her death Ariyoshi had written many novels and stories, as well as a number of plays that she had also directed. She had also won several literary awards.

Tomioka Taeko (1935–) began her career in the 1960s as a poet, turned to short stories and novels in the 1970s, and since then has produced screenplays, stage plays, radio scripts, essays, biographies, autobiographies, and even an album on which she sings some of her poems. Tomioka's best short stories draw on her early life as the daughter of a scrap dealer in Ōsaka. Her father abandoned the family when she was ten, but he continued to provide for her in some ways. While growing up, she developed an interest in *bunraku* and *kabuki* through an uncle who was a stage carpenter in Kyōto. After finishing a degree in English literature at the Ōsaka Women's College in 1958, she taught briefly before moving to Tōkyō. Married in 1969, she spent some time living in the United States before she produced her first story. "Facing the Hills They Stand" was published in 1971 to instant, and justifiable, acclaim. It is admired for its realistic image of life in the lower reaches of urban society during the first half of this century. Tomioka's prize-winning novella, *Family in Hell*, appeared in 1974. Her stories have a poetic quality that is both dreamlike and allusive, and they have been praised for their aesthetic sensibility and social acuity. Few of them, however, are available in English.

The cohort of women writers born and reared after the war has produced some of Japan's most fascinating and controversial writing. Their work reflects the greater freedom they enjoy in Japanese society, even though that freedom is by no means complete, as their writing testifies.

Tsushima Yūko (1947–), the daughter of Dazai Osamu, shares her father's ability to transform life into art. But she also has unique personal talents that make her one of the most astute observers of contemporary Japanese society and its changing mores.

Tsushima had already won acclaim for her writing before she graduated from college. Shortly afterward, she married and gave birth to a daughter. She divorced in 1976 and had a son out of wedlock in the same year. Her brother died when he was only fifteen, and her son died suddenly at the age of nine, events that heightened the pessimism and poignancy of her work.

Tsushima is best known for her short stories, eight of which appear in *The Shooting Gallery*. Two of her novels have also been translated, *Child of Fortune* (1978) and *Woman Running in the Mountains* (1980). On the surface, she seems to be writing about the problems of young women without husbands struggling to raise children in a society in which two-parent (if not fully functional) families are the norm. However, her work transcends these domestic issues to offer an acute vision of Japanese society as a whole. She is especially adept at portraying the culturally stifling and socially frenetic lives of Japanese men. The women in her works are aggressive, transgressive, progressive, and often — but not always — active agents of their own destinies.

Yamada Eimi (Amy) (1959–) has explored the life of the free woman in a radical and ostentatious way, as the titles of some of her translated works suggest: "When a Man Loves a Woman" (1987), "Kneel Down and Lick My Feet" (1988), "X-Rated Blanket" (1988), and *Trash* (1991). Yamada lived in many different places before her family settled near Tōkyō during her high school years. She entered the literature department at Meiji University but left during her third year to pursue a career as a cartoonist. Bored by this work, she found employment as a bar hostess, nude model, and "queen" at a sex club in Tōkyō. For several years, she also lived with a divorced African American soldier and his son. Yamada's first novel, *Bedtime Eyes* (1985), still untranslated, draws heavily on these experiences, as do her short stories. Her female figures are unmarried women driven by apparently insatiable sexual desires who fantasize about men and try to control them. Although Yamada's work caters to a broad audience in an affluent, media-oriented culture, it has also won critical approval and major prizes.

Yoshimoto Banana (1964–) is another young female writer who attracted a massive following beginning in the 1980s with the publication of her novella *Kitchen* (1989). An innocent romance that depicts the isolation and distress of two orphans, *Kitchen* attracted a wide audience, especially young women. Yoshimoto's talent is to sketch a society in which personal relations are weak to nonexistent, families are personal liabilities, and work and school are passing annoyances. She parodies Japanese customs in a way that highlights the anxieties of individuals striving to connect and find themselves in an anchorless world. Three other books have been translated: *NP* (1990), *Lizard* (1993), and *Amrita* (1994). (Also see the sections on culture in the Historical Narrative, and for comparisons, see Male Writers.)

PART III

Resource Guide

The Resource Guide lists three types of resources: printed, visual, and electronic. The first section contains an annotated bibliography of two hundred books, divided into five categories: General Works, Politics, Economics, Society, and Culture (the last four categories are the same as those in the Historical Narrative). The second section contains twenty-three annotated entries for visual resources, and the third section lists twenty electronic resources.

PRINTED RESOURCES

I selected printed resources on the basis of several criteria. First, I chose books spanning the period from 1850 to the late 1990s. I next picked the most authoritative works available for that period and usually the most recent works. In some cases, however, I cited books from the 1950s and 1960s, because they either have not been superseded in every respect or they remain the only reliable sources available in English.

General Works

SYNTHESES

Allinson, Gary D. *Japan's Postwar History*. Ithaca, N.Y.: Cornell University Press, 1997. (A balanced and integrated analysis of political, social, and economic history since 1932, showing the tensions accompanying Japan's ascent to affluence.)

Beasley, William G. *The Rise of Modern Japan*. 2d ed. New York: St. Martin's Press, 1993. (A detailed survey emphasizing domestic politics and foreign relations in the late 1800s.)

Gordon, Andrew, ed. *Postwar Japan as History*. Berkeley and Los Angeles: University of California Press, 1993. (Eighteen essays offering politically and topically wide-ranging interpretations of change in Japan from 1945 to 1990.)

Pyle, Kenneth. *The Making of Modern Japan*. 2d ed. Lexington, Mass.: Heath, 1995. (A concise history of Japan since 1600, stressing political, intellectual, and diplomatic themes since the 1870s.)

ENCYCLOPEDIAS

Huffman, James L., ed. *Modern Japan: An Encyclopedia of History, Culture, and Nationalism*. Hamden, Conn.: Garland, 1997. (A more current and more contemporary, one-volume supplement to the next entry.)

Itasaka, Gen, ed. *The Kodansha Encyclopedia of Japan*. 9 vols. Tokyo: Kodansha International, 1983. (The most detailed and comprehensive reference on all aspects of Japan and its history available in English.)

ATLAS

Editorial Department, Teikoku shoin. *Teikoku's Complete Atlas of Japan*. Tokyo: Teikoku shoin, 1996. (Contains nearly five thousand place-names and some fifty maps.)

DICTIONARIES

Hunter, Janet, comp. *Concise Dictionary of Modern Japanese History*. Berkeley and Los Angeles: University of California Press, 1984. (Besides 650 entries for political, social, and economic history, also includes many appendices and source citations.)

Iwao, Seiichi, ed. *Biographical Dictionary of Japanese History*. Trans. Burton Watson. Tokyo: Kodansha International, 1978. (About half the entries are for persons active after 1850.)

Lewell, John. *Modern Japanese Novelists: A Biographical Dictionary*. Tokyo: Kodansha International, 1993. (Based on English-language sources, contains biographical sketches, lists of translated works, and critical studies of fifty-seven authors.)

Mulhern, Chieko I., ed. *Japanese Women Writers: A Bio-Critical Sourcebook*. Westport, Conn.: Greenwood Press, 1994. (Biographies, critiques, and lists of works of fifty-eight women writers.)

BIBLIOGRAPHIES

Bibliography of Asian Studies. (Published annually since 1970 by the Association for Asian Studies, Ann Arbor, Mich. A list of books and articles in English on all fields of Japanese studies. Not annotated.)

Shulman, Frank J. *Japan*. Oxford: Clio Press, 1989. (The best, most authoritative, and most comprehensive single-volume guide to books on all fields of Japanese studies. Excellent annotations and useful cross-references.)

NEWSPAPERS

Japan Times. (Japan's main English-language daily newspaper. Published in Tokyo.)

Asahi Evening News. (An abbreviated, English-language version of one of Japan's most distinguished daily newspapers.)

PERIODICALS

Japan Echo (Tokyo). (Condensed translations of essays by prominent Japanese commentators that originally appeared in major Japanese publications.)

Japan Quarterly. (Published four times a year in Tokyo by the *Asahi shimbun*. Essays usually written by Japanese commentators on a wide variety of topics.)

Journal of Asian Studies. (Published four times each year by the Association for Asian Studies, Ann Arbor, Mich. Covers all of Asia and usually includes one or two scholarly articles on Japan, as well as numerous reviews of books about all aspects of Japan, in all periods.)

Journal of Japanese Studies. (Published twice a year by the Society for Japanese Studies, University of Washington, Seattle. Six to ten articles on Japan in each issue plus many reviews of books about Japan in all periods and disciplines.)

AUTOBIOGRAPHIES

Fukuzawa, Yukichi. *The Autobiography of Fukuzawa Yukichi*. Trans. Eiichi Kiyooka. New York: Schocken Books, 1972. (A somewhat self-serving depiction of Fukuzawa's life as the founder of Keiō Gijuku University and a major intellectual figure after the 1850s.)

Ishimoto, Shidzue. *Facing Two Ways: The Story of My Life*. Ed. Barbara Molony. Stanford, Calif.: Stanford University Press, 1984. (Ishimoto's early life before 1935 as the daughter of a noble family and the wife of a manager of the Miike Mines of Mitsui, whom she later divorced to marry a socialist politician.)

Katsu, Kokichi. *Musui's Story: The Autobiography of a Tokugawa Samurai*. Trans. Teruko Craig. Tucson: University of Arizona Press, 1988. (A candid autobiography by a low-ranking samurai in Edo illustrating how difficult life was for such men at the end of the Tokugawa era.)

Kuroyanagi, Tetsuko. *Totto-chan: The Little Girl at the Window*. Tokyo: Kodansha International, 1982. (A best-seller: a reminiscence by a famous television personality of her years as a student at a progressive elementary school between 1937 and 1945.)

Shibusawa, Eiichi. *The Autobiography of Shibusawa Eiichi: From Peasant to Entrepreneur*. Trans. Teruko Craig. Tokyo: University of Tokyo Press, 1994. (About a major figure in the business community for more than four decades after the Meiji Restoration, from 1840 to 1873.)

Tanizaki, Jun'ichirō. *Childhood Years: A Memoir*. Trans. Paul McCarthy. Tokyo: Kodansha International, 1988. (A famous novelist's early years in a merchant quarter of downtown Tokyo around the turn of the century.)

ACCOUNTS BY FOREIGN OBSERVERS

Alcock, Rutherford. *The Capital of the Tycoon: A Narrative of a Three Years' Residence in Japan.* 2 vols. London: Longman, Green, 1863. (Observations of Japan between 1859 and 1862 by Britain's first minister to Japan.)

Allen, G. C. *Appointment in Japan: Memories of Sixty Years.* London: Athlone Press, 1983. (Beginning with his teaching stint at a commercial high school in Nagoya in the early 1920s, the memoirs of the British economist Allen about his lifelong interest in Japan.)

Bird, Isabella L. *Unbeaten Tracks in Japan: An Account of Travels on Horseback in the Interior Including Visits to the Aborigines of Yezo and the Shrines of Nikko and Ise.* 2 vols. New York: Putnam, 1881. (A traveler's observations on her journeys in the 1870s.)

Emmerson, John K. *The Japanese Thread: A Life in the U.S. Foreign Service.* New York: Holt, Rinehart & Winston, 1978. (Emmerson's perceptions of Japan and its relations with the United States, based on service from the 1940s through the 1960s.)

Riesman, David. *Conversations in Japan.* New York: Basic Books, 1967. (The experience of a long-time sociologist at Harvard as a visitor to Tōkyō in the 1960s.)

von Baelz, Erwin O. E. *Awakening Japan: The Diary of a German Doctor.* Ed. Toku Baelz. New York: Viking, 1932. (The memoirs of a German physician who cared for the imperial family and taught at Tōkyō Imperial University between 1876 and 1905.)

Politics

TRANSITIONS

Beasley, William G. *The Meiji Restoration.* Stanford, Calif.: Stanford University Press, 1972. (A standard source on the Restoration emphasizing foreign relations and defining the event as a national revolution.)

Finn, Richard. *Winners in Peace: MacArthur, Yoshida, and Postwar Japan.* Berkeley and Los Angeles: University of California Press, 1992. (An assessment of the Occupation between 1945 and 1952 by a retired foreign service officer with long experience in Japan.)

Kawai, Kazuo. *Japan's American Interlude.* Chicago: University of Chicago Press, 1960. (One of the earliest systematic overviews of the Occupation, by a former journalist in Japan.)

Morley, James W., ed. *Dilemmas of Growth in Prewar Japan.* Princeton, N.J.: Princeton University Press, 1971. (Critical perspectives on the political economy of Japan in the decades before war.)

Najita, Tetsuo, and J. Victor Koschmann, eds. *Conflict in Modern Japanese History.* Princeton, N.J.: Princeton University Press, 1982. (Essays that analyze popular political action during two critical transitions, one around 1868 and the other around 1918.)

BIOGRAPHIES

Dower, John W. *Empire and Aftermath: Yoshida Shigeru and the Japanese Experience, 1878–1954*. Cambridge, Mass.: Council on East Asian Studies, Harvard University, 1979. (A political biography of an early postwar prime minister, plus Japan's prewar diplomacy and the postwar Occupation.)

Hackett, Roger F. *Yamagata Aritomo in the Rise of Modern Japan, 1838–1922*. Cambridge, Mass.: Harvard University Press, 1971. (The life and influence of a man at the center of Japanese politics from 1868 to 1922.)

Large, Stephen S. *Emperor Hirohito and Showa Japan: A Political Biography*. London: Routledge, 1992. (Both a biography of the Shōwa emperor and a political history of the years from 1921 through 1989.)

——. *Emperors of the Rising Sun: Three Biographies*. Tokyo: Kodansha International, 1997. (Short but highly informative sketches of the personal lives and political activities of the Meiji, Taishō, and Shōwa emperors between 1867 and 1989.)

Oka, Yoshitake. *Five Political Leaders of Modern Japan: Ito Hirobumi, Okuma Shigenobu, Hara Takashi, Inukai Tsuyoshi, and Saionji Kinmochi*. Trans. Andrew Frasier and Patricia Murray. Tokyo: University of Tokyo Press, 1986. (Anecdotal interpretations of five important personalities and their political accomplishments between the 1860s and 1940s.)

LAW AND THE CONSTITUTION

Akita, George. *Foundations of Constitutional Government in Modern Japan, 1868–1900*. Cambridge, Mass.: Harvard University Press, 1967. (Still the authoritative account of the framing of the Meiji constitution.)

Haley, John O. *Authority Without Power: Law and the Japanese Paradox*. New York: Oxford University Press, 1991. (An intriguing but controversial discussion of the relationships among law, authority, and power.)

Upham, Frank K. *Law and Social Change in Postwar Japan*. Cambridge, Mass.: Harvard University Press, 1987. (Interpretation of Japanese law regarding women, environmental protestors, industrial firms, and minority groups.)

POLITICAL PARTIES

Duus, Peter. *Party Rivalry and Political Change in Taisho Japan*. Cambridge, Mass.: Harvard University Press, 1968. (Assesses the powers of the established parties during the heyday of parliamentary politics in the 1920s.)

Fukui, Haruhiro. *Party in Power: The Japanese Liberal-Democrats and Policy-Making*. Berkeley and Los Angeles: University of California Press, 1970. (The conservative party's early years.)

Najita, Tetsuo. *Hara Kei in the Politics of Compromise, 1905–1915*. Cambridge, Mass.: Harvard University Press, 1967. (Pork-barrel politics as related to the powers of Hara Kei and the parties.)

Scalapino, Robert A. *Democracy and the Party Movement in Prewar Japan.* Berkeley and Los Angeles: University of California Press, 1962. (A still worthwhile seminal study, despite its age and the criticism it has suffered.)

BUREAUCRACY

Koh, B. C. *Japan's Administrative Elite.* Berkeley and Los Angeles: University of California Press, 1989. (An update of Kubota's earlier study.)

Kubota, Akira. *Higher Civil Servants in Postwar Japan.* Princeton, N.J.: Princeton University Press, 1969. (Patterns of organization, recruitment, and promotion in the bureaucracy in the early postwar period.)

Spaulding, Robert M. *Imperial Japan's Higher Civil Service Examinations.* Princeton, N.J.: Princeton University Press, 1967. (The authoritative account of the founding of the modern system of bureaucratic recruitment.)

ELECTORAL BEHAVIOR

Allinson, Gary D. *Suburban Tokyo: A Comparative Study in Politics and Social Change.* Berkeley and Los Angeles: University of California Press, 1979. (How suburban development between the 1920s and 1970s altered social structure and political behavior in two communities, Musashino and Fuchū, located to the west of downtown Tōkyō.)

Flanagan, Scott C., et al. *The Japanese Voter.* New Haven, Conn.: Yale University Press, 1991. (Essays relying heavily on voter surveys but the most detailed analysis of postwar electoral behavior.)

Gordon, Andrew. *Labor and Imperial Democracy in Prewar Japan.* Berkeley and Los Angeles: University of California Press, 1991. (Using evidence from a working-class district in Tōkyō between about 1900 and 1940, a provocative interpretation of popular politics and its affinities with fascism.)

Jain, Purnendra, and Takashi Inoguchi, eds. *Japanese Politics Today: Beyond Karaoke Democracy?* New York: St. Martin's Press, 1997. (Essays by a dozen Japanese, American, Australian, and English specialists on electoral politics and policymaking depicting the chaotic political environment of the 1990s.)

Steiner, Kurt, Ellis S. Krauss, and Scott C. Flanagan, eds. *Political Opposition and Local Politics in Japan.* Princeton, N.J.: Princeton University Press, 1980. (The electoral fortunes and political powers of the opposition parties during their heyday in the 1970s.)

POLICYMAKING

Allinson, Gary D., and Yasunori Sone, eds. *Political Dynamics in Contemporary Japan.* Ithaca, N.Y.: Cornell University Press, 1993. (Articles by six Japanese and six American scholars on how a more competitive and negotiated mode of politics arose after 1970, using case studies of finance, land policy, retail practices, and union reorganization.)

Garon, Sheldon. *The State and Labor in Modern Japan*. Berkeley and Los Angeles: University of California Press, 1987. (An analysis of the role of bureaucrats in labor policymaking from the 1910s to the 1950s.)

Hayao, Kenji. *The Japanese Prime Minister and Public Policy*. Pittsburgh: University of Pittsburgh Press, 1993. (The only systematic study of the role of the executive in postwar politics.)

Schwartz, Frank J. *Advice and Consent: The Politics of Consultation in Japan*. Cambridge: Cambridge University Press, 1998. (A perceptive analysis of recent policy processes, with case studies of finance, agriculture, and labor.)

Titus, David A. *Palace and Politics in Prewar Japan*. New York: Columbia University Press, 1974. (A reconstruction of the imperial politics of the prewar era.)

LOCAL GOVERNMENT

Steiner, Kurt. *Local Government in Japan*. Stanford, Calif.: Stanford University Press, 1965. (A description and analysis of local government between the 1870s and 1960s.)

DIPLOMACY

Barnhart, Michael. *Japan and the World Since 1868*. London: Arnold, 1995. (The most recent and comprehensive description of Japan's foreign relations in the modern era.)

Iriye, Akira. *Across the Pacific: An Inner History of American–East Asian Relations*. New York: Harcourt Brace & World, 1967. (A broad survey of American-Japanese relations by one of the leading authorities on the subject.)

Katzenstein, Peter J., and Takashi Shiraishi, eds. *Network Power: Japan and Asia*. Ithaca, N.Y.: Cornell University Press, 1997. (Eleven essays offering a comprehensive overview of Japan's relations with East and Southeast Asia during the twentieth century.)

Kennedy, Malcolm D. *The Estrangement of Great Britain and Japan, 1917–1935*. Berkeley and Los Angeles: University of California Press, 1969. (An analysis of a key relationship during a critical juncture, by a British officer with firsthand experience.)

IMPERIALISM

Beasley, William G. *Japanese Imperialism, 1894–1945*. Oxford: Clarendon Press, 1987. (A comprehensive, authoritative overview of Japan's colonial ventures in Asia during the half-century of its imperialism.)

McCormack, Gavan. *Chang Tso-lin in Northeast China, 1911–1928: China, Japan, and the Manchurian Idea*. Stanford, Calif.: Stanford University Press, 1977. (An analysis of Japanese encroachment on Chinese sovereignty.)

Morley, James W. *The Japanese Thrust into Siberia, 1918*. New York: Columbia University Press, 1957. (The nature of Japanese expansionism and the aggressiveness of the army well before the 1930s.)

Young, Louise. *Japan's Total Empire: Manchuria and the Culture of Wartime Imperialism*. Berkeley and Los Angeles: University of California Press, 1998. (How an empire in Manchuria shaped, and was shaped by, actions of the army, bureaucracy, political elites, intellectuals, and peasant emigrants.)

WAR AND THE MILITARY

Butow, Robert J. C. *Tojo and the Coming of the War*. Princeton, N.J.: Princeton University Press, 1961. (The decision-making process that led to war in 1941 against the United States, largely based on archives of the International Military Tribunal for the Far East.)

Committee for the Compilation of Materials on Damage Caused by the Atomic Bombs in Hiroshima and Nagasaki, comp. *Hiroshima and Nagasaki: The Physical, Medical, and Social Effects of the Atomic Bombings*. New York: Basic Books, 1981. (In detailed, clinical prose, the physical and psychological effects of the atomic bombs.)

Cook, Haruko Taya, and Theodore F. Cook. *Japan at War: An Oral History*. New York: New Press, 1992. (Mainly transcripts of interviews with survivors of the Pacific War, a study of the war's conduct and effects plus short summaries of the course of war.)

Dower, John W. *War Without Mercy: Race and Power in the Pacific War*. New York: Pantheon, 1986. (The differing perceptions of Americans and Japanese during the 1940s, based on visual and journalistic evidence.)

Hogan, Michael J., ed. *Hiroshima in History and Memory*. Cambridge: Cambridge University Press, 1996. (A summary by one Japanese and six American scholars of the latest assessments of the dropping of the atomic bomb and its long-term effects.)

Humphreys, Leonard A. *The Way of the Heavenly Sword: The Japanese Army in the 1920's*. Stanford, Calif.: Stanford University Press, 1995. (An analysis of the development of the modern Japanese army and its political role from 1868 to 1919 and during the 1920s.)

Economics

OVERVIEWS

Allen, G. C. *A Short Economic History of Japan*. Rev. ed. London: Allen & Unwin, 1972. (An analysis of Japan's modern economic history by a British economic historian.)

Cohen, Jerome B. *Japan's Economy in War and Reconstruction*. Minneapolis: University of Minnesota Press, 1949. (A description and analysis of Japan's economy during a critical and still poorly studied decade, based on materials now very hard to find.)

Lincoln, Edward J. *Japan: Facing Economic Maturity*. Washington, D.C.: Brookings Institution, 1988. (A shrewd, balanced analysis of Japan's economic dilemmas after the oil crises of the 1970s.)

Lockwood, William W. *The Economic Development of Japan: Growth and Structural Change, 1868–1938*. Rev. ed. Princeton, N.J.: Princeton University Press, 1968. (An early work but still the broadest and most detailed account of developments between 1868 and the 1930s.)

Ohkawa, Kazushi, and Henry Rosovsky. *Japanese Economic Growth: Trend Acceleration in the Twentieth Century*. Stanford, Calif.: Stanford University Press, 1973. (An early and still authoritative study of the rapid growth of Japan's economy after the 1880s.)

Patrick, Hugh. ed. *Japanese Industrialization and Its Social Consequences*. Berkeley and Los Angeles: University of California Press, 1976. (Essays by sixteen American and Japanese scholars on lifestyle, occupational change, poverty, inequality, and welfare in Japan after 1868.)

Yamamura, Kozo, ed. *The Economic Emergence of Modern Japan*. Cambridge: Cambridge University Press, 1997. (Essays by economists from Japan, Australia, and the United States; especially good on economic developments during the nineteenth century.)

AGRICULTURE

Beardsley, Richard K., John W. Hall, and Robert E. Ward, eds. *Village Japan*. Chicago: University of Chicago Press, 1959. (A collective study of all aspects of life in an agricultural village in western Japan around 1950.)

Dore, Ronald P. *Land Reform in Japan*. Oxford: Oxford University Press, 1959. (A detailed analysis of the postwar land reform and its effects in historical context.)

Francks, Penelope. *Technology and Agricultural Development in Prewar Japan*. New Haven, Conn.: Yale University Press, 1984. (An informative account of electrification, water control, and agrarian development.)

Nakamura, James. *Agricultural Production and the Economic Development of Japan, 1873–1922*. Princeton, N.J.: Princeton University Press, 1963. (A book that sparked a long-running controversy over growth rates and processes of agrarian development.)

Pratt, Edward. *Japan's Protoindustrial Elite: The Economic Foundations of the Gono, 1750–1900*. Cambridge, Mass.: Council on East Asian Studies, Harvard University, 1999. (The operations, powers, and fortunes of wealthy rural households across 150 years of turbulent change.)

Waswo, Ann. *Japanese Landlords: The Decline of a Rural Elite*. Berkeley and Los Angeles: University of California Press, 1977. (An analysis of not just landlords but also tenant relations and agricultural change during seven decades after 1868.)

FIRMS AND ENTERPRISES

Clark, Rodney. *The Japanese Company*. New Haven, Conn.: Yale University Press, 1979. (The operations of a small manufacturing firm in the broader context of the Japanese system of corporate relations.)

Cusumano, Michael A. *The Japanese Automobile Industry: Technology and Management at Nissan and Toyota*. Cambridge, Mass.: Council on East Asian Studies, Harvard University, 1985. (The evolution of the two leading firms in one of the postwar era's most important industries.)

Fruin, W. Mark. *The Japanese Enterprise System: Competitive Strategies and Cooperative Structures*. New York: Oxford University Press, 1994. (A detailed overview of the emergence of a distinctive style of corporate organization and affiliations.)

Hadley, Eleanor. *Antitrust in Japan*. Princeton, N.J.: Princeton University Press, 1970. (An authoritative analysis of the dissolution of the *zaibatsu* by an economist and participant in the Occupation.)

Havens, Thomas R. H. *Architects of Affluence: The Tsutsumi Family and the Seibu-Saison Enterprise in Twentieth-Century Japan*. Cambridge, Mass.: Council on East Asian Studies, Harvard University, 1994. (A description of the flamboyant Tsutsumi family and its far-flung transportation, retail, and entertainment empires.)

Whittaker, D. H. *Small Firms in the Japanese Economy*. Cambridge: Cambridge University Press, 1997. (The latest study of the small- and medium-size enterprise sector and its conditions at the end of the century.)

BUSINESS LEADERS

Hirschmeier, Johannes. *The Origins of Entrepreneurship in Meiji Japan*. Cambridge, Mass.: Harvard University Press, 1964. (How Japan found risk takers and business managers to lead its development after 1868.)

Marshall, Byron K. *Capitalism and Nationalism in Prewar Japan: The Ideology of the Business Elite, 1868–1941*. Stanford, Calif.: Stanford University Press, 1967. (The argument that business leaders drew on community-oriented Confucian values to justify their capitalist pursuits.)

Molony, Barbara. *Technology and Investment: The Prewar Japanese Chemical Industry*. Cambridge, Mass.: Council on East Asian Studies, Harvard University, 1990. (The meteoric career of Noguchi Jun, a chemist turned entrepreneur who played a major role in Japan's preparations for war.)

WORK RELATIONS

Dore, R. P. *British Factory—Japanese Factory: The Origins of National Diversity in Industrial Relations*. Berkeley and Los Angeles: University of California Press, 1973. (A classic study of two electrical manufacturers, highlighting the distinctiveness of labor relations in Japan.)

Gordon, Andrew. *The Evolution of Labor Relations in Japan: Heavy Industry, 1853–1955*. Cambridge, Mass.: Council on East Asian Studies, Harvard University, 1985. (The evolution of Japanese-style labor relations, based on the argument that workers played a major role in shaping outcomes.)

Kondo, Dorinne K. *Crafting Selves: Power, Gender, and Discourses of Identity in a Japanese Workplace*. Chicago: University of Chicago Press, 1990. (A fascinating glimpse of the lives of men and women employed in a small cake shop in a working-class district of Tōkyō around 1980.)

Kumazawa, Makoto. *Portraits of the Japanese Workplace: Labor Movements, Workers, and Managers.* Ed. Andrew Gordon. Boulder, Colo.: Westview Press, 1996. (A unique perspective on the labor movement and the plight of overworked employees in the 1980s by a Japanese scholar who specializes in labor relations.)

Rohlen, Thomas. *For Harmony and Strength: Japanese White Collar Organization in Anthropological Perspective.* Berkeley and Los Angeles: University of California Press, 1974. (Based on field research conducted in the late 1960s, a depiction of work relationships in a regional bank.)

Tsurumi, Patricia. *Factory Girls: Women in the Thread Mills of Meiji Japan.* Princeton, N.J.: Princeton University Press, 1990. (The horrendous working conditions of young textile hands between the 1880s and 1920s and a comparison of their lives with domestic servants and others.)

POLICYMAKING

Hein, Laura. *Fueling Growth: The Energy Revolution and Economic Policy in Postwar Japan.* Cambridge, Mass.: Council on East Asian Studies, Harvard University, 1990. (Hein's argument that postwar recovery was neither as smooth nor as consensual as Chalmers Johnson claims.)

Johnson, Chalmers. *MITI and the Japanese Miracle: The Growth of Industrial Policy, 1925–1975.* Stanford, Calif.: Stanford University Press, 1982. (The argument that Japan's success as a developmental state is attributable to the genius of the "economic bureaucracy.")

Okimoto, Daniel I. *Between MITI and the Market: Japanese Industrial Policy for High Technology.* Stanford, Calif.: Stanford University Press, 1989. (Okimoto's challenge to Chalmers Johnson's interpretation, emphasizing the role of corporate relationships, political interaction, and cultural norms.)

Smith, Thomas C. *Political Change and Industrial Development in Japan: Government Enterprise, 1868–1880.* Stanford, Calif.: Stanford University Press, 1955. (The short-lived fate of government-owned enterprises.)

TECHNOLOGY

Bartholomew, James R. *The Formation of Science in Japan: Building a Research Tradition.* New Haven, Conn.: Yale University Press, 1989. (A description of the evolution of policies and research practices in the biological sciences between the 1880s and the 1920s.)

Callon, Scott. *Divided Sun: MITI and the Breakdown of Japanese High-Tech Industrial Policy, 1975–1993.* Stanford, Calif.: Stanford University Press, 1996. (The demise of MITI's control over industrial policy, based on cooperative ventures in large-scale computing.)

Morris-Suzuki, Tessa. *The Technological Transformation of Japan: From the Seventeenth to the Twenty-First Century.* Cambridge: Cambridge University Press, 1994. (An overview of technology and economic development since the 1600s.)

Samuels, Richard J. *"Rich Nation, Strong Army": National Security and the Techno-logical Transformation of Japan.* Ithaca, N.Y.: Cornell University Press, 1994. (The contention that anxieties about military security have shaped economic production since the Meiji Restoration.)

Westney, D. Eleanor. *Imitation and Innovation: The Transfer of Western Organization-al Patterns to Meiji Japan.* Cambridge, Mass.: Harvard University Press, 1987. (A fas-cinating interpretation of Japan's adoption and adaptation of organizational tech-nology from Europe, through case studies of the postal system, police force, and newspapers in the late nineteenth century.)

INTERNATIONAL TRADE

Encarnation, Dennis J. *Rivals Beyond Trade: America Versus Japan in Global Compe-tition.* Ithaca, N.Y.: Cornell University Press, 1992. (An intriguing analysis of the re-lationship between foreign direct investment and international trade.)

Inoguchi, Takashi, and Daniel Okimoto, eds. *The Political Economy of Japan.* Vol. 2: *The Changing International Context.* Stanford, Calif.: Stanford University Press, 1988. (A comprehensive overview of Japan's international trade during the first four postwar decades.)

Yoshino, Michael Y., and Thomas B. Lifson. *The Invisible Link: Japan's Sogo shosha and the Organization of Trade.* Cambridge, Mass.: MIT Press, 1986. (One of the few works in English that explains the history and roles of Japan's international trading firms, such as Mitsui bussan and C. Itoh.)

Society

GENERAL WORKS

Hanley, Susan. *Everyday Things in Premodern Japan: The Hidden Legacy of Material Culture.* Berkeley and Los Angeles: University of California Press, 1997. (The ma-terial conditions of everyday life in the nineteenth century.)

Hashimoto, Akiko. *The Gift of Generations: Japanese and American Perspectives on Aging and the Social Contract.* Cambridge: Cambridge University Press, 1996. (A comparison of one city from each country, showing the differences in how people conceive of, and provide care for, the elderly.)

Lebra, Takie. *Above the Clouds: Status Culture of the Modern Japanese Nobility.* Berke-ley and Los Angeles: University of California Press, 1992. (The first and only study of the prewar aristocracy, emphasizing the family aspects of noble life.)

Mouer, Ross, and Yoshio Sugimoto. *Images of Japanese Society.* London: Methuen, 1986. (A revisionist work challenging the view of Japan as a harmonious and coop-erative society.)

Nakane, Chie. *Japanese Society.* Berkeley and Los Angeles: University of California Press, 1970. (An interpretation by an anthropologist who taught at Tōkyō University that exerted great influence over foreign views of Japan. Her book should be read together with Robert J. Smith's *Japanese Society*.)

Plath, David. *Long Engagements: Maturity in Modern Japan*. Stanford, Calif.: Stanford University Press, 1980. (An analysis of the lives of several men and women born before the war who had to deal with the turmoil, challenges, and opportunities of postwar society.)

Smith, Robert J. *Japanese Society: Tradition, Self and the Social Order*. Cambridge: Cambridge University Press, 1983. (A condensation of a lifetime of study of and reflection on Japanese society.)

Tipton, Elise K., ed. *Society and the State in Interwar Japan*. London: Routledge, 1997. (A multidisciplinary collection by scholars based in Australia that describes little-examined social groups and their political activities between about 1915 and 1945.)

Wagatsuma, Hiroshi, and George DeVos, eds. *Japan's Invisible Race: Caste in Culture and Personality*. Berkeley and Los Angeles: University of California Press, 1966. (A comprehensive description of the history and conditions of Japan's *burakumin*.)

FAMILY AND CLASS

Torrance, Richard. *The Fiction of Tokuda Shusei and the Emergence of Japan's New Middle Class*. Seattle: University of Washington Press, 1994. (A biography of a prewar novelist that also describes urban, middle-class life in Tōkyō before the war.)

Vogel, Ezra F. *Japan's New Middle Class: The Salary Man and His Family*. 2d ed. Berkeley and Los Angeles: University of California Press, 1971. (A classic study of the ideal urban family, based on field research undertaken in the late 1950s.)

COMMUNITY

Allinson, Gary D. *Japanese Urbanism: Industry and Politics in Kariya, 1872–1972*. Berkeley and Los Angeles: University of California Press, 1975. (A long-term study illustrating how the growth of the Toyota enterprise shaped political and social changes in Kariya and several small communities in central Japan.)

Ben-Ari, Eyal. *Changing Japanese Suburbia: A Study of Two Present-Day Localities*. London: Kegan Paul International, 1991. (Based on detailed research on two suburbs in the Kyōto area during the 1980s, this book is usefully read with Allinson's *Suburban Tokyo*.)

Bestor, Theodore C. *Neighborhood Tokyo*. Stanford, Calif.: Stanford University Press, 1989. (Based on lengthy residence and close knowledge of the community, an illustration of how a merchant neighborhood in southern Tōkyō does, and does not, bond together.)

Dore, Ronald P. *City Life in Japan: A Study of a Tokyo Ward*. Berkeley and Los Angeles: University of California Press, 1958. (Based on fieldwork conducted shortly after the war ended, a classic study of a small urban quarter near Ueno Park and a depiction of social life in Tōkyō at midcentury.)

Smith, Robert J. *Kurusu: The Price of Progress in a Japanese Village, 1951–1975*. Stanford, Calif.: Stanford University Press, 1978. (How a rural village changed under the pressures of urbanization and affluence.)

Smith, Robert J., and Ella Wiswell. *The Women of Suye Mura*. Chicago: University of Chicago Press, 1982. (Based on Wiswell's notes kept while living in a Kyūshū village, a revealing depiction of rural Japan in the 1930s.)

WOMEN

Bernstein, Gail Lee. *Haruko's World: A Japanese Farm Woman and Her Community*. Rev. ed. Stanford, Calif.: Stanford University Press, 1997. (The challenges facing a wife in a rural village, relying on participant observation in the early 1970s. The new edition carries the family's story into the 1990s.)

Bernstein, Gail Lee, ed. *Recreating Japanese Women: 1600–1945*. Berkeley and Los Angeles: University of California Press, 1991. (Essays portraying women in the modern era, as writers, company leaders, and factory workers, as well as wives and mothers.)

Brinton, Mary C. *Women and the Economic Miracle: Gender and Work in Postwar Japan*. Berkeley and Los Angeles: University of California Press, 1993. (A compelling view of women's roles in underwriting Japan's postwar economic growth.)

Hunter, Janet, ed. *Japanese Women Working*. London: Routledge, 1993. (Essays by nine scholars from Europe, the United States, and Japan on women's issues and women in various occupations during the twentieth century.)

Imamura, Anne, ed. *Re-Imaging Japanese Women*. Berkeley and Los Angeles: University of California Press, 1996. (Essays offering the latest view of women's multifaceted lives in contemporary Japan.)

Pharr, Susan J. *Political Women in Japan: The Search for a Place in Political Life*. Berkeley and Los Angeles: University of California Press, 1981. (How the few women active in Japanese politics managed to cross the hurdles they encountered.)

Sievers, Sharon L. *Flowers in the Salt: The Beginnings of Feminist Consciousness in Modern Japan*. Stanford, Calif.: Stanford University Press, 1983. (An overview of the early stages of the women's movement.)

Smith, Kazuko, trans. and ed. *Makiko's Diary: A Merchant Wife in 1910 Kyoto*. Stanford, Calif.: Stanford University Press, 1995. (Recollections of daily life accompanied by a useful introduction and photographs.)

DEMOGRAPHY

Coleman, Samuel. *Family Planning in Japanese Society: Traditional Birth Control in a Modern Urban Culture*. Princeton, N.J.: Princeton University Press, 1984. (The widespread use of abortion as the principal means of population control in the postwar era.)

Smith, Thomas C. *Nakahara: Family Farming and Population in a Japanese Village, 1717–1830*. Stanford, Calif.: Stanford University Press, 1977. (Population and birth control practices before the Meiji Restoration, based on demographic records.)

Taeuber, Irene B. *The Population of Japan*. Princeton, N.J.: Princeton University Press, 1958. (A comprehensive study of Japan's demographic changes between 1868 and 1955.)

EDUCATION

Cummings, William. *Education and Equality in Japan*. Princeton, N.J.: Princeton University Press, 1980. (A study of Japan's elementary schools, emphasizing their egalitarian nature.)

Hall, Ivan. *Mori Arinori*. Cambridge, Mass.: Harvard University Press, 1973. (A portrait of the founder of the modern system of public education and a description of the origins of the system itself.)

Marshall, Byron K. *Learning to Be Modern: Japanese Political Discourse on Education*. Boulder, Colo.: Westview Press, 1994. (The latest, most comprehensive overview of education in the modern era.)

Roden, Donald. *Schooldays in Imperial Japan: A Study in the Culture of a Student Elite*. Berkeley and Los Angeles: University of California Press, 1980. (The social and intellectual atmosphere among students in the elite "higher schools," or university prep schools, of the early twentieth century.)

Rohlen, Thomas. *Japan's High Schools*. Berkeley and Los Angeles: University of California Press, 1983. (A study of five high schools, emphasizing their inequalities.)

SOCIAL MOVEMENTS AND DISSENT

Bowen, Roger W. *Rebellion and Democracy in Meiji Japan: A Study of Commoners in the Popular Rights Movement*. Berkeley and Los Angeles: University of California Press, 1980. (An examination of three popular disputes in eastern Japan in the 1870s and 1880s, arguing that Japan did witness some democracy from below.)

Kelly, William. *Deference and Defiance in Nineteenth-Century Japan*. Princeton, N.J.: Princeton University Press, 1985. (A historical analysis of the shifting, contingent quality of peasant protest in the mid-nineteenth century.)

Koschmann, J. Victor, ed. *Authority and the Individual in Japan: Citizen Protest in Historical Perspective*. Tokyo: University of Tokyo Press, 1978. (Translated essays by Japanese scholars and an introduction by Koschmann, on Japanese perspectives on dissent.)

Lewis, Michael. *Rioters and Citizens: Mass Protest in Imperial Japan*. Berkeley and Los Angeles: University of California Press, 1990. (Concentrating on the rice riots of 1918, an interpretation of popular politics right before the 1920s.)

McKean, Margaret A. *Environmental Protest and Citizen Politics in Japan*. Berkeley and Los Angeles: University of California Press, 1981. (A view of the organizational forms and political consequences of citizen protests over environmental problems in the 1960s and 1970s.)

Packard, George R. *Protest in Tokyo: The Security Treaty Crisis of 1960*. Princeton, N.J.:

Princeton University Press, 1966. (An account of the protests, politics, and diplomacy surrounding the renewal of the security treaty.)

STATE-GUIDED ORGANIZATIONS

Garon, Sheldon. *Molding Japanese Minds: The State in Everyday Life*. Princeton, N.J.: Princeton University Press, 1997. (Case studies of religious suppression, women's organizations, and prostitution showing that the "state management" of everyday life has molded Japanese minds since 1868.)

Kasza, Gregory J. *The Conscription Society: Administered Mass Organizations*. New Haven, Conn.: Yale University Press, 1995. (A comparative analysis of mass organizations in Japan and elsewhere, illustrating how they mobilize support for war and authoritarian regimes.)

Smethurst, Richard J. *A Social Basis for Prewar Japanese Militarism: The Army and the Rural Community*. Berkeley and Los Angeles: University of California Press, 1974. (A description of the army's creation of state-guided organizations around 1900 and how it used them to promote cultural orthodoxy.)

Culture

IDEAS

Barshay, Andrew. *State and Intellectual in Imperial Japan: The Public Man in Crisis*. Berkeley and Los Angeles: University of California Press, 1988. (Prewar intellectual debates and the reasons that intellectuals did not oppose war.)

Gluck, Carol. *Japan's Modern Myths: Ideology in the Late Meiji Period*. Princeton, N.J.: Princeton University Press, 1985. (The ideas, organizations, and practices between 1890 and 1912 that prepared the groundwork for prewar cultural orthodoxy.)

Koschmann, J. Victor. *Revolution and Subjectivity in Postwar Japan*. Chicago: University of Chicago Press, 1997. (An examination of how the notion of subjecthood, or autonomy, was debated across academic disciplines and through the popular media between the 1920s and 1950s.)

Maruyama, Masao. *Thought and Behavior in Modern Japanese Politics*. Trans. Ivan Morris. Princeton, N.J.: Princeton University Press, 1972. (Essays about midcentury politics and ideas by one of Japan's most eminent intellectuals.)

Pincus, Leslie. *Authenticating Culture in Imperial Japan: Kuki Shuzo and the Rise of National Aesthetics*. Berkeley and Los Angeles: University of California Press, 1996. (A study of a European-educated philosopher, famous for his book on "style" or "dandyism" in the late Tokugawa period, describing the ideological atmosphere of the 1930s and the significance of aestheticism.)

Pyle, Kenneth. *The New Generation in Meiji Japan: Problems of Cultural Identity, 1885–1895*. Stanford, Calif.: Stanford University Press, 1969. (The shifts in intellectual fashions at a critical juncture in the Meiji era.)

Rimer, J. Thomas, ed. *Culture and Identity in Taisho Japan*. Princeton, N.J.: Princeton University Press, 1990. (A collection of essays offering a wide-ranging analysis of cultural behavior and disputation during the 1910s and 1920s.)

Rubin, Jay. *Injurious to Public Morals: Writers and the Meiji State*. Seattle: University of Washington Press, 1984. (The problems of censorship and the impediments to freedom of expression in the late nineteenth century.)

RELIGION

Davis, Winston. *Dojo: Magic and Exorcism in Modern Japan*. Stanford, Calif.: Stanford University Press, 1980. (A description of the many facets of a postwar new religion.)

———. *Japanese Religion and Society: Paradigms of Structure and Change*. Albany: State University of New York Press, 1992. (Analyses of the relationships among religious behavior, social structure, and values.)

Earhart, H. Byron. *Gedatsukai and Religion in Contemporary Japan*. Bloomington: Indiana University Press, 1989. (A case study of one of the new religions active in the postwar period.)

Guthrie, Stewart. *A Japanese New Religion: Rissho Kosei-kai in a Mountain Hamlet*. Ann Arbor, Mich.: Center for Japanese Studies, 1988. (An anthropological description of a major new religion in a rural setting.)

Hardacre, Helen. *Kurozumikyo and the New Religions of Japan*. Princeton, N.J.: Princeton University Press, 1986. (A study of a Shinto-inspired new religion founded in 1814, comparing the practices and beliefs of Kurozumikyo with those of other new religions.)

———. *Shinto and the State, 1868–1988*. Princeton, N.J.: Princeton University Press, 1989. (An overview of the evolution of the Shinto religion and its relationship with governing authorities after 1868.)

Kornicki, P. F., and I. J. McMullen, eds. *Religion in Japan: Arrows to Heaven and Earth*. Cambridge: Cambridge University Press, 1996. (Essays about contemporary pilgrimages, *mizuko kuyō* (memorial services for aborted fetuses and infants), and new-new religions.)

Reader, Ian. *Religion in Contemporary Japan*. Honolulu: University of Hawaii Press, 1991. (An introduction to all aspects of religion in the postwar era, including Shinto, Buddhism, Christianity, and new religions.)

Smith, Robert J. *Ancestor Worship in Contemporary Japan*. Stanford, Calif.: Stanford University Press, 1974. (The surprising persistence of ancestor worship even in urban families separated from home and family graves.)

POPULAR CULTURE

Ben-Ari, Eyal, Brian Moeran, and James Valentine, eds. *Unwrapping Japan: Society and Culture in Anthropological Perspective*. Honolulu: University of Hawaii Press,

1990. (Some of the earliest efforts to use anthropological theory to explore facets of popular culture in postwar Japan.)

Dalby, Liza Crihfield. *Geisha*. Berkeley and Los Angeles: University of California Press, 1983. (Based on the personal experiences of an American anthropologist, a description of the present and past practices of geisha in Japan's entertainment quarters.)

Plath, David. *The After Hours: Modern Japan and the Search for Enjoyment*. Berkeley and Los Angeles: University of California Press, 1964. (An analysis of a society with a greater sense of leisure.)

Skov, Lise, and Brian Moeran, eds. *Women, Media, and Consumption in Japan*. Honolulu: University of Hawaii Press, 1995. (Relations between media images and women's behavior across all age groups.)

Tobin, Joseph J., ed. *Re-Made in Japan: Everyday Life and Consumer Taste in a Changing Society*. New Haven, Conn.: Yale University Press, 1992. (A variety of perspectives on old practices and new curiosities.)

LITERARY BIOGRAPHY AND CRITICISM

Anderer, Paul, ed. and trans. *Literature of the Lost Home: Kobayashi Hideo—Literary Criticism, 1924–1939*. Stanford, Calif.: Stanford University Press, 1995. (The world of literature from 1890 to 1940.)

Bowring, Richard John. *Mori Ogai and the Modernization of Japanese Culture*. Cambridge: Cambridge University Press, 1979. (A condemnation of Ōgai's novels but praise for his work as a translator, critic, and short story writer.)

Copeland, Rebecca L. *The Sound of the Wind: The Life and Works of Uno Chiyo*. Honolulu: University of Hawaii Press, 1992. (A literary biography of Uno, translations of two of her stories, and an extraordinary essay about a puppet maker.)

Danly, Robert Lyons. *In the Shade of Spring Leaves: The Life and Writings of Higuchi Ichiyo, a Woman of Letters in Meiji Japan*. New Haven, Conn.: Yale University Press, 1981. (A biography plus translations of nine of Higuchi's best short stories, including "Child's Play.")

Fowler, Edward. *The Rhetoric of Confession: Shishosetsu in Early Twentieth-Century Japanese Fiction*. Berkeley and Los Angeles: University of California Press, 1988. (An interpretation of some of Japan's first I-novel authors.)

Gessel, Van C. *The Sting of Life: Four Contemporary Japanese Novelists*. New York: Columbia University Press, 1989. (An analysis of a group known as the Third Generation, which included Yasuoka Shōtarō and Endō Shusaku, to situate and critique their work in the early postwar period.)

—— *Three Modern Novelists: Soseki, Tanizaki, Kawabata*. Tokyo: Kodansha International, 1993. (An introduction to the lives and writings of three giants of modern Japanese literature.)

Ito, Ken K. *Visions of Desire: Tanizaki's Fictional World*. Stanford, Calif.: Stanford University Press, 1991. (A literary biography tracing Tanizaki's development as an author from his youth in Tōkyō to his old age in the Ōsaka area, relating his life to his writing.)

Keene, Donald. *Dawn to the West: Japanese Literature of the Modern Era.* 2 vols. New York: Henry Holt, 1984. (A study by one of the foremost students of the subject.)

Lyons, Phyllis I. *The Saga of Dazai Osamu: A Critical Study with Translations.* Stanford, Calif.: Stanford University Press, 1985. (A biography of a controversial writer that also includes translations of a novella and five short stories.)

McClellan, Edwin. *Two Japanese Novelists: Soseki and Toson.* Chicago: University of Chicago Press, 1969. (A study of two late-Meiji novelists famous for their works on families.)

Ryan, Marleigh Grayer. *Japan's First Modern Novel:* Ukigumo *of Futabatei Shimei.* New York: Columbia University Press, 1967. (An analysis of the works of the two men who laid the groundwork for the realist, psychological novel, including a translation of *Floating Clouds.*)

Schalow, Paul Gordon, and Janet A. Walker, eds. *The Woman's Hand: Gender and Theory in Japanese Women's Writing.* Stanford, Calif.: Stanford University Press, 1996. (A collection of the latest and most sophisticated critical commentary on Japanese women writers and their work.)

Seidensticker, Edward. *Kafu the Scribbler: The Life and Writings of Nagai Kafu, 1879–1959.* Stanford, Calif.: Stanford University Press, 1965. (A biography of a major author and translations of some of Kafū's best short stories.)

Suzuki, Tomi. *Narrating the Self: Fictions of Japanese Modernity.* Stanford, Calif.: Stanford University Press, 1996. (A critique of the I-novel, claiming that it is a product of retrospective criticism and not a uniform product of conscious intent.)

Tansman, Alan. *The Writings of Koda Aya: A Japanese Literary Daughter.* New Haven, Conn.: Yale University Press, 1993. (A literary biography of Kōda and translations of four of her best short stories from the 1950s.)

Ueda, Makoto. *Modern Japanese Writers and the Nature of Literature.* Stanford, Calif.: Stanford University Press, 1976. (An examination of the work of eight male writers: Sōseki, Kafū, Tanizaki, Shiga, Akutagawa, Dazai, Kawabata, and Mishima)

Vernon, Victoria V. *Daughters of the Moon: Wish, Will, and Social Constraint in Fiction by Modern Japanese Women.* Japanese Research Monograph no. 9. Berkeley: Institute of East Asian Studies, University of California, 1988. (A study of five female and two male writers of the twentieth century plus an analysis of Higuchi Ichiyō's "Child's Play.")

Walker, Janet A. *The Japanese Novel of the Meiji Period and the Ideal of Individualism.* Princeton, N.J.: Princeton University Press, 1979. (An examination of four writers active during the 1880s and later, revealing how "individualism" was conceived and debated.)

Washburn, Dennis C. *The Dilemma of the Modern in Japanese Fiction.* New Haven, Conn.: Yale University Press, 1995. (An examination of the works of such modern writers as Futabatei, Sōseki, Ōgai, Kafū, Shiga, Akutagawa, and Kawabata.)

VISUAL RESOURCES

Books About Films and Documentaries

Anderson, Joseph L., and Donald Richie. *The Japanese Film: Art and Industry.* Expanded ed. Princeton, N.J.: Princeton University Press, 1984. (An overview of the history of Japanese film from 1896 to the 1980s, with a lengthy commentary on the distinctive features of Japanese cinema.)

Bordwell, David. *Ozu and the Poetics of Cinema.* Princeton, N.J.: Princeton University Press, 1988. (Critical essays on fifty-five films, asserting that film director Ozu Yasujirō's work is highly varied thematically and not focused solely on family psychology.)

Burch, Noel. *To the Distant Observer: Form and Meaning in the Japanese Cinema.* Berkeley and Los Angeles: University of California Press, 1979. (An assessment of early Japanese films and film making, concentrating on film directors Ozu Yasujirō and Mizoguchi Kenji and the years from 1917 to 1945.)

Grilli, Peter, ed. *Japan in Film: A Comprehensive Catalogue of Documentary and Theatrical Films on Japan Available in the United States.* New York: Japan Society, 1984. (An annotated guide to 516 documentaries and 130 feature films.)

Richie, Donald. *The Films of Akira Kurosawa.* 3d ed. Berkeley and Los Angeles: University of California Press, 1996. (A commentary on twenty-six films by one of Japan's most famous directors.)

Feature Films on Video

An Autumn Afternoon. Directed by Ozu Yasujirō. 112 min. Color. Shochiku Company Ltd., 1962. New Yorker Films Artwork, 1991. (A depiction of progress toward a daughter's marriage amid nostalgic scenes of Tōkyō in the early 1960s.)

Black Rain. Directed by Imamura Shōhei. 123 min. Black and white. Toei Company, 1988. Fox Lorber Home Video, 1991. (Based on Ibuse Masuji's novel, an exploration of the dilemmas faced by victims of radiation sickness.)

Early Summer. Directed by Ozu Yasujirō. 135 min. Black and white. Shochiku Company Ltd., 1951. Sony Video Software Company, Inc., 1988. (A young woman facing the duty of marrying amid the social chaos of early postwar Tōkyō.)

The Family Game. (Kazoku geemu). Directed by Morita Yoshimitsu. 107 min. Color. 1983. Sony Video Software Company, Inc., 1987. (A scathing but still hilarious critique of a family overcome with anxieties about education, social mobility, and the prospect of failure.)

Fires on the Plain. Directed by Ichikawa Kon. 105 min. Black and white. Daiei Film Productions, 1959. Embassy Home Entertainment, 1987. (Based on the novel by Ōoka Shōhei, a film depicting the grisly nature of Japan's jungle warfare.)

The Funeral. Directed by Itami Jūzō. 124 min. Color. Itami Productions, 1987. Republic Pictures Home Video, 1988. (The death of a parent as an excuse to poke fun at a hapless middle-class family, the funeral industry, and Buddhist priests.)

Ikiru. Directed by Kurosawa Akira. 143 min. Black and white. Toho Limited, 1952. Public Media Home Vision. (One of Kurosawa's best movies, the portrayal of a man who can overcome the inertia of bureaucratic custom only when he faces death.)

The Makioka Sisters. (Sasameyuki). Directed by Ichikawa Kon. Toho eiga, 1983. Toho Company Ltd., 1983. (Based on the saga of Japanese family life by Tanizaki Jun'ichirō, a portrait of late prewar Japan.)

Rashōmon. Directed by Kurosawa Akira. 83 min. Black and white. Toho Ltd., 1952. RKO Radio Pictures, 1952. (A film version of the famous tale by Akutagawa Ryunosuke.)

Tampopo. Directed by Itami Jūzō. 114 min. Color. Itami Productions, 1987. Republic Pictures Home Video, 1988. (A spoof of the Japanese obsession with perfection in a "food flick" about the search for the perfect bowl of *ramen*.)

A Taxing Woman. Directed by Itami Jūzō. 127 min. Color. Itami Productions, 1987. Fox Lorber Home Video, 1994. (A parody of gender discrimination and the compulsive finance bureaucracy.)

Tokyo Story. Directed by Ozu Yasujirō. 139 min. Black and white. Shochiku Company Ltd., 1953. New Yorker Video. (The social costs of urbanization and their effects on two generations in the early postwar era.)

Woman in the Dunes. Directed by Teshigahara Hiroshi. 123 min. Black and white. 1964. Connoisseur Video Collection, 1991. (The film version of Abe Kōbō's award-winning novel, capturing its claustrophobic themes.)

Yōjimbo. Directed by Kurosawa Akira. 110 min. Black and white. Toho Company Ltd., 1962. Janus Films, 1986. (One of Kurosawa's most famous samurai films, the tale of a lone warrior who brings peace to warring factions in a Tokugawa-era village.)

Documentaries on Video

The Colonel Comes to Japan. WGBH, Boston. 30 min. Color. Learning Corporation of America, 1981. (An amusing depiction of Kentucky Fried Chicken's entry into Japan's fast-food market.)

Farm Song. Directed by John Nathan. 57 min. Color. New York: Japan Society, 1985. (A candid understanding of sexual and generational conflict in a farm family in the late 1970s.)

Full Moon Lunch. Directed by John Nathan. 57 min. color. New York: Japan Society, 1985. (A depiction of four generations in a family that ran a catering service in Tōkyō in the late 1970s.)

The Pacific Century. 10 videos of 60 min. each. Color. Pacific Basin Institute. South Burlington, Vt.: Corporation for Public Broadcasting, 1992. (A lengthy review of Asian history since 1800.)

ELECTRONIC RESOURCES

Library Catalogs

Harvard University:
 telnet: hollis.harvard.edu

Japan Documentation Center, Library of Congress:
 gopher: marvel.loc.gov:70/11/research/reading.rooms/jdc

Library of Congress:
 telnet: locis.loc.gov

National Diet Library:
 http://www.ndl.go.jp/index-e.html

University of California at Berkeley:
 telnet: gopac.berkeley.edu

Gateways to Information on Japan

Australian National University (Department of Asian Studies):
 http://coombs.anu.edu.au/WWWVL-AsianStudies.html

East Asian Libraries East Asian Cooperative World Wide Web:
 http://pears.lib.ohio-state.edu/

Japan Information Network (Japan Center for Intercultural Communications):
 http://jin.jcic.or.jp/

Japan Window (A joint product of Stanford University and NTT):
 http://jw.nttam.com/

University of New Mexico (U.S.-Japan Center):
 http://www.nmjc.org/jiap/

Japanese Government Worldwide Web Sites

Cabinet (of the Japanese Government):
 http://www.ntt.jp/japan/GOV/cabinet/cabinet.html

Ministry of Finance:
 http://www.mof.go.jp/english/index.html

Ministry of Foreign Affairs:
 http://www.nttls.co.jp/infomofa/

Ministry of International Trade and Industry (MITI):
 http://www.miti.go.jp/index-e.html

Prime Minister of Japan:
http://www.kantei.go.jp/

News on Japan (in English)

Asahi shimbun (a major Japanese newspaper):
http://www.asahi.com/english/enews/enews.html

Japan Times Online (Japan's major English-language daily):
http://www.japantimes.co.jp/

Kyodo News Service (an independent Japanese news agency):
http://www.kyodo.co.jp/

Mainichi shimbun Jam Jam (a major Japanese newspaper):
http://www.mainichi.co.jp/

NHK (Japan's public broadcasting system):
http://nhk.or.jp/index-e.html

PART IV

Appendix

This final part of the guide begins with six charters, rescripts, constitutions, and plans that have played a major role in shaping events and behavior in modern Japan. These are followed by a chronology of events, focusing primarily on political and economic affairs, and a list of the men who have served as prime minister since the creation of the modern cabinet system in 1885. The final segment of this appendix consists of a body of quantitative data dealing with population change, economic growth, exports and imports, and consumption. These written and numerical materials complement the Historical Narrative and the Topical Compendium and also provide further information.

DOCUMENTS

Document A: The Five-Article Imperial Covenant of 1868

This document, also referred to as the Meiji Charter Oath, is a short declaration in five parts that was issued by the Meiji emperor at a special ceremony on April 6, 1868. As one of the new government's first public manifestos, it can be compared in some ways with the U.S. Declaration of Independence, in that it spells out the goals of the new leaders. It is important for what it says, even though it is intentionally vague and ambiguous in its promises, and also important for its manner of announcement. This was the first time that the lower-ranking samurai leading the government exploited the ritual authority of the emperor to promote their political objectives.

Item. We shall determine all matters of state by public discussion, after assemblies have been convoked far and wide.

Item. We shall unite the hearts and minds of people high and low, the better to pursue with vigor the rule of the realm.

Item. We are duty bound to ensure that all people, nobility, military, and commoners, too, may fulfill their aspirations and not yield to despair.

Item. We shall break through the shackles of former evil practice and base our actions on the principles of international law.

Item. We shall seek knowledge throughout the world and thus invigorate the foundations of this imperial nation.[1]

Document B: *The Imperial Rescript to Soldiers and Sailors*

Promulgated in 1882, this rescript was issued by the emperor on behalf of Yamagata Aritomo, an army general who drafted the document in order to inculcate proper behavior in the new army. The precepts were drummed into new recruits, and many officers knew the five articles by heart. Like the Imperial Rescript on Education which was promulgated just eight years later, this one emphasizes the need for duty, loyalty, self-control, and sincerity in comparably elevated language. Given the Japanese army's conduct during the 1930s and 1940s, Yamagata's injunctions in article 3 are prescient.

. . . Soldiers and Sailors, We are your supreme Commander in Chief. Our relations with you will be most intimate when We rely upon you as Our limbs and you look up to Us as your head. Whether We are able to guard the Empire, and so prove Ourself worthy of Heaven's blessings and repay the benevolence of Our Ancestors, depends upon the faithful discharge of your duties as soldiers and sailors. If the majesty and power of Our Empire be impaired, do you share with Us the sorrow; if the glory of Our arms shine resplendent, We will share with you the honor. If you all do your duty, and being one with Us in spirit do your utmost for the protection of the state, Our people will long enjoy the blessings of peace and the might and dignity of Our Empire will Shine in the World. As We thus expect much of you, Soldiers and Sailors, we give you the following precepts:

1. The soldier and sailor should consider loyalty their essential duty. Who that is born in this land can be wanting in the spirit of grateful service to it? No soldier or sailor, especially, can be considered efficient unless this spirit be strong in him. A soldier or a sailor in which this spirit is not strong, how-

---

[1] John Breen, "The Imperial Oath of April 1868: Ritual, Politics, and Power in the Restoration," *Monumenta Nipponica* 51:4 (Winter 1996): 410.

ever skilled in art or proficient in science, is a mere puppet; and a body of soldiers or sailors wanting in loyalty, however well ordered and disciplined it may be, is in an emergency no better than a rabble. Remember that as the protection of the state and the maintenance of its power depend upon the strength of its arms, the growth or decline of this strength must affect the nation's destiny for good or for evil; therefore neither be led astray by current opinions nor meddle in politics, but with single heart fulfil your essential duty of loyalty, and bear in mind that duty is weightier than a mountain, while death is lighter than a feather. Never by failing in moral principle fall into disgrace and bring dishonor upon your name. . . .

2. The soldier and the sailor should show proper respect to superiors and consideration to inferiors. . . .

3. The soldier and the sailor should esteem valor. . . . To be incited by mere impetuosity to violent action cannot be called true valor. The soldier and the sailor should have sound discrimination of right and wrong, cultivate self-possession, and form their plans with deliberation. Never to despise an inferior enemy or fear a superior, but to do one's duty as soldier or sailor — this is true valor. Those who thus appreciate true valor should in their daily intercourse set gentleness first and aim to win the love and esteem of others. If you affect valor and act with violence, the world will in the end detest you and look upon you as wild beasts. Of this you should take heed. . . .

4. The soldier and the sailor should highly value faithfulness and righteousness. . . .

5. The soldier and the sailor should make simplicity their aim. If you do not make simplicity your aim, you will become effeminate and frivolous and acquire fondness of luxurious and extravagant ways; you will finally grow selfish and sordid and sink to the last degree of baseness, so that neither loyalty nor valor will avail to save you from the contempt of the world.

These five articles should not be disregarded even for a moment by soldiers and sailors. Now for putting them into practice, the all-important thing is sincerity. These five articles are the soul of Our soldiers and sailors, and sincerity is the soul of these articles. If the heart be not sincere, words and deeds, however good, are all mere outward show and can avail nothing. If only the heart be sincere, anything can be accomplished. Moreover, these five articles are the "Grand Way" of Heaven and earth and the universal law of humanity, easy to observe and to practice. If you, Soldiers and Sailors, in obedience to Our instruction, will observe and practice these principles and fulfill your duty of grateful service to the country, it will be a source of joy, not to Ourself alone, but to all the people of Japan.[2]

Document C: The Meiji Constitution

Promulgated on February 11, 1889, this constitution prevailed in Japan for the next fifty-eight years. Bestowed by the emperor on the people, the document is rich with the condescending political rhetoric of the mid-Meiji period. The constitution was written by a small group of high-ranking government leaders under the direction of Itō Hirobumi and did not need to be ratified by a broad, popular assembly of any kind. Accordingly, the constitution grants sweeping powers to the emperor and sharply limits the rights of the people. The following excerpts include the entire preamble and key passages dealing with the emperor, the people (referred to as "the subjects"), the Diet, the cabinet and Privy Council, and the judiciary.

Preamble

Having, by virtue of the glories of Our Ancestors, ascended the Throne of a lineal succession unbroken for ages eternal; desiring to promote the welfare of, and to give development to the moral and intellectual faculties of Our beloved subjects, the very same that have been favored with the benevolent care and affectionate vigilance of Our Ancestors; and hoping to maintain the prosperity of the State, in concert with Our people and with their support, We hereby promulgate, in pursuance of Our Imperial Rescript of the 12th day of the 10th month of the 14th year of Meiji, a fundamental law of State, to exhibit the principles, by which We are to be guided in Our conduct, and to point out to what Our descendants and Our subjects and their descendants are forever to conform.

The rights of sovereignty of the State, We have inherited from Our Ancestors, and We shall bequeath them to Our descendants. Neither We nor they shall in future fail to wield them, in accordance with the provisions of the Constitution hereby granted.

We now declare to respect and protect the security of the rights and of the property of Our people, and to secure to them the complete enjoyment of the same, in the extent of the provisions of the present Constitution and of the law.

The Imperial Diet shall first be convoked for the 23rd year of Meiji and the time of its opening shall be the date when the present Constitution comes into force.

When in the future it may become necessary to amend any of the provisions of the present Constitution, We or Our successors shall assume the ini-

---

[2] Based on the official translation, published in Tokyo in 1913.

tiative right, and submit a project for the same to the Imperial Diet. The Imperial Diet shall pass its vote upon it, according to the conditions imposed by the present Constitution, and in no otherwise shall Our descendants or Our subjects be permitted to attempt any alteration thereof.

Our Ministers of State, on Our behalf, shall be held responsible for the carrying out of the present Constitution, and Our present and future subjects shall forever assume the duty of allegiance to the present Constitution.

Chapter 1: The Emperor

Article 1. The Empire of Japan shall be reigned over and governed by a line of Emperors unbroken for ages eternal.

Article 2. The Imperial Throne shall be succeeded to by Imperial male descendants, according to the provisions of the Imperial House Law.

Article 3. The Emperor is sacred and inviolable.

Article 4. The Emperor is the head of the Empire, combining in Himself the rights of sovereignty, and exercising them, according to the provisions of the present Constitution.

Article 5. The Emperor exercises the legislative power with the consent of the Imperial Diet.

Article 6. The Emperor gives sanction to laws and orders them to be promulgated and executed.

Article 7. The Emperor convokes the Imperial Diet, opens, closes and prorogues it, and dissolves the House of Representatives.

Article 8. The Emperor, in consequence of an urgent necessity to maintain public safety or to avert public calamities, issues, when the Imperial Diet is not sitting, Imperial Ordinances in the place of law.

Such Imperial Ordinances are to be laid before the Imperial Diet at its next session, and when the Diet does not approve the said Ordinances, the Government shall declare them to be invalid for the future. . . .

Article 11. The Emperor has the supreme command of the Army and Navy.

Article 12. The Emperor determines the organization and peace standing of the Army and Navy.

Article 13. The Emperor declares war, makes peace, and concludes treaties. . .

Chapter 2: Rights and Duties of Subjects

Article 18. The conditions necessary for being a Japanese subject shall be determined by law.

Article 19. Japanese subjects may, according to qualifications determined in laws or ordinances, be appointed to civil or military or any other public offices equally.

Article 20. Japanese subjects are amenable to service in the Army or Navy, according to the provisions of law.

Article 21. Japanese subjects are amenable to the duty of paying taxes, according to the provisions of law.

Article 22. Japanese subjects shall have the liberty of abode and of changing the same in the limits of law.

Article 23. No Japanese subject shall be arrested, detained, tried, or punished, unless according to law.

Article 24. No Japanese subject shall be deprived of his right of being tried by the judges determined by law.

Article 25. Except in the cases provided for in the law, the house of no Japanese subject shall be entered or searched without his consent.

Article 26. Except in the cases mentioned in the law, the secrecy of the letters of every Japanese subject shall remain inviolate.

Article 27. The right of property of every Japanese subject shall remain inviolate.

Measures necessary to be taken for the public benefit shall be provided for by law.

Article 28. Japanese subjects shall, in limits not prejudicial to peace and order and not antagonistic to their duties as subjects, enjoy freedom of religious belief.

Article 29. Japanese subjects shall, in the limits of law, enjoy the liberty of speech, writing, publication, public meetings, and associations.

Article 30. Japanese subjects may present petitions, by observing the proper forms of respect, and by complying with the rules specially provided for the same. . . .

Chapter 3: The Imperial Diet

Article 33. The Imperial Diet shall consist of two Houses, a House of Peers and a House of Representatives.

Article 34. The House of Peers shall, in accordance with the Ordinance concerning the House of Peers, be composed of the members of the Imperial Family, of the orders of nobility, and of those persons who have been nominated thereto by the Emperor.

Article 35. The House of Representatives shall be composed of Members elected by the people, according to the provisions of the Law of Election. . . .

Chapter 4: The Ministers of State and the Privy Council

Article 45. The respective Ministers of State shall give their advice to the Emperor, and be responsible for it.

All Laws, Imperial Ordinances and Imperial Rescripts of whatever kind, that relate to the affairs of the State, require the countersignature of a Minister of State.

Article 56. The Privy Councillors shall, in accordance with the provisions for the organization of the Privy Council, deliberate upon important matters of State, when they have been consulted by the Emperor.

Chapter 5: The Judicature

Article 57. The Judicature shall be exercised by the Courts of Law according to law, in the name of the Emperor.

The organization of the courts of Law shall be determined by law.

Article 58. The judges shall be appointed from among those who possess proper qualifications according to law.

No judge shall be deprived of his position, unless by way of criminal sentence or disciplinary punishment.

Rules for disciplinary punishment shall be determined by law.

Article 59. Trials and judgments of a Court shall be conducted publicly. When, however, there exists any fear that such publicity may be prejudicial to peace and order, or to the maintenance of public morality, the public trial may be suspended by provision of law or by the decision of the Court of Law.

Article 60. All matters that fall in the competency of a special Court shall be specially provided for by law.

Article 61. No suit at law, which relates to rights alleged to have been infringed by the illegal measures of the administrative authorities and which shall come in the competency of the Court of Administrative Litigation specially established by law, shall be taken cognizance of by a Court of Law. . . .[3]

Document D: *The Imperial Rescript on Education*

Promulgated in 1890, the Imperial Rescript on Education touched the lives of millions of Japanese for the next fifty-six years. Amid strict rituals conducted to drive home the import of the document, the edict was either read aloud or recited from memory in school classrooms throughout Japan, often daily. The message conveyed was designed to cultivate loyalty to the emperor, obedience

---

[3] Based on the official government translation of 1889.

to one's parents, compliance with social norms, and commitment to the nation and its goals. It had a powerful impact on the political socialization of two generations of Japan's citizenry. The somewhat Victorian English of the original translation captures the rather stiff quality of Meiji-era Japanese.

Know ye our subjects:

Our Imperial Ancestors have founded Our Empire on a basis broad and everlasting, and have deeply and firmly implanted virtue; Our subjects ever united in loyalty and filial piety have from generation to generation illustrated the beauty thereof. This is the glory of the fundamental character of Our Empire, and herein also lies the source of our education. Ye, Our subjects, be filial to your parents, affectionate to your brothers and sisters; as husbands and wives be harmonious, as friends true; bear yourselves in modesty and moderation; extend your benevolence to all; pursue learning and cultivate arts, and thereby develop intellectual faculties and perfect moral powers; furthermore, advance public good and promote common interests; always respect the constitution and observe the laws; should emergency arise, offer yourselves courageously to the State; and thus guard and maintain the prosperity of Our Imperial Throne coeval with heaven and earth. So shall ye not only be Our good and faithful subjects, but render illustrious the best traditions of your forefathers.

The Way here set forth is indeed the teaching bequeathed by Our Imperial Ancestors, to be observed alike by Their Descendants and their subjects, infallible for all ages and true in all places. It is Our wish to lay it to heart in all reverence, in common with you, Our subjects, that we may all attain the same virtue.[4]

Document E: The 1947 Constitution of Japan

The postwar constitution differs from the Meiji Constitution in many obvious ways, especially in substance and language. The reasons for these differences are easily explained. American legal specialists in the Allied occupying forces drafted the postwar constitution, which although it was reviewed by Japanese legal scholars and debated in the Diet, was barely changed. Therefore, the current constitution has a strongly Anglo-American tone and flavor, as the preamble immediately reveals. Following the full preamble are brief excerpts from the constitution pertaining to the emperor, war, the people, the Diet, the

---

[4] Based on the official government translation of 1890.

cabinet, and the judiciary, each of which is quite different from the Meiji Constitution of 1889.

Preamble

We, the Japanese people, acting through our duly elected representatives in the National Diet, determined that we shall secure for ourselves and our posterity the fruits of peaceful cooperation with all nations and the blessings of liberty throughout this land, and resolved that never again shall we be visited with the horrors of war through the action of government, do proclaim that sovereign power resides with the people and do firmly establish this Constitution. Government is a sacred trust of the people, the authority for which is derived from the people, the powers of which are exercised by the representatives of the people, and the benefits of which are enjoyed by the people. This is a universal principle of mankind upon which this Constitution is founded. We reject and revoke all constitutions, laws, ordinances and rescripts in conflict herewith.

We, the Japanese people, desire peace for all time and are deeply conscious of the high ideals controlling human relationships, and we have determined to preserve our security and existence, trusting in the justice and faith of the peace-loving peoples of the world. We desire to occupy an honored place in an international society striving for the preservation of peace, and the banishment of tyranny and slavery, oppression and intolerance for all time from the earth. We recognize that all peoples of the world have the right to live in peace, free from fear and want.

We believe that no nation is responsible to itself alone, but that laws of political morality are universal; and that obedience to such laws is incumbent upon all nations who would sustain their own sovereignty and justify their sovereign relationship with other nations.

We, the Japanese people, pledge our national honor to accomplish these high ideals and purposes with all our resources.

Chapter 1. The Emperor

Article 1. The Emperor shall be the symbol of the State and of the unity of the people, deriving his position from the will of the people with whom resides sovereign power.

Article 2. The Imperial Throne shall be dynastic and succeeded to in accordance with the Imperial House Law passed by the Diet.

Article 3. The advice and approval of the Cabinet shall be required for all acts of the Emperor in matters of state, and the Cabinet shall be responsible therefor.

Article 4. The Emperor shall perform only such acts in matters of state as are provided for in this Constitution, and he shall not have powers related to government. . . .

Chapter 2. Renunciation of War

Article 9. Aspiring sincerely to an international peace based on justice and order, the Japanese people forever renounce war as a sovereign right of the nation and the threat or use of force as means of settling international disputes.

In order to accomplish the aim of the preceding paragraph, land, sea, and air forces, as well as other war potential, will never be maintained. The right of belligerency of the state will not be recognized.

Chapter 3. Rights and Duties of the People

Article 11. The people shall not be prevented from enjoying any of the fundamental human rights.

These fundamental human rights guaranteed to the people by this Constitution shall be conferred on the people of this and future generations as eternal and inviolate rights.

Article 12. The freedoms and rights guaranteed to the people by this Constitution shall be maintained by the constant endeavor of the people, who shall refrain from any abuse of these freedoms and rights and shall always be responsible for utilizing them for the public welfare.

Article 13. All of the people shall be respected as individuals. Their rights to life, liberty, and the pursuit of happiness shall, to the extent that it does not interfere with the public welfare, be the supreme consideration in legislation and in other governmental affairs.

Article 14. All of the people are equal under the law, and there shall be no discrimination in political, economic, or social relations because of race, creed, sex, social status, or family origin.

Peers and peerage shall not be recognized.

No privilege shall accompany any award of honor, decoration, or any distinction, nor shall any such award be valid beyond the lifetime of the individual who now holds or hereafter may receive it.

Article 15. The people have the inalienable right to choose their public officials and to dismiss them.

All public officials are servants of the whole community and not of any group thereof.

Universal adult suffrage is guaranteed with regard to the election of public officials

In all elections, secrecy of the ballot shall not be violated. A voter shall not be answerable, publicly or privately, for the choice he has made. . . .

Article 20. Freedom of religion is guaranteed to all. No religious organization shall receive any privileges from the State nor exercise any political authority.

No person shall be compelled to take part in any religious act, celebration, rite, or practice.

The State and its organs shall refrain from religious education or any other religious activity.

Article 21. Freedom of assembly and association as well as speech, press, and all other forms of expression are guaranteed.

No censorship shall be maintained, nor shall the secrecy of any means of communication be violated. . . .

Article 24. Marriage shall be based only on the mutual consent of both sexes, and it shall be maintained through mutual cooperation with the equal rights of husband and wife as a basis.

With regard to choice of spouse, property rights, inheritance, choice of domicile, divorce, and other matters pertaining to marriage and the family, laws shall be enacted from the standpoint of individual dignity and the essential equality of the sexes. . . .

Article 28. The right of workers to organize and to bargain and act collectively is guaranteed. . . .

Article 37. In all criminal cases, the accused shall enjoy the right to a speedy and public trial by an impartial tribunal.

He shall be permitted full opportunity to examine all witnesses, and he shall have the right of compulsory process for obtaining witnesses on his behalf at public expense.

At all times the accused shall have the assistance of competent counsel who shall, if the accused is unable to secure the same by his own efforts, be assigned to his use by the State. . . .

Chapter 4. The Diet

Article 41. The Diet shall be the highest organ of state power and shall be the sole lawmaking organ of the State.

Article 42. The Diet shall consist of two Houses, namely, the House of Representatives and the House of Councillors.

Article 43. Both Houses shall consist of elected members, representatives of all the people.

The number of members of each House shall be fixed by law. . . .

Article 60. The budget must first be submitted to the House of Representatives.

Upon consideration of the budget, when the House of Councillors makes a decision different from that of the House of Representatives, and when no agreement can be reached even through a joint committee of both Houses, provided for by law, or in the case of failure by the House of Councillors to take final action in thirty days, the period of recess excluded, after the receipt of the budget passed by the House of Representatives, the decision of the House of Representatives shall be the decision of the Diet.

Chapter 5. The Cabinet

Article 65. Executive power shall be vested in the Cabinet.

Article 66. The Cabinet shall consist of the Prime Minister, who shall be its head, and other Ministers of State, as provided for by law.

The Prime Minister and other Ministers of State must be civilians.

The Cabinet, in the exercise of executive power, shall be collectively responsible to the Diet. . . .

Chapter 6. Judiciary

Article 76. The whole judicial power is vested in a Supreme Court and in such inferior courts as are established by law. . . .[5]

Document F: The Income-Doubling Plan

Issued in late 1960 at the behest of Prime Minister Ikeda Hayato, the Income-Doubling Plan was both a political manifesto and an economic guide. Politically, the plan implied that the government would concentrate on economic matters that would draw the nation together in the wake of some acrimonious strikes and demonstrations. Economically, the plan set forth a series of ambitious targets for growth in individual incomes, gross national product, and exports. In addition, the plan was attentive to the allocation of resources, laying out a blueprint to equalize the distribution of wealth in Japan among both geographic areas and socioeconomic groups. Ever since, politicians and bureaucrats, and even private-sector actors have used this blueprint to shape the way Japan's economy has evolved, especially during the years of rapid growth in the 1960s and 1970s.

1. Objectives of This Plan

---

[5] Based on the official government translation of 1947.

The plan to double the individual income must have as its objectives the doubling of the gross national product, attainment of full employment through expansion in employment opportunities, and raising the living standard of our people. We must adjust differentials in living standard and income existing between farming and nonfarming sectors, between large enterprises and small- and medium-size enterprises, between different regions of the country, and between different income groups. We must work toward a balanced development in our national economy and life patterns.

2. Targets to Be Attained

The plan's goal is to reach 26 trillion yen in GNP (at fiscal year 1958 prices) in the next ten years. To reach this goal, and in view of the fact that there are several factors highly favorable to economic growth existing during the first part of this plan, including the rapid development of technological changes and an abundant supply of skilled labor forces, we plan to attain an annual rate of growth of GNP at 9 percent for the coming three years. It is hoped that we shall be able to raise our GNP of 13.6 trillion yen (13 trillion yen in fiscal year 1958 prices) in fiscal year 1960 to 17.6 trillion yen (in 1960 prices) in fiscal year 1963 with the application of appropriate policies and cooperation from the private sector.

3.Points to Be Considered in Implementing the Plan and Directions to Be Followed

The plan contained in the report of the Economic Council [an advisory body to the Ministry of International Trade and Industry that issued its report on November 1, 1960] will be respected. However, in its implementation we must act flexibly and pay due consideration to the economic growth actually occurring and other related conditions. Any action we undertake must be consistent with the objectives described above. To do so, we shall pay special attention to the implementation of the following:

a. Promotion of Modernization in Agriculture. . . .
b. Modernization of Small- and Medium-Size Enterprises. . . .
c. Accelerated Development of Less Developed Regions. . . .
d. Promotion of Appropriate Locations for Industries and Reexamination of Regional Distribution of Public-Sector Projects. . . .
e. Active Cooperation with the Development of the World Economy....[6]

---

[6] Based on the English-language version of the Income-Doubling Plan issued by the Economic Planning Agency in 1960.

CHRONOLOGY

Periods in Japan's Modern History

Tokugawa era, 1600–1868

Meiji era, 1868–1912

Taishō era, 1912–1926

Shōwa era, 1926–1989

Heisei era, 1989–

A Chronology of Political and Economic Events

1850–1851: The Tokugawa house struggles to resolve a succession crisis.

1853: Commodore Matthew Perry arrives in Japanese waters for the first time.

1854: Japan signs the Treaty of Friendship with the United States; the ports of Shimoda and Hakodate are opened to foreign trade.

1856: Townsend Harris arrives in Japan to negotiate a commercial treaty.

1858: Japan concludes a commercial treaty with the United States and, later, four European nations. Extraterritoriality begins, and tariff autonomy is lost.

1859: *Bakufu* executes Yoshida Shōin, a Chōshū samurai.

1860: Ii Naosuke (a *bakufu* official who signed the commercial treaty) is assassinated.

1863: British vessels bombard castle town of Satsuma domain.

1864: Foreign powers bombard port of Shimonoseki, near Chōshū domain.

1866: Satsuma and Chōshū domains join to overthrow Tokugawa house.

1867: Tokugawa house cedes authority to emperor.

1868: Meiji Restoration: Emperor resumes governing authority. Edo is renamed Tōkyō, and Tōkyō becomes the nation's capital.

1869: Domains cede authority to the new government.

1871: Domains are abolished, and prefectures are established. The Iwakura mission begins.

1872: Old system of four legal classes is abolished. The government opens Tomioka silk mill.

1873: The government conducts land survey and introduces land tax reforms. The government splits in dispute over Korean policy. The Daiichi Bank is founded, and Mitsubishi shōji is established.

1874: Domestic political opposition expands. The government sends an expedition to Taiwan, and Mitsubishi opens a shipping route to Shanghai.

1875: Japan signs a territorial treaty with Russia.

1876: Japan signs a treaty with Korea, expanding its rights there. The government ends its financial support of former samurai and abolishes their right to wear swords. Mitsui enterprise opens bank and trading company.

1877: The government crushes samurai rebellion on Kyūshū. Teikoku daigaku (later Tōkyō University) is established. Ashio copper mine opens.

1878: Tōkyō Stock exchange opens, and Chamber of Commerce is established.

1879: Japan incorporates Ryūkyū Islands as Okinawa Prefecture. Yasuda Bank opens.

1880: Popular rights movement strengthens.

1881: The government promises a constitution in ten years. Finance Minister Matsukata introduces deflationary policies.

1882: Bank of Japan opens. Japan Spinners' Association forms.

1884: The government establishes a peerage of five ranks and begins selling public firms to private interests.

1885: A formal system of cabinet government is established.

1886: Imperial University Law announced. Mitsubishi establishes central holding company.

1887: The government issues Income Tax Law. Mitsubishi purchases a government shipyard in Nagasaki.

1888: Privy Council is established. Mitsui opens Miike Mines.

1889: The government promulgates Meiji Constitution on February 11. Meiji emperor begins to designate *genrō*. New system of local government is established. Kanegafuchi Spinning is incorporated.

1890: First general election is held, and the new Diet opens. Imperial Rescript on Education is promulgated. Mitsubishi purchases former army grounds in Marunouchi district of downtown Tōkyō.

1891: Environmental problems appear at Ashio copper mines.

1892: Second general election is held amid violent clashes at some voting sites.

1893: Civil service examination system is inaugurated.

1894: Sino-Japanese War begins. Japan concludes treaty with Great Britain that will eventually end terms of "unequal" treaties.

1895: Treaty of Shimonoseki ends the Sino-Japanese War. Triple Intervention by Russia, France, and Germany forces Japan to alter terms of the treaty.

1896: Kawasaki Heavy Industries is established.

1897: First national labor association is formed.

1898: Ōkuma Shigenobu forms a party-based cabinet opposed to the Satsuma-Chōshū clique. Civil code is promulgated and employed until 1945.

1900: First socialist party is formed but disbanded in 1904. Itō Hirobumi establishes the Seiyūkai. Peace Police Law is passed, imposing severe restrictions on political activities. Tsuda Umeko establishes Tsuda English Academy.

1901: Yahata steel mills begin production. Patriotic Women's League is established.

1902: Anglo-Japanese Alliance is concluded.

1903: Disputes with Russia over Korea intensify.

1904: War breaks out in Korea with Russia.

1905: Russo-Japanese War ends with Treaty of Portsmouth; Japan gains a military and political foothold in northeastern China. Riots begin in Hibiya district and spread throughout Tōkyō. Japan makes Korea a protectorate.

1906: Nationalization law creates Japan National Railways (JNR). South Manchurian Railway Corporation is established.

1907: Labor disputes erupt, involving some six thousand workers in fifty-seven incidents.

1908: Recession leads to higher taxes on sake and sugar.

1909: Itō Hirobumi is assassinated in Manchuria.

1910: Japan colonizes Korea. Imperial Reservists' Association and Imperial Agricultural Society are established. The government cracks down on socialists.

1911: Twelve socialists executed for participating in high treason incident. Japan recovers full tariff autonomy.

1912: The Meiji emperor dies and the Taishō emperor ascends throne. General Nogi commits suicide. Proposal for universal manhood suffrage passes the lower house but dies in the upper house. New labor organization, the Yuaikai, is formed.

1914: World War I begins, and Japan takes control of German territories in East Asia and the Pacific. Natsume Sōseki's *Kokoro* is published.

1915: Japan issues its Twenty-One Demands to China.

1916: The Kenseikai is formed.

1917: Japan Industrial Club is opened.

1918: Riots over high rice prices spread throughout country. Japan sends expeditionary force to Siberia. Hara Kei, a nonpeer, forms a party cabinet under the Seiyūkai majority. World War I ends.

1919: Kyōchōkai forms to promote labor-management harmony. Saionji Kinmochi represents Japan at the Versailles Peace Conference. China's Shandong Peninsula becomes a Japanese protectorate.

1920: Japan conducts first modern, nationwide census. Many organizations form to promote interests of workers, tenants, women, and *burakumin*. Keiō Gijuku University and Waseda University are formalized under New University Law. Hitachi is incorporated.

1921: Labor disputes spread as postwar recession deepens. Japan Communist Party is organized, briefly, secretly, and illegally.

1922: Washington Naval Limitation Treaty is concluded, setting a 5:5:3 ratio on naval ships for Great Britain, the United States, and Japan, respectively. Japan withdraws its expeditionary forces from Siberia.

1923: Tōkyō area experiences severe earthquake, killing as many as 150,000.

1924: Political instability fosters greater pressure for universal manhood suffrage. United States prohibits further immigration from Japan.

1925: Diet passes universal manhood suffrage law and severe Peace Preservation Law. Japan restores diplomatic relations with the Soviet Union. Japan makes its first radio broadcast. Greater Japan Alliance of Youth Organizations is established.

1926: The Taishō emperor dies, and the Shōwa emperor (Hirohito) ascends throne. Economic problems worsen, especially in rural areas.

1927: The Minseitō arises to challenge the Seiyūkai, after the Kenseikai breaks apart. Japanese military actions in Manchuria provoke wider opposition in China. Bank failures cause financial crisis.

1928: First lower house election held under universal manhood suffrage law; the Seiyūkai wins narrow victory over the Minseitō. Zhang Zoulin, a Manchurian warlord, is killed under suspicious circumstances; Chinese opposition to Japanese actions deepens.

1929: Japan prohibits gold exports and adopts deflationary policies. Worldwide depression begins with crash on Wall Street.

1930: Japan returns to the gold standard. Depression deepens, prices fall, and unemployment rises.

1931: Japanese army in Manchuria, the Kantō army, provokes incident and expands zone of control. Gold exports permitted again.

1932: Japan establishes puppet state of Manchuria. Right-wing terrorists assassinate minister of finance and Dan Takuma of Mitsui. Prime Minister Inukai is assassinated in coup attempt; party cabinets are ended.

1933: Japan leaves League of Nations. Reflationary policies spur economic recovery, especially in heavy and military-related industries.

1934: Nissan auto firm is incorporated. Poor harvests deepen rural poverty.

1935: Right-wing groups intensify their ideological attacks. Matsushita Kōnosuke incorporates his electrical enterprises.

1936: Finance Minister Takahashi dies in coup attempt by young military officers. Japan allies with Germany and Italy under defense accord.

1937: Japanese army in Manchuria invades north China. The government establishes Cabinet Planning Board. Toyota Motors is incorporated.

1938: Diet passes National Mobilization Act. Japanese forces in China occupy Wuhan cities, Guangzhou. General Araki becomes minister of education.

1939: Japanese military invades Hainan Island and engages Russian forces in the Nomonhan incident. Price control laws are issued. Tōkyō Electric and Shibaura Works merge to form Toshiba.

1940: Greater Japan Patriotic Industrial League forms, and Imperial Reserve Assistance Association is established. Japan signs Tripartite (Axis) Pact with Germany and Italy. Japanese military forces invade Indochina.

1941: Japan concludes neutrality agreement with the Soviet Union. General Tōjō Hideki becomes prime minister. Japan launches sea and air attack on Pearl Harbor.

1942: Japanese home economy begins to falter. The government directs formation of industrial control associations. Greater Japan Women's Association is formed. Allied victory in Battle of Midway arrests Japan's southward advance. The Allies bomb Japanese cities for the first time.

1943: Domestic consumption levels steadily decline. Ministry of Munitions is established. The government conscripts schoolchildren to aid production effort.

1944: Allies are victorious in Philippines. Air attacks on Japanese cities begin in earnest. Bretton Woods agreement is concluded.

1945: Air attacks on Japanese cities intensify, and millions flee to rural areas. United States drops A-bombs on Hiroshima and Nagasaki. Emperor Hirohito announces surrender. Allied Occupation begins and institutes the first reforms.

1946: Allied authorities purge politicians, business leaders, bureaucrats, and others. Occupation forces abolish Ministry of Army and Ministry of Navy. Land reform begins. Emperor renounces his divine status.

1947: New constitution goes into effect. General Douglas MacArthur prohibits general strike. A socialist-led government rules briefly. Local Autonomy Law is enacted, and the Ministry of Labor is established.

1948: The "reverse course" begins. The National Civil Service Law is passed, withdrawing from public workers the right to strike.

1949: Dodge Line goes into effect. The Ministry of International Trade and Industry (MITI) is created. Shoup Plan calls for financial reforms. Yen is stabilized at 360 to $1.

1950: Sōhyō labor federation is formed. Korean War begins, stimulating economic recovery. "Red purge" takes place. Local Civil Service Law is enacted.

1951: San Francisco Peace Treaty and the U.S.-Japan Security Pact are signed.

1952: Allied Occupation officially ends.

1953: Japanese government begins to revise Occupation reforms.

1954: Self-Defense Forces and Self-Defense Agency are established.

1955: Economic Planning Agency is established. Japan joins the General Agreement on Tariffs and Trade (GATT). The Liberal Democratic Party (LDP) is formed. Period of high-speed growth begins in earnest.

1956: Japan and the Soviet Union renew diplomatic relations. Japan enters the United Nations.

1957: Prime Minister Kishi Nobusuke pursues conservative agenda.

1958: National Police Law revision sparks sharp partisan conflict. Small radio manufacturer in Tōkyō renames itself the Sony Corporation.

1959: Democratic Socialist Party (DSP) is formed.

1960: Renewal of Security Treaty provokes mass demonstrations. Kishi cabinet is forced out, and Ikeda Hayato forms new cabinet devoted to economic development and doubling of incomes. Strikes at Miike Mines, longest in postwar era, finally end.

1961: Basic Agricultural Law passed.

1962: Japan concludes trade agreement with People's Republic of China.

1963: Basic Law for Small and Medium Enterprises is passed. Environmental problems worsen.

1964: International Olympics are held in Tōkyō. Mitsubishi Heavy Industries reconsolidates. Japan is invited to enter International Monetary Fund (IMF) and Organization for Economic Cooperation and Development (OECD).

1965: Average life expectancy for men reaches sixty-eight years.

1966: Major Japanese auto firms consolidate to compete internationally.

1967: The government implements capital liberalization. Clean Government Party (CGP) wins first seats in House of Representatives (HOR).

1968: Japan's GNP ranks second in world after the United States.' Long period of trade conflict begins. Era of the Three Cs: car, air conditioner, and color TV.

1969: Urban Redevelopment Law is passed. Japan becomes the world's top TV maker. Rice surpluses begin to mount.

1970: Ōsaka hosts World Exposition.

1971: United States agrees to return Okinawa to Japan.

1972: Nixon "shock" causes yen to appreciate to 272 to $1. Prime Minister Tanaka Kakuei restores normal relations with People's Republic of China.

1973: Organization of Petroleum Exporting Countries (OPEC) drives up oil prices; worldwide economic slowdown begins. Diet passes Large-Scale Retail Stores Law.

1974: Period of high inflation; real growth in GNP declines slightly. The LDP's power wanes, and period of conservative-progressive parity begins.

1975: Cutbacks take place in textile and shipbuilding industries; unemployment rises.

Progressive governors take power in Tōkyō, Ōsaka, and Kanagawa. Public-sector labor unions conduct politically unpopular right-to-strike actions.

1976: Lockheed scandal is revealed, and Prime Minister Tanaka Kakuei is arrested. The LDP retains a precarious hold on power.

1977: The LDP stages a recovery in upper house election. Trade disputes and problems widen. Average Japanese life expectancy (men: seventy-three years) surpasses Sweden's to become longest in the world.

1978: The MITI establishes voluntary trade restraints on auto exports. Yen rises to 185:$1. Diet passes Structurally Depressed Industries Law.

1979: The LDP wins close victory in the House of Representatives (HOR) election. Japan and United States settle nagging trade disputes over textiles.

1980: Prime Minister Ohira Masayoshi dies just ten days before HOR election; the LDP wins with sympathy vote.

1981: The government establishes the Commission on Administrative Reform, and the privatization movement advances. Special Administrative Reform Law passes. Japan concedes to voluntary trade restraints on auto exports to the United States.

1982: Diet passes Health Law for the Elderly. Commission on Administrative Reform recommends privatization of three public corporations. Prime Minister Nakasone Yasuhiro begins five-year term characterized by many conservative policy initiatives.

1983: Structural Reform Law for Specified Industries passes. The LDP bargains to retain narrow majority in the HOR.

1984: Nissan announces plans to build a factory in England. Japan and United States conclude agreements on citrus and meat imports.

1985: Toyota announces plans to build factory in United States. Equal Employment Opportunity Act is passed. Japan and United States conclude agreement on steel trade. National Pension Law is revised. Telecommunications and tobacco monopolies are privatized.

1986: Doi Takako becomes first woman to head a political party, the Japan Socialist Party. The LDP wins large majorities in both the HOR and the House of Councillors (HOC), marking the height of the conservative resurgence.

1987: A new union federation (Rengō) is formed. The Japan National Railway is broken up and privatized after eighty-one years as a government enterprise. The government approves a defense budget that surpasses 1 percent of GNP.

1988: Japan records its highest ever trade surplus with the United States. Japan's foreign direct investment is world's highest for third straight year. Japan settles disputes over construction industry with United States.

1989: Shōwa emperor (Hirohito) dies, and the Heisei emperor (Akihito) ascends throne. Recruit Scandal taints many political leaders. Government implements highly unpopular consumption tax. The LDP's political problems deepen.

1990: The speculative economic bubble of the 1980s bursts; the economic slowdown begins; and Japan retreats from overseas investments. The LDP clings to power with a narrow victory in upper house.

1991: Japanese government is embarrassed at home and abroad by disputes surrounding its role in the Gulf War.

1992: Severe economic downturn begins in earnest. The first of the 1990s "reform" parties forms and runs candidates in the HOC election.

1993: More "reform" parties emerge. The LDP is defeated in HOR election, and non-LDP coalition government takes office. Japanese peacekeeping units are sent to Cambodia.

1994: Major political reform bill is passed. Two non-LDP coalition governments fall, and a new coalition, including the LDP and the Socialists, forms cabinet. The DSP, CGP, and some "reform" parties dissolve to form a single party. Japan ends voluntary trade restraints on autos.

1995: Severe earthquake strikes Kobe area. Economic problems continue to worsen, and the yen reaches a postwar high of 79:$1.

1996: First HOR election held under new electoral system. The LDP emerges as the largest single party and forms government.

1997: Banking crises impede economic upturn. Shinshintō disbands.

1998: Corruption in financial system revealed. Economic downturn worsens.

LIST OF PRIME MINISTERS

From 1885 to the End of the Pacific War

Itō Hirobumi: 1885–1888

Kuroda Kiyotaka: 1888–1889

Yamagata Aritomo: 1889–1891

Matsukata Masayoshi: 1891–1892

Itō Hirobumi: 1892–1896

Matsukata Masayoshi: 1896–1898

Itō Hirobumi: 1898

Ōkuma Shigenobu: 1898

Yamagata Aritomo: 1898–1900

Itō Hirobumi: 1900–1901

Katsura Tarō: 1901–1906

Saionji Kinmochi: 1906–1908

Katsura Tarō: 1908–1911

Saionji Kinmochi: 1911–1912

Katsura Tarō: 1912–1913

Yamamoto Gonnohyōei: 1913–1914

Ōkuma Shigenobu: 1914–1916

Terauchi Masatake: 1916–1918

Hara Kei (Takashi): 1918–1921

Takahashi Korekiyo: 1921–1922

Katō Tomosaburō: 1922–1923

Yamamoto Gonnohyōei: 1923–1924

Kiyoura Keigo: 1924

Katō Takaaki: 1924–1926

Wakatsuki Reijirō: 1926–1927

Tanaka Giichi: 1927–1929

Hamaguchi Osachi: 1929–1931

Wakatsuki Reijirō: 1931

Inukai Tsuyoshi: 1931–1932

Saitō Makoto: 1932–1934

Okada Keisuke: 1934–1936

Hirota Kōki: 1936–1937

Hayashi Senjurō: 1937

Konoe Fumimaro: 1937–1939

Hiranuma Kiichiō: 1939

Abe Nobuyuki: 1939–1940

Yonai Mitsumasa: 1940

Konoe Fumimaro: 1940–1941

Tōjō Hideki: 1941–1944

Koiso Kuniaki: 1944–1945

Suzuki Kantarō: 1945

Since the Pacific War

Prince Higashikuni: 1945

Shidehara Kijūrō: 1945–1946

Yoshida Shigeru: 1946–1947

Katayama Testsu: 1947–1948

Ashida Hitoshi: 1948

Yoshida Shigeru: 1948–1954

Hatoyama Ichirō: 1954–1956

Ishibashi Tanzan: 1956–1957

Kishi Nobusuke: 1957–1960

Ikeda Hayato: 1960–1964

Satō Eisaku: 1964–1972

Tanaka Kakuei: 1972–1974

Miki Takeo: 1974–1976

Fukuda Takeo: 1976–1978

Ohira Masayoshi: 1978–1980

Suzuki Zenkō: 1980–1982

Nakasone Yasuhiro: 1982–1987

Takeshita Noboru: 1987–1989

Uno Sōsuke: 1989

Kaifu Toshiki: 1989–1991

Miyazawa Kiichi: 1991–1993

Hosokawa Morihiro: 1993–1994

Hata Tsutomu: 1994

Murayama Tomiichi: 1994–1996

Hashimoto Ryutarō: 1996–1998

Obuchi Keizō: 1998–

QUANTITATIVE DATA

Population of Japan

YEAR	POPULATION IN THOUSANDS
1870	32,718
1880	36,649
1890	39,902
1900	43,847
1910	49,184
1920	55,963
1930	64,450
1940	71,933
1950	83,200
1960	93,419
1970	103,720
1980	117,060
1990	123,611

SOURCE: Asahi shimbun, ed., *Asahi Shimbun Japan Almanac: 1994* (Tokyo: Asahi Shimbun Co., 1993), pp. 274–277. Based on government census figures.

Gross National Product of Japan

YEAR	IN HUNDRED MILLIONS OF YEN
1930	139
1940	394
1950	39,467
1960	159,980
1970	731,884
1980	2,400,985
1990	4,274,692

Source: Asahi shimbun, ed., *Asahi Shimbun Japan Almanac: 1994* (Tokyo: Asahi Shimbun Co., 1993), pp. 278–279. Based on official data from and estimates by the Economic Planning Agency.

Distribution of Labor Force by Sector, in Percentages

YEAR	I	II	III
1880 (estimate)	80	10	10
1920	54	21	25
1940	44	26	30
1960	33	29	38
1980	11	34	55

Note: I = Primary sector: Agriculture, forestry, and fishing. II = Secondary sector: Manufacturing, mining, and construction. III = Tertiary sector: All other occupations.
Source: Yano Tsuneta Kinenkai, ed., *Sūji de miru Nihon no hyakunen* (A statistical view of one hundred years of Japan) (Tokyo: Kokuseisha, 1991), p. 79.

Japan's Changing Trade Patterns

Percentage of Japanese Exports by World Area

EXPORTS TO	1900	1940	1960	1990
All of Asia	48	68	36	34
Europe (except USSR)	22	5	12	22
North America	29	16	30	34
All other areas	1	11	22	10

Percentage of Japanese Imports by World Area

IMPORTS FROM	1900	1940	1960	1990
All of Asia	30	44	30	42
Europe (except USSR)	45	6	9	18
North America	23	38	39	26
All other areas	2	12	22	14

Source: Yano Tsuneta Kinenkai, ed., *Sūji de miru Nihon no hyakunen* (A statistical view of one hundred years of Japan) (Tokyo: Kokuseisha, 1991), pp. 323, 324.

Diffusion of Consumer Commodities

COMMODITY	1965	1990
Sewing machines	79	81
Washing machines	72	100
Refrigerators	62	98
Cameras	58	88
Electric vacuum cleaners	41	99
Radios and cassette players	18	75
Stereo equipment	17	60
Automobiles	9	76
Pianos	5	23
Room air-conditioners	2	66
Color television sets	0	99
Microwave ovens	0	71

Note: Figures equal the percentage of all nonfarm households that possessed the commodity in a given year.

Source: Adapted from Yano Tsuneta Kinenkai, ed., *Sūji de miru Nihon no hyakunen* (A statistical view of one hundred years of Japan) (Tokyo: Kokuseisha, 1991), table 9–9, p. 479.

Maps

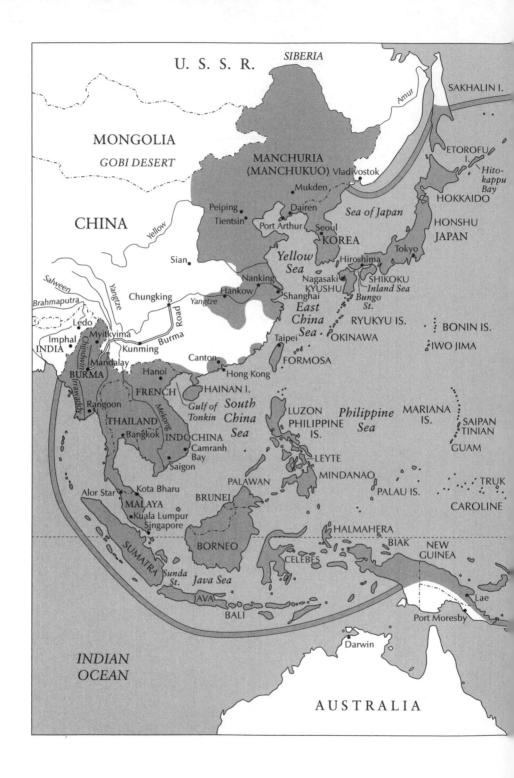

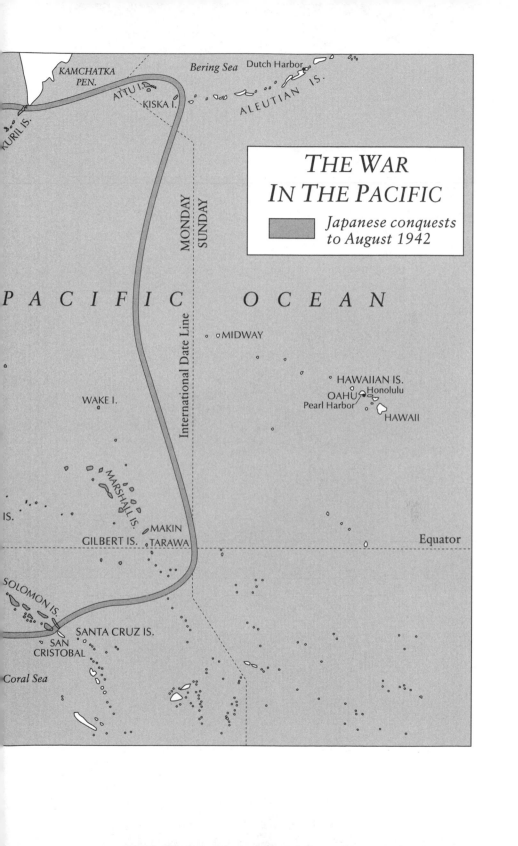

KAMCHATKA
PEN.

Bering Sea Dutch Harbor

ATTU I.

KURIL IS.

KISKA I.

ALEUTIAN IS.

THE WAR
IN THE PACIFIC

*Japanese conquests
to August 1942*

MONDAY
SUNDAY

P A C I F I C   O C E A N

International Date Line

MIDWAY

HAWAIIAN IS.
OAHU Honolulu
Pearl Harbor
HAWAII

WAKE I.

MARSHALL IS.

IS.

MAKIN

GILBERT IS. TARAWA

Equator

SOLOMON IS.

SANTA CRUZ IS.

SAN
CRISTOBAL

Coral Sea

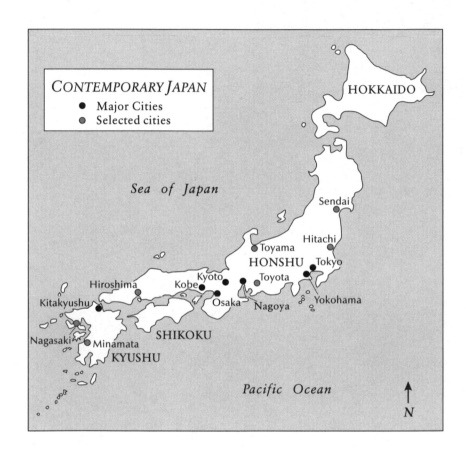

CONTEMPORARY JAPAN

● Major Cities
● Selected cities

HOKKAIDO

Sea of Japan

Sendai

Hitachi

Toyama

HONSHU

Tokyo

Kyoto

Kobe

Toyota

Hiroshima

Osaka

Nagoya

Yokohama

Kitakyushu

Nagasaki

Minamata

SHIKOKU

KYUSHU

Pacific Ocean

N

INDEX

DATE DUE

DEC 1 0 1997			
FEB 2 3 2010			